cfw

THE BROADSIDE BALLAD

"I love a ballad in print, a'life: for then we are sure they are true."

MOPSA (*Winter's Tale*—SHAKESPEARE)

(Collections of broadside ballads) ". . . veritable dunghills, in which, only after a great deal of sickening grubbing, one finds a very moderate jewel."

PROFESSOR FRANCIS JAMES CHILD

"I may, however, hint at the difference, not always attended to, betwixt legendary poems and real imitations of the old ballad; the reader will find specimens of both in the modern part of this collection."

SIR WALTER SCOTT (Introduction to
Minstrelsy of the Scottish Border)

"There was never ane o' ma sangs prentit till ye prentit them yoursel' and ye hae spoilt them a' thegither. They were made for singing and no for reading, but ye hae broken the charm now and they'll never be sung mair. And the warst thing o' a', they're nouther right spell'd, nor right setten down."

MRS. HOGG (of Sir Walter Scott's
Minstrelsy of the Scottish Border)

"Popular poetry cannot lose its value. Being founded on what is permanent and universal in the heart of man, and now by printing put beyond the danger of perishing, it will survive the fluctuations of taste, and may from time to time serve, as it notoriously did in England and Germany a hundred years ago, to recall a literature from false and artificial courses to nature and truth."

PROFESSOR FRANCIS JAMES CHILD

THE BROADSIDE BALLAD

A Study in Origins and Meaning

By

LESLIE SHEPARD

FOLKLORE ASSOCIATES
HATBORO, PENNSYLVANIA

LONDON : HERBERT JENKINS

First Published by
Herbert Jenkins Limited
3 Duke of York Street
London, S.W.1
1962

MADE AND PRINTED IN GREAT BRITAIN
BY COX AND WYMAN LTD., LONDON,
READING AND FAKENHAM

FOREWORD

by
A. L. LLOYD

WE have grown used to thinking of folk-song as an essentially rural kind of song passed on by word of mouth. In doing so, we ignore the influence of town and print. True, our great folk-song collectors of half a century ago came on most of their finds among country singers, but that is no evidence that the songs weren't at one time also current in the cities; perhaps it only shows that the folk Muse lingered among the hedgerows after she had withdrawn from the taverns of the towns. True, too, orality is a special characteristic of folk-song transmission, but besides being passed on from mouth to mouth, thousands of songs were spread among the folk by means of writing and reading. The idea of "the folk" as an autonomous social category alien to book learning and mechanical industry, and evolving their own unwritten culture in isolation, is a senti-mental abstraction, particularly where Western Europe is con-cerned. As the present study illustrates, song- and ballad-texts in the form of street literature were being sold widely in the British Isles for nearly four hundred years, and in the main the buyers were precisely the class of people among whom the bearers of the folk-song tradition were to be found.

London was the centre of the song-sheet trade, but it also came to flourish in industrial towns such as Birmingham, Manchester, Preston and Newcastle. Printed on leaflets of various sizes, at times adorned with woodcuts of remarkable incongruity, the song-texts were sold from cheapjack stalls, or carried from door to door in pedlars' satchels, along with ribbons, papers of pins, and boxes of pills, or hawked in the streets and on the fairgrounds by bawling "chaunters". Apprentice boys would paste these fugitive leaves in the lids of their clothes-chests, seamen would fasten them in the back of log-books, milkmaids would paper the dairy walls with them, and learn the songs by heart as they churned: and after a

5

while the dairy would be whitewashed and a new set of song-sheets pasted up, and so through the years layer on layer of song would accumulate.

Of course, by no means all the song-texts on the broadsides were of the stuff that makes folk-song. Some were crude versifications of passing events that failed to secure a grip on the popular imagination. Others, sung by pleasure-garden or stage singers before they reached the common folk, never lost their professional shape to acquire the character, elusive yet unmistakable, of folk-song. But many of the texts were taken ready-made from the stock of orally-traditional song, and many were author-made pieces destined to enter the folk-song tradition and remain there tenaciously. On the broadsides, one may find effusions that have long lost their savour, if they ever had any. One may also find versions of some of the masterpieces of folk poetry. Generally, the customer did not discriminate between ephemeral pot-poem, stage-lyric and folk-song, any more than did the ballad hawker or publisher. Just so, to this day, the village singer will pour out traditional song, music-hall song and aspidistra ballad without any finicky concern about categories. From the broadsides, the singers took any song that caught their fancy; and if it wasn't already a folk-song, they quite often turned it into one. Perhaps the greatest value of Mr. Shepard's work is to remind us of the valiant part played by the despised broadside in the shaping of our native tradition of song.

The despised broadside? It is true that, compared with the best models from oral tradition, the poetry of the song-sheets is generally flat, colourless, lacking in secret or surprise. Often in the broadside prints, the magic has ebbed from the ballad, preoccupation with daily affairs has replaced the passions of mythology, and shadowy larger-than-life heroes are reduced in stature as they are bathed in the light of everyday. The very homeliness of the broadside has encouraged scholarly contempt; but in fact these humble pieces of street literature have performed an important task. To my mind—and here, perhaps, Mr. Shepard would not agree with me—the broadsides should not be seen simply as a sign of the decline of folk memory and of oral tradition. For the last six hundred years or so—the years during which our folk-song has taken on the shapes we recognize—even remote parts of the

countryside have not remained entirely unaffected by book culture. Nor is a condition of exclusive orality necessarily a healthy
one for the artistic creativeness of the folk. A community so back-
ward that its culture is entirely oral may turn out to be leading too
worried a life to think very hard about creating music and poetry.
This has been the experience in some East European villages
where, in pre-1914 days, even such astute and diligent folklorists
as Bartok found only a tiny depressed repertory of song, with no
evidence of any new creation for some centuries past; yet in the
period between the World Wars, with the establishment of bus
services, the growth of literacy, the advent of radio and the
expansion of village economy, folk balladry positively bloomed
among communities almost barren of song; and now, in these
same areas, the present generation of villagers are renowned for
their musical creativity, and for their ability to absorb into their
local tradition songs from other areas, whether learnt from record,
radio or print. In the process of digesting these "foreign" songs into
the local repertory, many of the texts and tunes have become much
improved. It is not impossible that something of the sort may have
happened, in the past, in Britain. We have no evidence to suggest
that the oral folk-song repertory was larger in, say, 1300, before
the days of print, than in 1700, when broadside-ballads had been
on sale for some centuries. Possibly the contrary is the case. Far
from being a symptom of the shrinking of folk-song tradition, the
broadside may originally have been a sign of its expansion.
Unaided by print, many of our folk-songs had only very limited
diffusion, and some of the finest have been recovered only once,
from a single singer, and never again encountered in a "natural"
state (*Brigg Fair*, for instance). There can be little doubt that the
broadside was a powerful instrument for helping the spread of a
song, and chaunter and chapman ensured wide diffusion for many
fine ballads that might otherwise have withered away in their
native locality after a relatively brief and restricted life.

It is good, then, that Mr. Shepard does honour to the humble
broadside. His well-documented exposition speaks for itself. Here
and there, the reader may be taken along paths that seem a little
remote from the territory of the penny ballad-sheet, and perhaps
the long-song seller, with his stubbly chin and battered stovepipe

hat, cuts an odd figure at the mouth of that shadowy cave that reverberates with the primordial and world-creating syllable: AUM. But it is time we took a fresh look at our folk traditions, and it is salutary to have our presuppositions challenged and our thinking given new directions by the enlarged documentation and penetrating comment to be found in a volume such as this.

A. L. LLOYD

Greenwich, London.

PREFACE

by
KENNETH S. GOLDSTEIN

THERE have been numerous volumes of broadside ballads published; there are several broadside ballad indexes; and now, finally, there is a book *about* broadside ballads. It is not the definitive book—rarely is an introductory work ever so encompassing as to warrant the title definitive—but it is a volume which will remain a standard text for a long time to come.

In a letter to this writer, Leslie Shepard modestly described his work as ". . . something of a blueprint—an extended essay, rather than an all-inclusive summation of the subject." The comparison of this extended essay to a *blueprint* is an excellent one, for blueprints are the first stages in any building operation. And with this blueprint, the author has built a broad and firm base for future study of and commentary on the broadside ballad.

Britain continues to supply the English-speaking world with "lay" scholars; excellent scholarly treatises on various aspects of folklore have been published by private, non-academically-connected scholars from all walks of British life. And this is as it should be, for scholarship is the domain of those rare intelligent beings who combine brilliant insight with the broadest imaginable knowledge of their subject. Academics may fill such a description, but often the very nature of academic life stultifies creativity and imprisons insight. Mr. Shepard is his own man—no fetters bind either his creativity or his insight. It is this very freedom of thought and expression which results in the author seeking for the meaning, in addition to the form, of the ballad, broadside or traditional.

It is this emphasis on *meaning*—the interpretation of data in relation to the human situation (as compared with the academic study *in vacuo*)—which is Mr. Shepard's main contribution. For him a study of the broadside ballad and its origins is a step towards the clarification of the main aspects of the human situation—

9

metaphysics and materialism, religion and politics, the trivial and the profound, heroic origins and everyday preoccupations.

There will be those scholars who will find something to complain about in Mr. Shepard's use of metaphysical interpretations and insights in explaining ballad origins and tradition. And, indeed, he is a brave man for publishing his thoughts on these matters when man is at the edge of the space-age and less and less receptive to philosophical commentary on the secret of existence itself. In developing his thesis about the primordial and sometimes mysterious archetypal images and situations of the ballad, he has drawn on the awe-inspiring profundity and subtlety of ancient Hindu literature and philosophy. For those who do not know Mr. Shepard and would question his qualifications for such discourse, suffice it to say that he has spent half a lifetime of study, in and out of India, absorbing and digesting the most complex body of philosophy and literature in the world.

But there is more meat on the bone. Even those who reject some of the author's interpretations will find a vast store of information on the broadside ballad's origin, history and scholarship. And for those who properly view culture as a continuum, there is a final chapter on the survival and extension of the broadside medium into modern times.

Leslie Shepard's THE BROADSIDE BALLAD is a small book. Its contribution is in inverse proportion to its size.

KENNETH S. GOLDSTEIN

Hatboro, Pennsylvania

CONTENTS

metrie/she myght mesure in alle maistryes/ffor by mesure was the world made, and alle thinges hye, lowe & deep,

Here folo: weth of mu: syque/capi:

The fir: ste of the vij scie: ces is called musyque / the whiche fourmeth hym of Arsmetryque/Of this science of mu: syque cometh alle attemperaunce, And of this arte pro:

An early illustration of Ballad Singers, from *Mirrour of the World*, printed by W. Caxton, Westminster, 1481

LIST OF PLATES

(Original size of specimens reproduced is shown in parentheses.)

13

INTRODUCTION

THIS study is designed as an introduction to a fascinating field that
links together a number of separate studies, ranging from English
Literature to the Social Sciences. Few subjects offer such a rich
variety as Broadside Balladry. The antiquary pores over precious
broadside collections, the lover of traditional music compares the
oral and printed versions, the student of history, economics and
sociology discovers how ordinary people lived and thought in
other times.

In the past, there has been much confusion on the relative importance of various kinds of balladry, and a tendency to isolate one
aspect at the expense of another. It is not unusual to find that
studies on the Broadside Ballad barely notice the traditional sort,
whilst writers on the Traditional Ballad affect distaste for the
broadside variety. The present work provides a context for both
partisans. The antiquarian specialist in printed broadsides may
discover a richer ancestry in the traditional background. Purists for
the traditional ballad may despise the street songs, but they will
find their ballads on printed sheets as much as on the lips of the
people.

This book attempts to place the whole subject in perspective,
and thus provide a general basis for more specialized studies.
There are familiar quotations, unavoidable for those who write on
this subject, but there is much original material. As I have drawn
sparsely upon existing works, the books listed in the selected
bibliography will provide fascinating material for further study.
In general, the emphasis is on meaning rather than data, and an
attempt has been made to communicate the essential intangible
qualities of balladry that should animate the data. Proper studies
should enrich our understanding of life rather than lead to solemn
academic abstraction. An essential key to ballad study is the oral
tradition—a complex elusive aspect that cannot be captured by
books. Listening to the gramophone recordings classified at the
end of this book will give a deeper understanding than formal

discussion of textual questions. Experience of the living voice of singers in the traditional idiom brings a literary study to life.

Books on broadsides should also familiarize one with the appearance of the actual sheets. All the examples illustrated have been selected from my own collection of broadsides, and are part of a group that is being prepared for exhibition. The choice has been difficult as the field is a vast one, but I have tried to do justice to the themes that underlie the broadside phenomenon, in particular the interaction between religion and politics that gives the broadside wider meaning. As collections of ballads are difficult of access for the general reader as apart from the student, the illustrations should provide something in the nature of a portable exhibition.

Every writer in this field should acknowledge the immense debt that English ballad study owes to American scholarship, to specialists like Professor Hyder E. Rollins, and universities like Harvard where the subject has been a tradition since the days of the great Professor Francis James Child. Much scholarship has been expended on the first two centuries of broadside ballads, following upon the cataloguing and reprinting of the great "Black-Letter" collections of Roxburghe, Bagford and Pepys. It is hoped that the present book will attract attention to the relatively virgin field of the Whiteletter Ballad.

ACKNOWLEDGEMENTS

My grateful thanks to the following for kind permission to reproduce:

The British Museum, for the illustration from Caxton's *Mirrour of the World*.

The *Evening News* and *Evening Standard* for their front pages.

Chappell & Co. for the song cover *Robin Hood by Carl Sigman*.

Evangelical Tract Distributors Inc., Canada, for the tract *He Had No Song*.

Free Church Federal Council Inc. for *Wayside Pulpit No. 335*.

Felix McGlennon Ltd. for *Record Song Book No. 175*.

Walton's Piano and Musical Instrument Galleries, Dublin, for the song *The Battle of Baltinglass* (by Sylvester Gaffney).

Fleetway Publications Ltd. for *Robin Hood Told in Pictures*.

Eric Winter for cover of *Sing* Magazine, Vol. 6, No. 4, and broadsheet *Songs for the March for Life*.

Sydney Carter for *Every Star Shall Sing a Carol* on the cover of *Sing* magazine.

John Brunner and Fred Dallas for songs on the cover of *Songs for the March for Life*.

John Manifold, Australia, for the broadside *Wild Colonial Boy* in the *Bandicoot Ballads* series.

John Foreman, the Broadsheet King, for various broadsides.

Ewan MacColl for the song *Go Down, You Murderers*, on a John Foreman broadside.

Siegfried Sassoon for permission to quote one verse from his poem *Every One Sang*.

The Clarendon Press, Oxford, for a quotation from *The Ballad of Tradition* by Gordon H. Gerould.

My personal thanks to A. L. Lloyd, Kenneth S. Goldstein, Barry Duncan, Mrs. Nan Fried, Hans Fellner and Eric Winter for help and encouragement; my apologies to John Foreman for not having space to include some of his excellent recent productions.

THE BROADSIDE

CHAPTER ONE

THE BROADSIDE

THE story of broadside ballads is a most romantic one of flimsy sheets of paper finding their way through four centuries. Although great libraries have been destroyed by religious or political prejudice, there is something in the very format of a book that inspires respect and careful preservation. Broadsides, however, were single sheets of paper with no pretensions to permanence. They were discarded after reading; at best they might be pasted up on walls, on cupboard doors, or put in albums. The broadside was essentially printed for the day, as ephemeral as yesterday's newspaper or a handbill given in the streets, yet somehow a great many of these precious sheets have been miraculously preserved and lovingly studied. They give valuable information about bygone days, and simple pleasure to the song-lover and the antiquary. Much of the fascination of broadside ballads is the way in which they throw light upon so many different studies—history, folklore, religion, politics, economics and sociology. In a much wider sense these sheets may be correlated with oral traditions of folklore as part of the history of civilization.

Properly speaking, the term "broadside" covers many different kinds of popular street literature—handbills, proclamations, advertisements, religious documents, as well as ballads and songs. A broadside is simply a sheet of paper with printing on one side. The term "broadsheet" has often been used instead of "broadside", usually in relation to ballad broadsides. However, the modern trend in American bibliography assigns a special meaning. According to MACMURTRIE (*Instructions for the Description of Broadsides*, American Imprints Inventory, 1939):

"The Broadsheet is a single sheet of paper printed on *both* sides. Except for the fact that the text is carried over to a second page a broadsheet is similar to a broadside. In the collections of broadsides in various important collections throughout the country it is the practice to include among the broadsides single printed sheets with one fold (4 page folders)."

The distinction is further clarified by a quotation from CHARLES EVANS (*American Bibliography*):

"First the broadside. If the printed matter is on the recto, or face, of an unfolded sheet, only, it is, bibliographically a broadside, in folio, quarto, octavo, or sixteenmo size, as the printed sheet of paper may be. The proclamation, sheet calendar, handbill, advertisement, and the political squib, whose design is to be posted up for general information, are all of this description.

"Second, the broadsheet. If the printed matter overruns the recto of an unfolded sheet, and the verso is also printed upon, it then becomes a broadsheet, and is bibliographically described as consisting of pp. (2), folio, quarto, octavo, or whatever size the single sheet of paper may be. The circular letter, and short political address, belong to this description. Dictionaries and encyclopaedias make the two terms, broadside and broadsheet, synonymous; bibliographically they are not, but differentiated in the manner stated."

These are valuable definitions in a field that suffers from confusing terminology. For general purposes it is often convenient to refer to printed broadside ballads as "balladsheets".

Inevitably the student of broadside ballads who is not a rigid purist will find his attention straying to the broadsides of royal proclamations and other public notices. These may be compared side by side with the histories in song, helping to build up a picture of their times.

Some of the early forms of popular newspaper were simply single printed sheets; while these gave topical items in prose, the broadside ballads would give news in verse. Need we be too pedantic about the difference between a ballad and a newspaper? It is obviously very difficult to draw a hard and fast line in such matters when early balladsheets told topical news in song. Here is a typical title of a seventeenth century broadside ballad:

"THE TRAGEDY OF DOCTOR *Lambe*,
The great supposed Conjurer, who was wounded to
death by Saylers and other Lads, on Fryday the

14, of June, 1628. And dyed in the Poultry Counter,
neere Cheap-side, on the Saturday morning following.
To the tune of *Gallants come away*."[1]

Much historical interest is attached to such news ballads when viewed against the background of their times. Dr. Lambe, a famous magician, was actually mobbed on June 13th, not the 14th, but the ballad particulars of his pursuit and brutal death are very close to the facts. However, the real reason for this unpopularity may have been less his alleged trafficking with the Devil in his conjurations than the belief that by his magic his patron the Duke of Buckingham was able to seduce innocent women. It is certainly true that Buckingham instigated Charles I to threaten the city of London with a £6,000 fine and loss of its charter for the crime. Buckingham, however, was assassinated a couple of months later; the city of London was actually fined 1,500 marks.[2]

This ballad, typical of many sold and sung in the streets, served the function of newspaper, and has probably as much accuracy in reporting as the popular newspaper of today.

In fact, if you assemble all the different types of subject of the broadsides from the sixteenth to the nineteenth centuries, you will find the unvarying make-up of the modern newspaper—Royalty, Murders, Topical News, Politics, Sport, Humour and Advertisements. The only item which has declined in popularity as a subject is religion, but what the modern newspaper does not print may still be seen today as broadside texts and exhortations on advertisement hoardings, while religious handbills are still given to you in the streets of cities. The relationship between religious and secular subject-matter in the history of the broadside is an important one, and will be dealt with in more detail later in this study.

In the field of the broadside, we find that both subject-matter and format change in a manner that defies rigid distinctions. If we keep strictly to the definition of a broadside as a piece of paper printed on one side, the varieties of prose and verse issued in this form must constitute separate studies. Thus, the history of street ballads becomes a separate study from the history of royal proclamations, and so on. But what happens when the printer puts

---

[1] See ROLLINS, *A Pepysian Garland*, pp. 276–282.
[2] Details from ROLLINS, *A Pepysian Garland*.

additional matter on the back of the sheet, and suppose the sheets are folded? And what about handwritten sheets? The student of street ballads will find his subject changing format in such a way as to render the terms "broadside" and "broadsheet" irrelevant except for library classification.

For example, many popular ballads were written by hand before the invention of printing; some were probably sold in the streets in the same way as printed broadsides. Then, too, in the late period of broadsides, some printers added advertisements to the back of the sheet. Some balladsheets are even printed on both sides, but are hardly the less broadsides on this account.

During the early years of printing in England, the distinction of sheets printed only on one side was largely one of trade convenience. Printers were licensed by the Stationers' Company, London (incorporated 1556), and if they did not keep to their agreed field of printing they could be fined. "Things printed on one side" of a sheet were usually licensed to the poorer printer members.

From a general point of view, the broadside is really concerned with the ebullition of popular street literature, prose and verse, in the format of cheap printing. If we can accept this close connection between the different kinds of broadsides, from proclamations to balladsheets, we need not limit the field to such things printed only on one side of a sheet of paper.

The broadside sheet, folded once, twice, or more, makes a small pamphlet. In this format were published collections of songs and ballads, as well as stories, sermons, jests and almanacks. These "chapbooks", as they were called ("cheap-books"), became the universal popular cheap literature of poor people between the sixteenth and nineteenth centuries. They are the forerunners of the cheap "paperbacks" which have come into favour again in modern times.

Travelling pedlars called "chapmen" moved from village to village selling ballads and chapbooks as well as the various useful knick-knacks that are still sold in street markets nowadays. Shakespeare has portrayed a chapman in the character of Autolycus in the *Winter's Tale*: "He hath songs for man, or woman, of all sizes; no milliner can so fit his customers with gloves. He has the prettiest love songs for maids; so without bawdry, which is strange ..." Such pedlars are not wholly extinct even in the twentieth century. You can still find itinerant vendors of cheap wares in London's West End, ready to shut their cases or trays as soon as a policeman appears. They do not sell ballads, but recall the seventeenth century definition of Cotgrave in his *Dictionarie of the French and English Tongues*: "A paultrie Pedlar, who in a long packe or maund (which he carries for the most part open, and (hanging from his necke) before him) hath Almanacks, Bookes of News, or other trifling ware to sell."

The stallholder in the markets of towns and cities today is a legitimate descendant of the travelling pedlar, now anchored respectably but still magically beguilding with his tongue and crafty in his business methods. In the old days when balladsheets were sold from the stalls at market fairs, broadsides came to be known as "stall copies".

Chapbooks should be distinguished from Tracts, the political and religious pamphlets of the sixteenth, seventeenth and eighteenth centuries.[1] These were more scholarly and substantial pamphlets, circulating, for the most part, amongst the intellectual and influential sections of the community. Moreover, many of the tracts vigorously denounced balladsheets and ballad-singers, as the following title shows:

"A LAMENTATION OVER THE CITY OF GRONINGHEN.
Containing
An answer to Four Papers written against
the People called *Quakers*, Two by the Magistrates,
and Two Lies sung in the Street, by the Wild and
Ungodly Ballet-Singers, which shews that the Spi-
rit of Persecution and Mockery comes all from one
Ground ...
LONDON, Printed by T. Sowle, 1694."

Some of the earliest printed collections of songs and ballads in pamphlet form were known as "Garlands". They often included poems, and since they might have as many as thirty or more pieces they could be considered books. In 1584, Richard Jones printed *A Handefull of pleasant delites* which contains the famous ballad *A*

---

[1] The term *tract* is often loosely used for any early broadsheet or pamphlet.

New Courtly Sonet of the Lady Greensleeves as well as lesser known ballads, songs and poems. *Tottel's Miscellany* of 1557 contains poems, by the Earl of Surrey, Sir Thomas Wyatt, Nicholas Grimald and others. In those days, ballads and poems were not always clearly distinguished, because popular broadside ballads might be written by eminent poets and courtiers as well as by the tavern minstrels of the street. As we shall see later, the term "ballad" has been loosely applied to a variety of verse forms. Even *Greensleeves* was described as a sonnet.

The sixteenth and early seventeenth century garlands bore extravagant titles like: *The Paradise of Dainty Devises* (1576), *The Princely Garland of Golden Delites*, *The Gorgeous Gallery of Gallant Inventions* (1578), *The Phœnix Nest* (1593). Almost any collection of poetry or song has been called a Garland, but a less confusing term for these early collections is "poetical miscellanies".

Towards the end of the eighteenth century, the term "garland" was even being applied to individual poems, ballads, and prose narratives![1] Typical titles from single sheets are: "The Bristol Garland", "The Doating Mother's Garland", "The Factor's Garland". In general, the word "garland" is best reserved for a collection of love songs in pamphlet form.

Broadside and chapbook activity was not confined to England. With the invention of cheap printing, popular literature of this sort spread throughout Europe. The same conventions of Broadside format may be found in Holland, France, Italy, Spain and Germany—the sheets with a crude woodcut illustration and phrases like "A New Song . . .", "To be sung to a New Tune", and so on. From the seventeenth century onwards, English broadsides found their way to America, and many songs and ballads from these sheets were reprinted locally; some gave rise to new oral traditions of American balladry. A comparative study of foreign broadsides and the political and religious influence exerted by them would require a separate book.

For the present, we should note that the newspaper proper had its origin in Italy, where collections of news were first written by

---

[1] Probably the great number of Garlands published in chapbook format led to "garland" and "chapbook" becoming synonymous, thereafter a "garland" became the sort of piece found in chapbooks.

hand. These Venetian "gazettas" were imitated by other govern-
ments, and the very name "Gazette" is still with us. The idea of the
newspaper is perhaps even older, as we are told that Cicero used
shorthand writers to record the speeches of Cato for a daily report
of debates in the Roman Senate.

The earliest surviving newspapers in the English language were
printed in Holland from 1620 until 1621, when the privilege to
publish was granted to London printers. These *Corantos* ("Courants
of News") began as broadsheets, printed on both sides of a single
sheet; later on they became small pamphlets—"books-of-news".
(The *English Mercurie* of 1588, once cited as an early newspaper, is
a famous forgery of the Earl of Hardwicke and Phillip Birch.)

Newspapers remained well beyond the general public for two
centuries, and the popular newspaper of today has evolved from
the broadside rather than the Venetian *gazetta*, the news pamphlet
or the literary journal.

The broadside ballad is a key focal point in a much wider and
more intangible trend than mere classification would suggest. As
we shall see later, the ballad ancestry of the broadside reaches back
to remote antiquity. With the growth of towns and cities in sixteenth century England, the popular need for topical news and
opinion ran side by side with fading memories of traditional tales
and songs.

So the broadside ranges from verse to prose, shades off into garland, chapbook and tract on a variety of subjects, finally culmina-
ting in the ephemeral form of the popular newspaper and the more
permanent form of the book. The story of this transition from folk
memory to printed sheet, from sheet to pamphlet and book is a
fascinating one. No true lover of ballad broadsides will be able to
resist at least a passing glance at the proclamations and tracts, at
the evolution of printing type and display, the use of the woodcut
illustration. The student of engraving will find work by Bewick and
Cruikshank on street balladsheets, while modern commercial
artists have learnt to revive many of the decorative types and borders from broadsides. The historian and sociologist will find valuable source material in broadsides, garlands, chapbooks and tracts.
These are all near relations, and our search for ballads need not be
restricted to the single-sided sheet.

For that matter, if we were to be at all purist about broadside
ballads, we should find great difficulty in defining just what *is* a
ballad! Many different classes of musical and poetical composition
are covered by the same term, and at one time or another most of
these various types of ballad have all been printed on broadsides
and in garlands and chapbooks.

" London's Gazette here "

THE BALLAD

CHAPTER TWO

THE BALLAD

IT has been well said that a ballad is a song that tells a story. This definition is wide enough to include most kinds of ballad. Beyond this point, however, certain distinctions need to be made. For convenience, we can distinguish four main groups: the Traditional Ballad, the Broadside Ballad, the Literary Ballad, and the Drawing-room Ballad.

These divisions, although accepted terms, are far from precise. The pieces printed on broadsides, for example, do not belong to one distinct metrical, poetical or musical form, as the sheets have included traditional ballads side by side with popular songs and poems. Again, the traditional ballad is not a fixed form, being the result of the shaping of folk cultures over a long period of time. In the case of Literary Ballads, the authors of these poems often had confused ideas as to what constituted ballad form.

The Traditional Ballad is usually defined with reference to Professor Francis James Child's monumental collection of three hundred and five *English and Scottish Popular Ballads*, completed in 1898. Since that date relatively few additional specimens have been been added by other experts. It is convenient for scholars to refer to ballads by the number allocated by Child in his classification. This collection is the definitive work on the subject. It is possible to dispute the inclusion of some pieces and the exclusion of others, but there is no doubt that this tremendous compilation, with its perceptive comparison of foreign analogues and themes from ancient folk-tales has resolved the field for all subsequent ballad scholars.

In general, the traditional ballad is a dramatic or humorous story in song, usually impersonal, derived from past folk culture and learnt by ear rather than from literature. Generations of oral tradition in singing have preserved certain ancient tones and inflexions, while reshaping certain formal aspects of the story. At one time or another new names and topical circumstances have become associated with older stories; for this reason ballads are more concerned with poetic insight than with historical fact.

Folk Songs, as distinct from ballads, are usually shorter, more lyrical and personal. The ballad singer is an impartial narrator of a story, whereas the singer of folk-songs expresses moods and events from his own experience. These distinctions are not absolute, and in the final analysis are only useful labels attached to stages of development of folk poetry. For general purposes, it suffices to say that ballads are things like: *Sir Patrick Spens*, *Earl Brand*, *The Two Sisters*, *The Cruel Brother*, whereas folk-songs are pieces like *The Seeds of Love*, *The Waggoner's Lad*, *The Cuckoo*, *The Foggy Dew*.

Perhaps it is really a good thing that rigid classification breaks down in this field. It is precisely the shifting changing nature of the ballad that throws light upon the evolution of musical and poetical forms and their meaning in the long life of mankind. Ballad themes, images and situations precede the ballad form itself, and are found in mythology, primitive religion, folk tales, epics, sagas, troubadour poetry, and nursery rhymes. In turn, the period of the oral tradition preceded the urban existence that generated the broadside form; the poems, songs and recitations of folk memory changed into the fixed compositions of the printed page. In one sense, broadsides are very much part of the folklore of cities.

Historically, the traditional ballad is a form of popular folk poetry that crystallized towards the end of the Middle Ages. With the decline of folk memory and the oral tradition, the broadside ballad grew out of the remains of traditional balladry, flourishing between the sixteenth and nineteenth centuries and absorbing popular poetry and song. In the eighteenth century, cultured literary interest in broadside and traditional balladry resulted in the injection of a robust and romantic strain into a poetry and literature that had become anaemic.

The period of the printed broadside ballad marks a curious exchange between two social strata. While the ballad brought romance and folk imagery into stilted literary forms, the broadside soon took over the worst affectations of polite poetry.

The Literary Ballad developed as a form in the German romantic movement led by Herder, and in Britain by Scott, Burns, Wordsworth and Coleridge. *The Rime of the Ancient Mariner* has caught much of the feeling of the old traditional ballad, although Wordsworth's "Lyrical Ballads" contain compositions nearer to a plodding broadside idiom. Indeed one wonders whether there is anything on broadsides quite so bathetic as *Simon Lee the Old Huntsman*. The main literary influence on broadsides is, of course, the high-toned Colins, Strephons and Floras of the eighteenth century sheets, and the catchpenny "culture" journalism of the nineteenth century. *I Stood Amid the Glittering Throng* is headed: "This song, which is the same as created so great a sensation at the Evening Concerts of Lady ——, but a few nights past, is set to one of the most touching and plaintive melodies ever composed by Bishop, who appears to have exerted more than his usual talent in giving effect to a Ballad, which like '*Oh,! no, we never mention her*', has been, we are told, the result of feeling on the part of its author. Madame Vestris, Miss Inverarity, Mrs. Wood, Mrs. Waylett, Miss Somerville, and Miss H. Cawse, are the ladies by means of whose most sweet warbling it will make its debut before the public."

Many of the imitations of the ballad by Scott and others now seem false and contrived, but later poets have often captured the mood and images of the ballad, notably Keats (*La Belle Dame sans Merci*), Morris (*Two Red Roses Across the Moon*), Sylvia Townsend Warner (*The Image*), W. H. Auden and Walter de la Mare.

During the nineteen-thirties, the Poetry Bookshop in London printed a series of *Poetic Broadsides*, some with designs by McKnight Kauffer; these were, however, artistic revivals and had nothing in common with the broadside ballad tradition. Modern poets like Paul Potts attempted to revive a broadside tradition by printing poems on single sheets and selling them in the street. More recently supporters of the Campaign for Nuclear Disarmament have produced and sold broadsides and garlands in traditional style.

The degeneration of the ballad form occurs in the Victorian *Drawing-room Ballads*, genteel sentimental solos characteristic of the period. Many of them were reprinted on broadsides and sung in the streets, but they were poor things by traditional standards and lacked even the robust crudity of the earlier broadsides. "I stood amid the Glittering Throng" is typical. From 1867 onwards many

"Ballad Concerts" were held in London, when genteel compositions were sung together with refined versions of old folk-songs.
Even today, such concert performances of bowdlerized folk-songs
are often mistaken for the real thing. Favourite pieces are duets like
Oh No, John! and *The Keys of Heaven,* or the clever folk-song settings
of Benjamin Britten. They are usually sung to a mannerized piano
accompaniment with impossibly coy and arch gestures from the
singers. Transitional forms between the spontaneous and the highly
sophisticated often suffer from a clash of idiom. Tones, rhythms,
singing line and mannerisms that are charming in lieder become
ridiculous in arranged folk-song sung by trained singers.

It is difficult to be impartial in assessing a hybrid form like the
drawing-room ballad. In fact, it is a valid genre in an over-refined
society; the error lies in regarding it as, in any sense, "folk" or
"traditional". There is something incongruous in a situation where
genteel singers would blush to know the frankly bawdy implications
of some of their innocent pieces.

Another amusing misconception is seen in the nineteenth
century appointment of Arthur Sullivan, famous for his collabora-
tion in the "Gilbert and Sullivan Operas", as "Professor of Piano-
forte and Ballad Singing" at the Crystal Palace School of Art . . .

Yet throughout the centuries the ballad has been a vital influence in the complex interaction of form in changing cultures.
Sometimes aristocratic, often vulgar, mysterious and beautiful,
humorous or simply topical, it has persisted. Its true history is
older than the specific forms in which it has been defined at
different dates.

Much controversy still surrounds certain questions of traditional
ballad origin. The main issues are those relating to individual
versus communal authorship, actual antiquity of the ballad form,
the relationship between versions of the same ballads in different
countries, and the connections between ballad and dance. These
questions cannot be satisfactorily settled by formal evidence.
Documentary support for various theories is too scanty for definitive
proof, and the atmosphere of scholastic interpretation and debate
is alien to real understanding of the ballad. It is true that informed
and accurate scholarship is essential in ballad study, but it must be
brought to life by actual experience of folk tradition. More can be

learnt from listening to a traditional ballad singer than by studying texts, and active participation in singing and dancing adds a new dimension to academic study. Furthermore, some philosophical and metaphysical background is essential in a field that constantly reflects the changing beliefs of past generations. If we can learn how to experience what lies at the heart of the ballad we shall resolve many questions that harass academic study.

The origin of the term "ballad" is bound up with dance, as well as song and dramatic recitation. The Latin *ballare* means "to dance", and Dance Ballads still survive in Scandinavian countries. In England, folk singing and folk dancing have gone separate ways for centuries, although the classical ballet of today is still a story told in dance. The word *ballet* has lingered over four centuries as the name for a written or printed copy of a popular song; it is the early name for a song broadside, and was still in use by isolated communities in Kentucky, U.S.A. in the early twentieth century.

The word "carol", as applied to religious folk ballads, derives from the Old French term *carole*,[1] a ring-dance such as survives in children's nursery games. Although some carols are secular, the majority are religious in subject or intention.[2]

There is no real distinction between early carols and ballads in essence, insofar as both express deep religious feeling by chant, song or dance. Some of the folk carols are nominally Christian, but their images belong to pagan religion. Most of the ballads are nominally secular, but their sturdy humour and dark dramatic stories of love and death are profound allegories of the human situation. Whatever contemporary historical references have attached themselves to ballads, there can be little doubt that the characters are supernatural beings, larger than lifesize, and the play of action springs from deep intuitive understanding of the meaning and purpose of life. These are more than everyday tales of heroes and heroines of their time. The dominant element of tragic love in the ballads and songs, as with the stylizations of the troubadour poets, hints at an original dynamic of spiritual rather than physical passion. In the traditional ballads, life is interpreted

---

[1] Mentioned in medieval romances, such as *The Chatelaine of Vergi* (translated by Alice Kemp Welch, London, 1908).

[2] Of 474 medieval carols listed by Dr. R. L. Greene (*Early English Carols*, Oxford 1935) 397 are religious.

through a cosmic tragi-comedy of archetypal images and situations.

It is this metaphysical aspect of ballad origin that has confused those scholars who are forced to value pedantry higher than intuition. Many have felt instinctively that ballads were "ancient" and used the term indiscriminately even when it was manifest that the ballad form was not earlier than the Middle Ages. But long before the ballad form itself there were epics, sagas, minstrelsy, folk tales, myths and rituals, that carried the same essential story in forms appropriate to the folk culture of their times. It is in the primal dancing and singing of the Mysteries that ballad had its birth.

Some controversy stems from a too literal interpretation of the historical evidence prior to the Middle Ages. It does not greatly matter that some ballads appear to have been written by minstrels, others by priests, and some composed by the folk. All these are aspects of an earlier tradition in which the essential quality of the ballad is an *attitude of mind* rather than a specific form. This attitude takes different forms at different periods of history.

The key to the ballad is a metaphysical one—the secret of existence itself which runs parallel with the scientific materialism which catalogues and makes use of natural phenomena. Modern interest in balladry of all kinds is unquestionably a romantic one— as life becomes more materialistic we salvage the fragments from a metaphysical past and try to find good respectable scientific reasons for doing so. Yet this materialist attitude itself defeats discovery of the metaphysical secret which cannot be expressed in material and intellectual terms.

Again, what fascinates the student of folk ballads and songs is not merely the words and the verse form, but the *manner of singing*. Certain tones and inflexions have great antiquity, and the oral tradition is a living unwritten history in itself. It may be assembled from fragments of singing style, equally from city street singers, from country folk, even from the chanting of children's nursery rhymes. At one time or another, these tones and inflexions have passed between priest, minstrel and peasant; they have an uncanny power, just as did the magic spells from ancient times.

In the British Isles there were Bards and Skalds and Gleemen from earliest history. They were the musicians and poets, and music and poetry were the arts of religion, although the gods were pagan in those days. When Christianity came, the pagan cults were christianized, and remnants of this may be found in some old folk carols where the power of pagan images still dominates a nominally Christian form, as in the various versions of *Down in Yon Forest* (*The Falcon Hath Bourn My Make Away*):

> "Lully, lulley, lully, lulley,
> The falcon hath bourn my make away.
>
> He bare him up, he bare him down,
> He bare him into an orchard brown.
>
> In that orchard there was a hall
> That was hanged with gold and pall.
>
> And in that hall there was a bed,
> It was hanged with gold so red.
>
> And in that bed there lieth a knight,
> His woundes bleeding day and night.
>
> By that bedside kneeleth a may,
> And she weepeth both night and day.
>
> And by that bedside there standeth a stone
> Corpus Christi written thereon."
>
> (*From the Hill Manuscript—Balliol, MS. 354*)

The unearthly power and beauty of some of the folk ballads and songs is due to the combination of ancient oral style with the archetypal images of birth, death, the changing seasons, and the human situation.

There are many complex elements in the growth, diffusion and elaboration of religion and ancient minstrelsy. Even at an early date, two distinct sorts of Minstrel began to emerge—the Bard proper, with an aristocratic background of bardic colleges, and the *jongleur*, or travelling minstrel. In the development of feudal forms of society, minstrels were given place of honour as entertainers to kings and nobles, yet at the same time a more popular type of minstrel would travel throughout the country singing for the common people who had not yet lost contact with their own traditions. Meanwhile, the specifically religious subject-matter of songs and ballads had become secularized, and stories of the old gods were overshadowed by histories of heroic warriors, praises for the patron and his wife, or even political satires. Later on, traditional songs and the newer forms of popular topical ballad tended to become more preoccupied with the contemporary social scene, in all its growing diversity, than with the religious mysteries of existence.

This is, of course, the world process. Religion becomes politics— not only the politics of contending parties, but of policy, expediency and establishment. As Stevenson says: "The very saints, in the exercise of living, become less dainty, and take on the tone of their surroundings."—(*Markheim*).

Throughout ballad history, religious and secular subject-matter have run side by side. If the ancient world lived too much in the clouds, perhaps the modern world is too preoccupied with practical affairs. Ballad study itself can become an empty museum of titles, versions, names and dates, unless restored by living tradition.

The primal origin of the oral tradition itself, the dynamic of all traditional utterance, belongs to mythology and religion. In many religious concepts the world is an emanation from one primordial sound—the Word of God in the Gospel of St. John, the Tetragrammaton of the Greeks and Hebrews, the Parabrahman "AUM" of the Hindus.

In India, *Sangita*, the triple art of Music, Dance and Drama, was born from the gods. We know that the Mysteries were danced by the Greeks, and the *choros* of their tragedies was a group dance-song. The Greek modes, taken over by European church music and still used by folk singers, are fractions of the tremendously complex musical culture of India, and can be equated with the secondary *ragas* of the Karnatic system. Many of the epic poems of India contain images and themes that have persisted in folk tales throughout Europe, as far as Scandinavia. Familiar situations from balladry take on startling clarity when seen in the context of ancient Indian metaphysical literature. For example, the questions and answers of "Riddles Wisely Expounded" (Child No. 1) have primary significance viewed in the light of the seventy riddles of the Rakshasi *Karkati* in the "Yoga Vasishtha-Maharamayana" of Valmiki.

The dominant elements in ballad survival are undoubtedly vestiges of the great Aryan migrations of ancient times, stemming from the common source of Indo-European tradition. If this should seem a more far-fetched antiquity than the speculations of eighteenth century antiquaries like Bishop Percy, it is only necessary to point to two astounding parallels.

The first is from the *Rig-Veda*, one of the most ancient Hindu scriptures. Some Indologists believe these hymns to date from the twelfth century B.C.; Indian scholars have calculated an alternative date five thousand years before the Christian era. Undoubtedly the verses of oral tradition are earlier than any date assigned by scholars for their collation by the sage Vyasa.

> "Purusha (Lord) has a thousand heads, a thousand eyes, a thousand feet. . . . From that universal sacrifice sprang the Ric and Saman verses, the metres and Yajush (*i.e.* all scripture, etc.). From it sprang horses, and all animals . . .; kine sprang from it. . . . When (the gods) divided Purusha, into how many parts did they cut him up? What was his mouth? What arms had he? . . ."
>
> (Abbreviated from *Rig-Veda*, x,90;
> MUIR, *Sanskrit Texts*, 2nd edition, i.9)

Compare the whole complex of European magical and humorous folk-songs of the *Derby Ram, Cutty Wren, Jolly Herring, Wonderful Crocodile* type, where monstrous animals are hunted, killed and divided; it will be noted that the form of such songs is often question and answer relating to the manifold applications of the parts of such mythical creatures. A version of the "Cutty Wren" chanted in Carmarthenshire in the nineteenth century runs:

> "O, what will you cut her up with? says Milder to Malder,
> O, I cannot tell, says Festel to Fose,
> With knives and forks, says John the Red Nose,
> With knives and forks, says John the Red Nose . . ."
> (From MASON, M. H., *Nursery Rhymes and
> Country Songs*, 1877, p. 47)

Frazer's *Golden Bough* contains many examples of sacrificial hunting; it is perhaps ironic that the central Mystery of killing the divine animal should descend through the centuries to a children's nursery rhyme.

The second quotation is from *Brihadaranyaka Upanishad*, another Hindu scripture, and elaborates a similar theme to the *Rig-Veda* extract:

"In the beginning this was Self alone, in the shape of a person (Purusha). He looking round saw nothing but his Self. He first said, 'This is I'; therefore he became I by name . . . But he felt no delight. Therefore a man who is lonely feels no delight. He wished for a second. He was so large as man and wife together. He then made this his Self to fall in two, and thence arose husband and wife. Therefore Yajnavalkya said: 'We two are thus (each of us) like half a shell.' Therefore the void which was there, is filled by the wife. He embraced her, and men were born. She thought, 'How can he embrace me, after having produced me from himself? I shall hide myself.' She then became a cow, the other became a bull and embraced her, and hence cows were born. The one became a mare, the other a stallion; the one a male ass, the other a female ass. He embraced her, and hence one-hoofed animals were born. The one became a she-goat, the other a he-goat; the one became a ewe, the other a ram. He embraced her, and hence goats and sheep were born. And thus he created everything that exists in pairs, down to the ants. . . ."

(1st adhyaya, 4th brahmana; from MÜLLER,
Sacred Books of the East)

Compare with the ballad "The Two Magicians" (Child No. 44) and its numerous analogues in folk tales like "Farmer Weathersky" (DASENT: *Popular Tales from the Norse*):

"She turnd hersell into a hare,
    To rin upon yon hill,
And he became a gude grey-hound,
    And boldly he did fill.
        O bide, lady, bide, &c.

Then she became a gay grey mare,
    And stood in yonder slack,
And he became a gilt saddle,
    And sat upon her back.

Was she wae, he held her sae,
    And still he bade her bide;
The rusty smith her leman was,
    For a' her muckle pride. . . ."

(Text collected by PETER BUCHAN: *Ballads of
the North of Scotland*, Edinburgh, 1828)

Both the themes and some of the form of these extracts from ancient Hindu scriptures have been preserved in European folk tale, song and ballad. These themes—miraculous emanations, and magical transformations from copulation—are aspects of the same primordial story; they are Creation myths. . . .

The story of mankind is that of the emergence of infinite variety from singularity—from the first creative acts come the animal, mineral and vegetable kingdoms, from the earliest human parents come the million millions of the human family, the myriad data and inter-relationships of the cosmos. This is the story chronicled by myths, epics and sagas, by hundreds of ballads and thousands of songs, traditional and topical. The form and subject-matter change and expand, but the authentic tones of the minstrel can still be heard in the street. The costermonger, the newspaper-seller, the cheapjack and entertainer of the market-place share an oral history with the priest and politician.

Some of the sacred sounds of priests may today be no more than a cry in the streets. Magic from an old clothes man or a porter on British Railways! . . .

THE BROADSIDE BALLAD

"Ye Maidens and Men, come for what you lack,
and buy the Fair Ballads I have in my pack"

CHAPTER THREE

THE BROADSIDE BALLAD

THE cry in the streets that has sustained religions and unseated kings has travelled the centuries in many forms; it has also reached the antiquary in his study, poring over the history of past times.

"Fine ballads! New ballads, what lack ye?"[1]
"Come buy of me, come; come buy, come buy!"[2]
"Ballads! My masters, ballads!
Will you ha' o' the newest and truest matter
in all London? I have of them for all choices,
and over all arguments too. Here be your
story-ballads, your love-ballads, and your
ballads of good-life . . ."[3]

It is the antiquary who has preserved the evidence of these flimsy sheets, but the voices of the singers and the crowds are far off. There are great collections of broadsides in the libraries of the world and much scholarship has been expended on them, but one essential element is lacking in the studies—the living sound of the times. . . .

It was a centuries-old tradition of minstrels and country folk singing traditional songs and ballads that was channelized into the Broadside Ballad of the sixteenth century. A certain number of these songs and ballads found their way on to the printed sheets, since they were old favourites, especially to city-dwellers losing touch with their own folk heritage. At this date, however, *any* popular or topical verse that could be sung to a new or old tune began to be called a "ballad". Indeed, Coverdale's Bible of 1535 even describes the Song of Solomon as "Salomon's Balettes".

[1] From *Dodsley's Old Plays*, quoted by ROLLINS in *The Black-Letter Broadside Ballad*.
[2] SHAKESPEARE, *The Winter's Tale*.
[3] From *The Exchange in all its Humour* . . . quoted by ROLLINS in *The Black-Letter Broadside Ballad*.

We have seen that the Broadside Ballad combined two elements —the Broadside, a printed sheet of paper, and the Ballad, once a special traditional song, but now any kind of popular or topical verse. Dating from the early days of cheap printing, each sheet usually contained the words only, together with a decorative wood-cut illustration; these sheets satisfied equally the need for news and the nostalgia for tradition. Near-relations of the broadside ballad, valuable for supplementary study, are the various proclamations, garlands, chapbooks, almanacks, religious and political pamphlets which embodied the same spirit of the times in a modified format. In order to sell their sheets, ballad-sellers would sing them loudly in the streets and at country fairs. Most people remembered the old tunes, and the sheet of words would call up the new pieces.

Thus we see that the broadside ballad brings together many different strains. The true past history includes the ballads that were *not* written down or printed but sung and learnt traditionally, and the perennial popular interest in such "song histories" was the mainspring for the successful form of the printed ballad. Traditional and topical ballads were sung side by side, and some topical ballads even became "folk" by passing into oral tradition.

Although the general trend of broadside balladry was towards everyday topics and trivia, the broadsides never completely lost contact with the impulse to understand the meaning of life and the human situation, the urge that had dominated ancient myth and ritual and helped to shape the traditional ballad. In the broadside period the focus had shifted from a mystical background to material affairs, yet there were echoes of older heroic outlines of wonder, terror and uncertainty in the mundane marvels, moralizing and doctrinaire clashes of religious and political formality. The broadside was not a new phase of human activity but rather a convenient chapter in an ageless story. The act of printing was, so to speak, merely superimposed on an oral tradition that had already found new directions.

*   *   *

Much obscurity surrounds the date of the first printed sheets. We do not know how many of these flimsy pieces of paper may have been destroyed during the centuries, how many may have met the fate originally destined for the famous Percy Folio Manuscript of the first part of the eighteenth century. Bishop Percy discovered this unique collection of ballads and songs, written down around 1650, being used by the maids to light fires at the house of his friend Mr. Humphrey Pitt.

Manuscript collections of ballads existed before the invention of printing. In a book by the Rev. S. Baring-Gould there is an illustration of two ballad singers captioned "from a Broadside". A man is playing a pipe, while a woman with a balladsheet under her arm is singing. It is not possible to tell whether the balladsheet is meant to be manuscript or print, but the illustration itself is one which first occurred in Caxton's *Mirrour of the World*, printed in 1481.[1] Doubtless manuscript balladsheets were offered by sale by early street singers. In contrast one remembers the deception of the earliest printers, when the Bibles of Gutenburg and his associates were hawked around at bargain prices without disclosing that they were not manuscript productions! One of our earliest religious ballads comes from a thirteenth century manuscript; this is the ballad of "Judas" (Child No. 23).

We know that broadsides were printed in the fifteenth century, but so far as we can trace, these were all ecclesiastical documents (papal bulls, licences to confessors and indulgences). Some of the earliest German printing consisted of single sheets bearing a woodcut of a saint; one of these picture broadsides is dated 1423. The earliest printed broadsides in England were the work of Caxton, one issued in 1477 is an advertisement for a book, the *Sarum Ordinale*.

Ballad broadsides were undoubtedly printed in the early part of the sixteenth century. How many we cannot tell. Few sheets ever bore a printed date, so there is some uncertainty about those that have survived, apart from any that *may* have been in existence.

Broadsides were very useful as wastepaper, particularly in bookbinding, so it is possible that there are still rare sheets waiting to be discovered in the covers of early books.

Amongst the earliest printed ballads, we should give pride of place to "The Ballade of the Scottysshe Kynge", which was found in stripping off the cover of *The Romance of Huon of Bordeaux*. The

---

[1] Reproduced on page 12.

D

book was printed in Paris in 1513, but the binding had been done in England. The ballad was written by John Skelton, Poet Laureate to Henry VIII; it concerns the Battle of Flodden Field which took place on September 9th, 1513, so we are fairly safe in dating the ballad for that year.

There is also a long poem called "The Nut Browne Mayde" printed around 1503. This might be considered a ballad, but as it forms part of a book miscellany we cannot class it as a broadside. It was reprinted in 1718 by Matthew Prior to demonstrate how he had improved it in his poem of "Henry and Emma", and it was adversely criticized by Dr. Johnson. In 1760, however, it was republished in its own right in Capell's *Prolusions, or Select Pieces of Antient Poetry*.

Much nearer to the broadside format is *A Lytel Geste of Robyn Hode*, circa 1506. This is an early pamphlet printed by Wynken de Worde, now in the University Library, Cambridge. There is another undated copy of this long Robin Hood ballad, printed in Antwerp between 1510 and 1515. It is in a volume of ten other pieces in the National Library, Edinburgh, all *circa* 1508. One is from an unknown printer, and nine are from the first Scottish press of Chepman and Myllar, Edinburgh. There is a version of (*Sir*) *Eglamour*, a "Ballade" beginning "In all oure gardyn growis thare na flouris", a metrical romance of *Golagrus and Gawain*, and ballad type poems by John Lydgate and William Dunbar.

These are sparse fragments, but we know from manuscript sources of other ballads that were being sung up and down the land. Special mention should be made of *Ladye Bessiye* (Percy Folio MSS. iii, p. 319), a beautiful and poignant piece of history with all the best of traditional ballad style. Skelton's ballad of Flodden can be supplemented with two manuscript pieces: *Scotish Feilde* and *Flodden Feilde* (Percy Folio i, p. 199, and p. 313).

The printed sheets date from the latter period of Henry VIII's reign, but long before that, political and religious ballads were exercising great influence upon public opinion. As far back as the fourteenth century, the popularity of ballads of Robin Hood and other outlaws reflected a growing anti-clericalism. In the fifteenth and early sixteenth centuries the tremendous religious upheavals before and after the Reformation were to be echoed in the broadsides.

There are tantalizing gaps in our broadside history. In 1520, John Dorne, a bookseller of Oxford, sold from his shop more than one hundred and ninety unnamed ballads. We do not know their titles or format, and no ballad broadsides have been discovered until a good fifteen or twenty years after that date.

The earliest surviving sheets are religious ones: *Luther, The Pope, and a Husbandman* was printed about 1535, and *A Ballad on the Downfall of Thomas Lord Cromwell* in 1540. In 1533 a proclamation was issued for the suppression of "fond books, ballads, rhimes, and other lewd treatises in the English tongue", and it is known that in 1537 a certain John Hogon was arrested for singing a political ballad. Many repressive measures against ballads, ballad-singers and printers were to follow, yet the broadside grew and multiplied.

Cromwell was Henry VIII's minister during the campaigns against the Church of Rome; his fall from grace delighted the papal party. Other ballads were published supporting the Protestant party, and this broadside ballad warfare is reflected in a group of eight balladsheets in the collection of the Society of Antiquaries, London.

So the broadside ballad was born, in a period of social upheaval, with religion and politics as its main preoccupations, with the ecclesiastical edict and the royal proclamation as its immediate ancestors. Soon the range of subject-matter rapidly expanded to include marvellous signs and wonders, monstrous births, merry love songs, and all the gossip of the day.

The popularity of the new street ballads coincided with the steady decline of the traditional and professional minstrel, and by the period of Elizabeth I, minstrels had become legally ranked with rogues, vagabonds and beggars. The printed balladsheet must have contributed largely to the downfall of ancient traditional balladry in favour of new popular street songs. Who would pay a minstrel to sing long old-fashioned ballads of far-off times when you could buy a smart up-to-date broadside for one penny? Besides, in a period of great changes the emphasis was on topicality.

The popularity of street ballads was the subject of stern comment from the church, and "spiritualization" of ballads began at an early date. A typical example is Miles Coverdale's *Goostly Psalmes and Spirituall Songes* of 1538. Coverdale complained:

> "Wolde God that our Mynstrels had none other thynge to play upon, neither our carters and plowmen other thynge to whistle upon, save psalmes, hymns, and such like godly songes. . . . And if women at the rockes (flax distaffs), and spinnynge at the wheles, had none other songes to pass their tyme withall, than such as Moses' sister . . . songe before them, they should be better occupied than with 'Hey, nonny, nonny—Hey, trolly, lolly,' and such like fantasies."

So spiritually elevating songs were written to the tune of bawdy street ballads, a practice that has left traces in modern times when the Salvation Army still sing hymns to popular song melodies. As Wesley and others have remarked: "Why should the devil have the best tunes?" . . .

In 1543, an Act was passed "for the advancement of true religion, and for the abolishment of the contrary". It stated that "froward and malicious minds, intending to subvert the true exposition of scripture, have taken upon them, by printed ballads, rhymes, etc., subtilly and craftily to instruct his highness' people, and specially the youth of this his realm, untruly. For reformation whereof, his majesty considereth it most requisite to purge his realm of all such books, ballads, rhymes, and songs, as be pestiferous and noisome . . ." It is notable, however, that a number of books printed before 1540 (including *Canterbury Tales* and other works by Chaucer) were exempted from this prohibition. It is somewhat surprising that in face of repeated harsh legislation the ballad continued to make steady headway.

We move on safer ground in the dating of early broadside ballads from 1556 onwards, when the Stationers' Company was incorporated and began to require legal registration of ballads in the following year. The fee for a ballad was fourpence. Although many ballad-printers ignored registration, the Company's registers give us a representative survey of popular street ballads from 1557 to 1709, the first great chapter in broadside ballad history. There are over three thousand entries. These records are fascinating, reminding us of many songs that still survive as an oral tradition in the countryside.

An entry for March 4th, 1588, reads:

"John Wolfe to print 3 ballads,
one is 'Goe From My Window, Goe'."

This is a particularly interesting song, still sung in the West Country in the late nineteenth century. It has also been collected as a *cante-fable*, a folk-tale with interpolated song sequences. A spiritualized version was circulated in 1590 in *Ane Compendious Booke of Godly and Spirituall Songs*, a famous religious collection of such pieces. The original song was very popular in the reign of Elizabeth I and frequently quoted in plays; it is mentioned in Beaumont and Fletcher's *Knight of the Burning Pestle* and also in Heywood's *Rape of Lucrece*.

December 14th, 1624, was an interesting date, when no fewer than one hundred and twenty-eight ballads were licensed, including many familiar titles, such as:

"THE BLIND BEGGAR (OF BETHNAL GREEN)"
"(LORD) BATEMAN"
"THE KING AND THE SHEPHERD"
"SIR JOHN BARLEY CORNE"
"JANE SHORE"
"GEORGE BARNWELL"
"CHEVIE CHASE" (probably first written in 1548)
"JERUSALEM, MY HAPPIE HOME"
"THE KING AND THE TANNER"
"THE LORD OF LORNE"
"SPANISH LADY"
"FORTUNE MY FOE" (this was sung to the tune of "GREENSLEEVES")...

Many of these are good traditional ballads. Others are the cheap newspapers of their period, hastily printed and circulated amongst eager crowds that have long passed away. Some of the sheets remain but many have been lost. Here are a few typical titles from the press of the Widow Toye, wife of Robert Toye the printer who died around 1555:

"THE DAY OF THE LORDE YS AT HANDE"
"WOMEN BESTE WHEN THEY BE AT RESTE"
"THE MURNYNGE OF EDWARDE DUKE OF BUCKYNGHAM"

"A MAYDE THAT WOLDE MARY WITH A SERVING MAN"
"AN EPYTAPH UPON THE DEATH OF KYNGE EDWARD YE SIXTE"
"I WILL HAVE A WIDOW YF EVER I MARYE"

Broadside ballads are of enormous importance for the light they throw upon the everyday interests, activities, events and opinions of the common people over several centuries. Textbook history is so often a matter of great names and dates and ruling monarchs. The broadsides show us a *living* history. William of Malmesbury, in his account of Athelstan, says: "Thus far relating to the King, I have written from authentic testimony: that which follows I have learned more from old ballads, popular through succeeding times, than from books written expressly for the information of posterity. I have subjoined them, not to defend their veracity, but to put my readers in possession of all that I know."[1]

John Aubrey, seventeenth-century author of the delightful and curious *Miscellanies*, mentions that his nurse could repeat the history of England from the Conquest to the time of Charles I in ballads.

There are several aspects to be considered in relating ballads to history. Traditional ballads tended to romanticize and falsify history by building topical references into earlier dramatic situations. Their value, like that of myth, is metaphysical and poetical, not factual.

Some of the newly composed broadside ballads presented clear, reasonably accurate reports, others were written to excite public opinion and did not hesitate to stretch facts to support a partisan view. Sometimes the incidental detail of a ballad may interest the historian as much as the foreground action. In the ballad of *Ladye Bessiye* there is a line: "the shott of guns were soe ffree", which illustrates the use of artillery at the battle of Bosworth Field, 1485.[2]

It is not possible to give here a detailed analysis of the interconnections between broadsides and the historical events of their period. This has been done elsewhere with fine scholarship by Chappell, Firth, Rollins and others. A few general points can be mentioned.

[1] *Gesta regum Anglorum, Lib. II*, trans. Rev. John Sharpe, London, 1815.
[2] See FIRTH, *The Ballad History of the Reigns of Henry VII and Henry VIII*, London, 1908

Religion and politics were popular, if dangerous, subjects throughout the dramatic and colourful periods of social change between Henry VIII and the Commonwealth of 1649. Between them, topical street broadsides and old country songs helped to create popular journalism. Even the titles of many pieces read like newspaper headlines:

"AN ANSWER TO A PAPISTICALL BYLL, CAST IN THE STREETES OF NORTH-AMPTON, AND BROUGHT BEFORE THE IUDGES AT THE LAST SYSES, 1570"

"A WARNING TO LONDON BY THE FALL OF ANTWERP"

"A VERY LAMENTABLE AND WOFUL DISCOURS OF THE FIERCE FLUDS, WHICHE LATELY FLOWED IN BEDFORDSHIRE, IN LINCOLNSHIRE, AND IN MANY OTHER PLACES, WITH THE GREAT LOSSES OF SHEEP AND OTHER CATTEL. The v. of October, Anno Domini 1570"

"THE DESCRIPTION OF A RARE OR RATHER MOST MONSTROUS FISHE TAKEN ON THE EAST COAST OF HOLLAND THE XVII. OF NOVEMBER, ANNO 1566"

Here are a few more titles that demonstrate the typical range of subject-matter:

"THE WONDERS OF ENGLAND, 1559"

"THE DESCRIPTION OF A MONSTROUS PIG, THE WHICH WAS FARROWED AT HAMSTED BESYDE LONDON, 1562"

"THE VAILLIANTE ACTS OF GUY OF WARWICK" (1592)

"THE MERCHANTE'S DAUGHTER OF BRISTOLE" (1595)

"SIR WALTER RALEIGH'S LAMENTATION" (1618)

"THIS MAID WOULD GIVE TEN SHILLINGS FOR A KISS"

"DAMNABLE PRACTISES OF THREE LINCOLNSHIRE WITCHES"

"A MERRY NEW SONG HOW A BRUER MEANT TO MAKE A COOPER CUCKOLD, AND HOW DEERE THE BRUER PAID FOR THE BARGAINE"

"GOOD ALE FOR MY MONEY"

"CELIA'S COMPLAINT FOR THE LOSS OF HER VIRGINITY"

"THE SOULES PETITION AT HEAVEN GATE"

Towards the end of the sixteenth century there appeared a curious marriage between ballad, drama and dance—the Jig. This was usually in the form of a dance dialogue, often of a bawdy nature, and would be performed at the conclusion of a play. The words were printed and sold on broadsides. The Jig (or Droll) perhaps represents the last echo of the early connection between ballad and dance. . . .

Broadsides suffered a temporary setback during the Common-wealth period, when stage players and ballad singers risked the pillory and whipping post, or worse. None the less, the Puritan repression of popular music and dance has been sometimes overemphasized. In Queen Elizabeth's reign an act had prescribed that convicted minstrels be "grievously whipped and burned through the gristle of the right ear with a hot iron of the compass of an inch about", and third offence could entail "death without benefit of clergy or privilege of sanctury". Yet the street ballad flourished during the Elizabethan period! Furthermore Playford's *Introduction to the Skill of Musick* was published during the Puritan period, and his *English Dancing-Master* first appeared in 1650. The Restoration period is, of course, marked by greater freedom of expression in song and drama, and many bawdy ballads date from that time.

* * *

Who wrote the street ballads? At first, poets and authors like John Skelton and John Heywood, priests like William Forrest and Leonard Stopes. Many others—poets, courtiers and churchmen—wrote anonymously. Soon arose a class of professional balladist, and while some writers risked extreme penalties for circulating their chronicles, others secured favour by pandering to patrons and popular sentiment in a kind of broadside journalism. Of the latter class were writers like William Elderton and Thomas Deloney. Elderton, sixteenth century actor, comedian and ballad writer was famous for his love of liquor, and his red nose was as celebrated as Tom D'Urfey's long one. A fellow-scribbler of Elderton's composed these lines:

> "Will Elderton's red nose is famous everywhere,
> And many a ballet shows it cost him very dear;
> In ale, and toast, and spice, he spent good store of coin;
> Ye need not ask him twice to take a cup of wine.
> But though his nose was red, his hand was very white,
> In work it never sped, nor took in it delight;
> No marvel therefore 'tis, that white should be his hand,
> That ballets writ a score, as you will understand."

D'Urfey, friend of Charles II, will be remembered as the editor of the famous *Wit and Mirth, or Pills to Purge Melancholy*, an important collection of songs and ballads which has always excited violently conflicting opinions. Addison wrote in *The Guardian* (No. 67): "I must heartily recommend to all young ladies, my disciples, the case of my old friend, who has often made their grandmothers merry, and whose sonnets have perhaps lulled to sleep many a pleasant toast, when she lay in her cradle." The otherwise broad-minded Rev. S. Baring-Gould, many years later, comments: "The fun so commended by the pious and grave Addison is filth of the most revolting description" . . .[1]

In the sixteenth and seventeenth centuries it was fashionable for poets and playwrights to disparage popular ballad writing and singing. Shakespeare has made many such references in his plays. However, one need not take these witticisms too seriously, since both playwright and balladist wrote to please the people. Ben Johnson's remark that "a poet should detest a ballad-maker" is perhaps answered by D'Urfey's comment a generation later: "The Town may da-da-damn me for a Poet, but they si-si-sing my Songs for all that."

The tavern poet was a natural target for the sarcasm of more aspiring writers, but he remained the backbone of broadside balladry right down to comparatively modern times. A typical early judgement is that of William Webbe in his *A Discourse of English Poetrie*, published 1586:

"If I let passe the uncountable rabble of ryming Ballet makers and compylers of sencelesse sonets, who be most busy, to stuffe every stall full of grosse devises and unlearned Pamphlets: I trust I shall with the best sort be held excused. Nor though many such can frame an Alehouse song of five or sixe score verses, hobbling upon some tune of a Northen Iygge, or Robyn hoode, or La lubber etc. . . . yet if these might be accounted Poets (as it is sayde some of them make meanes to be promoted to ye Lawrell) surely we shall shortly have whole swarmes of Poets: and every one that can frame a Booke in Ryme, though for want of matter, it be but in commendations of Copper noses whose pottical poeticall (I should say) heades, I would wyshe, at their worshipfull commencements might in steede of

[1] BARING-GOULD, S., *Songs of the West* (intro.), London, 1905.

Lawrell, be gorgiously garnished with fayre greene Barley, in token of their good affection to our Englishe Malt."

Yet these men often swayed the loyalties of the multitude from the scribble of an Elizabethan tavern as much as the modern journalist from a Fleet Street pub. Even the inaccuracies and exaggerations of the ballad writers show us how public opinion was formed in the social movements of the times. In 1703, Andrew Fletcher wrote the following shrewd comments, as an account of a conversation:

". . . Even the poorer sort of both sexes are daily tempted to all manner of lewdness by infamous ballads sung in every corner of the streets. One would think, said the Earl, this last were of no great consequence. I said, I knew a very wise man so much of Sir Christopher's sentiment, that he believed if a man were permitted to make all the ballads, he need not care who should make the laws of a nation. And we find, that most of the antient legislators thought they could not well reform the manners of any city without the help of a lyric, and sometimes of a dramatic, poet . . ."

*   *   *

The eager, jostling living tide of humanity that surged through the streets and houses has passed away, leaving, with the dying echo of many voices, only a few scraps of paper. These have become the prize of the antiquary and the scholar. The sheets once priced at one penny have become precious and costly testaments— "antique ballads, sung to crowds of old, now cheaply bought for thrice their weight in gold."

Most of the broadsides of the sixteenth and seventeenth centuries were printed in the quaint old Gothic type known as **Black-Letter.** Judging by the surviving specimens, the size of the folio sheets varied considerably, ranging from 14 to 16 inches by 8½ to 10 inches, usually somewhat larger than a modern foolscap. The broadsides in many famous collections have been closely trimmed and do not give a reliable indication of their original size.

Early sheets often had the verses printed in four columns, and were sometimes cut into two separate leaves; individual leaves being sold separately. Some balladsheets with very long pieces were sold serially in two sheets, the continuation carrying the formula "The Second Part, to the same tune". Many seventeenth and early eighteenth century sheets printed the verse in three wide columns; some examples are illustrated in the present collection.

Ballad titles were displayed over a crude woodcut, the lettering often being a pleasant mixture of Gothic and Roman type, sometimes a larger type than the verse. In the body of the ballad, proper names were often printed in roman letters with the rest of the text in Black-Letter. Some sheets exhibited from one to four crude woodcuts, and produced an artistic effect by the use of decorative borders. At the end of the sheet was the name and address of the printer—those romantic colophons beloved by balladsheet collectors:

> "Printed for P. Brooksby, at the Golden Ball, in West Smithfield."
> "Printed for J. Deacon at the Angel in Guilt-Spur-street, without Newgate."
> "Printed by M. F. for Tho: Lambert, and are to be sold at the signe of the Horse shooe in Smithfield."
> "Printed by C. Bates at the Sun and Bible in Pye-Corner."

Black-Letter Ballads held a peculiar fascination for antiquaries and great collections were made, one of the most famous being that of Samuel Pepys. This was a continuation of an early collection begun by John Selden. It is now housed in the Pepysian Library at Magdalene College, Cambridge; it contains 1,800 ballads, of which 1,376 are in Black-Letter.

Another great collection is the Roxburghe Ballads, commenced by Robert Harley, Earl of Oxford, who died in 1773. The collection passed through various hands, notably those of John, Duke of Roxburghe in 1788. It contains more than thirteen hundred broadsides, mostly in Black-Letter, and is at present in the care of the British Museum, London. Celebrated though the Roxburghe Collection is, it should be said that the beautifully mounted sheets are in poorer condition than lesser-known collections, and have all been trimmed to fit the page.

There is also in the British Museum a small collection of 225 Black-Letter Ballads with the Shelf-Mark C.22,f. 6. These are in superb condition and the sheets are untrimmed. Many of the ballads are merry and bawdy ones, from which I quote:

"you'l never get her up, Or Love in a Tree,
Being a pleasant new Song, shewing how a Maid
was got with Child without lying with a Man.
        To the tune of, Buggering Oats prepare thy Neck."
"the lancashire cuckold: or, the
Country Parish-Clark betray'd by a Conjurer's
Inchanted Chamber-pot.
        To the tune of, Fond Boy, &c."
"virginity grown troublesome: or,
The Younger Sisters Lamentation for want of a Husband.
Being a most pleasant and delightful New Song
much in Use, &c."

Appropriately enough, the gilt Royal Arms stamped on the
cover of the red leather binding bears the motto "Honi Soit Qui
Mal y Pense" . . .

Undoubtedly much of the fascination of eighteenth-century
ballad collection was due to the great number of such lusty and
bawdy ballads on the Black-Letter sheets. In an age of genteel
literature, ballad collection might rank as a secret vice! Perhaps
the antiquary is the best person to assess the morals of a past age
without false prudery. In the late nineteenth century, under the
auspices of the Ballad Society, London, the Rev. Joseph Woodfall
Ebsworth dedicated himself to the reprinting of the Roxburghe
and Bagford Ballads, unexpurgated, and spent his own time and
money in brilliant scholarship, albeit in a field somewhat ambi-
guous for a parson. His introductions abound in special pleading
for his unconventional enthusiasms:

> "The Editor is willing to defy misconstruction, as to his motive in
> giving back to the world these 'shady' memorials. That he was re-
> quested to do so, might exonerate him sufficiently. But there is a
> stronger defence. The social anatomist is justified in dealing with a
> morbid subject for the preservation of health. No sympathy need be
> felt with sickly squeamishness, or with prurient prudery . . ."

This spirited defence was prefixed to the reprint of *The Poor
Whore's Complaint to the Apprentices of London* and similar pieces.

Ebsworth, Vicar of Molash by Ashford, was an unusual character, fond of gypsies and vagabonds in the manner of George Borrow,
and with a romantic attachment to Charles II and the Cavalier

cause. Apart from his devoted work for the Ballad Society, Ebsworth had another connection with the ballad tradition as brother-in-law of Sam Cowell, the famous comic singer who immortalized "The Ratcatcher's Daughter" . . .

In the eighteenth century, Addison was one of the earliest writers to express a genuine interest in what he called "the darling songs of the common people". In his periodical, *The Spectator*, he wrote:

"... for it is impossible that any thing should be universally tasted and approved by a Multitude, tho' they are only the Rabble of a Nation, which hath not in it some peculiar Aptness to please and gratify the Mind of Man."

If this sounds a little condescending, it must be remembered that it was written in 1710, fifty-five years before the publication of Bishop Percy's *Reliques of Ancient English Poetry*. Percy's genuine enthusiasm for ballads, whatever his shortcomings as an editor, crystallized a growing literary trend away from artificiality towards the robust beauty of popular and traditional balladry. Literary figures of the past gave ballads a special place in their affections. As Addison wrote:

"The old song of CHEVY-CHASE is the favourite Ballad of the common People of England, and Ben Johnson used to say he had rather been the Author of it than of all his Works. Sir Philip Sidney in his Discourse of Poetry speaks of it in the following words: 'I never heard the old Song of Piercy and Douglas, that I found not my Heart more moved than with a Trumpet; and yet it is sung by some blind Crowder (minstrel) with no rougher Voice than rude Stile; which being so evil apparelled in the Dust and Cobweb of that uncivil Age, what would it work trimmed in the gorgeous Eloquence of Pindar?' For my own part I am so professed an Admirer of this antiquated Song, that I shall give my reader a Critick upon it, without any further Apology for so doing . . ."

The great Dr. Johnson remarked of this same ballad of *Chevy-Chase* that it was a masterpiece of "chill and lifeless imbecility", but in spite of this and other caustic condemnations of the ballad form he was a good friend of Bishop Percy and approved the publication of his collection.

One of the earliest and most important published collections of broadside ballads is the three volume work ascribed to Ambrose Phillips, printed between 1723 and 1725: *A Collection of Old Ballads. Corrected from the best and most Ancient Copies Extant. With Introductions Historical and Critical.* The title page quotes from Rowe's drama of "Jane Shore":

> "Let no nice Sir despise the hapless Dame;
> Because Recording BALLADS chaunt her Name.
> Those Venerable Ancient Song-Enditers
> Soar'd many a Pitch above our modern Writers . . ."

In a somewhat tongue-in-cheek introduction to the second volume, the editor praises Addison and comments: "And I cannot but observe here, that when the Great Sir Philip Sidney commends the Old Song of Chevy-Chase, his Commendation is in a much ruder Stile than the Ballad itself . . ."

The influence of Percy's *Reliques* was considerable, but ultimately it led to the collection and appraisal of traditional ballads and songs rather than to study of the broadside. Yet by a strange misunderstanding, the imitations of the ballad, like the appraisals of Addison, were invariably related to the broadside form. It is astonishing to think that Percy's noblest ballads should have as companions such offerings as Shenstone's *Jemmy Dawson* or Grainger's *Bryan and Pereene. A West Indian Ballad!*

From the eighteenth century onwards, cultured interest in the ballad grew, but it was not until the period between Sir Walter Scott and Professor Francis James Child that clear distinctions between broadside ballads and traditional ballads began to evolve. In more modern times, the period of great folk-song collectors like the Rev. S. Baring-Gould and Cecil Sharp is notable for laying proper emphasis on the *music* of the ballads and the singing style, instead of the literary form of the words.

There are some strange and ironic tangles in the story of the ballad in its many forms. While collectors were hoarding their precious Black-Letter sheets, and learned scholars like Percy and Ritson fiercely disputed the accuracy of old manuscripts, many of the pieces were still being sung in the countryside by people with more feeling for a good song than an old piece of paper.

Many of the songs and ballads still current in the twentieth century are probably from broadsides of two centuries back which, in their time, had copied old country pieces!

There is a beautiful folk song in oral tradition in England and America which is usually called *Ten Thousand Miles* ("The True Lover's Farewell"). One version runs:

> "Now fare thee well, my own true love,
> Now fare thee well for a while.
> 'Though I go far away I will surely come again,
> 'Though I go Ten Thousand Miles, my dear,
> 'Though I go Ten Thousand Miles. . . ."

Now there is a broadside in the famous *Osterley Park Collection* called "The Unkind Parents, or The Languishing Lamentation of two Loyal Lovers". The first verse is as follows:

> "Now fare thou well my Dearest Dear,
> And fare thou well a while,
> Altho' I go I'll come again;
> if I go ten thousand mile, Dear Love;
> if I go ten thousand mile. . . ."

(There is also a literary working over of this theme by Robert Burns in "My love is like a red, red rose".)

Now the broadside version was printed between 1690 and 1702, and may well be based on a folk-song of the period. Yet the modern oral tradition is too close to be other than an offshoot of the broadside. We already know from Walton's *Compleat Angler* (1653) that country folk assimilated printed texts at an early period:

> "I entered into the next field, and a second pleasure entertained me: 'twas a handsome milk-maid, that had cast away all care, and sung like a nightingale; her voice was good, and the ditty fitted for it; 'twas that smooth song which was made by Kit Marlow, now at least fifty years ago; and the milk-maid's mother sung an answer to it, which was made by Sir Walter Raleigh in his younger dayes."

(This must have been *The Passionate Shepherd to his Love*—"Come live with me and be my love", with Raleigh's *The Nymph's Reply to the Shepherd*—"If all the world and love were young".)

Country people always loved a good song, and a popular poem

that caught their fancy stood a chance of continuing side by side
with ancient traditional pieces, sometimes being reshaped into a
truer folk idiom by generations of singers. Walton tells how the
milkmaid's mother says to him:

> "If you will but speak the word, I will make you a good sillabub,
> and then you may sit down in a hay-cock and eat it, and Maudlin
> shall sit by and sing you the good old song of the *Hunting in Chevy-
> Chase*, or some other good ballad, for she hath good store of them:
> Maudlin hath a notable memory."

The fresh open air of the countryside and the voice of the milkmaid are a long way from the musty air of the antiquary's study.
Some of the greatest collections of Black-Letter ballads were
undoubtedly those which were stuck on the walls of cottages and
inns. The good-humoured Walton says: "I will now lead you to an
honest ale-house where we shall find a cleanly room, lavender in
the window, and twenty ballads stuck about the wall." Addison
confessed: "I cannot for my heart leave a room before I have
thoroughly studied the walls of it, and examined the several printed
papers which are usually pasted upon them."

Yet there is a strange charm in the manias of antiquaries. One
can hardly fail to be infected by the gushing enthusiasm of biblio-
philes like the Rev. T. F. Dibdin, who will be remembered for his
bold attempt surreptitiously to list the titles of the Percy Folio
Manuscript at a time when it was kept away from the public eye.
In his *Library Companion; or, The Young Man's Guide, and the Old
Man's Comfort, in the Choice of a Library* (1825) he enthuses over a
rare collection of Christmas Carols:

> "Nearly approaching the preceding in rarity, and of considerably
> greater interest from its contents, both in quantity and character, is
> the UNIQUE copy of Christmas Carols, possessed by Francis Freeling,
> Esq., from the press of that 'cunning' typographical wight, *Richard
> Kele*. . . . It is a very small doudecimo volume, containing, in the
> whole, twenty-four leaves; and has been pretty fully described in the
> *Typ. Antiq.* vol. iv., page 304. . . . See also the *Bibliographical Mis-
> cellanies*, Oxon, 1813, 4to, page 48, where copious extracts from it
> appear. Ah, that 'longe shop' of Master Richard Kele!—there be
> many of my acquaintance who would make '*short work*' with its con-

tents, could they now be collected into one tangible form! Think, amongst other things, of those pretty little Skeltonic 'bits' printed in three parts (mentioned as in the library at Ham House, p. 661, *ante*) which produced, at the sale of Mr. Bindley's library, the sum of 31*l*. 10*s*."

The Black-Letter type was discontinued on broadsides about 1700, and with its passing went also much of the enthusiasm of collectors, in spite of the fact that ballads were still being printed. The title-page of the Pepys Collection reads:

"My Collection of Ballads. Vol. I. Began by M[r] Selden; improv'd by y[e] addition of many Pieces elder thereto in Time; and the whole continued to the year 1700. When the Form, till then peculiar thereto, viz[t] of the Black Letter with Picturs, seems (for cheapness sake) wholly laid aside, for that of the White Letter without Pictures."

The "White Letter" is roman type, but there is a curious misunderstanding in the suggestion that ballads subsequent to 1700 did not have woodcuts. Such illustrations continued to flourish right up to the end of the nineteenth century.

The original two volumes of the Roxburghe Collection, collected by Robert, Earl of Oxford, before the addition of the Duke of Roxburghe and others, also concluded in the year 1700, as may be seen from the title:

"ANCIENT SONGS AND BALLADS:
Written on Various Subjects, And
Printed between the Year MDLX and MDCC. . . ."

With the passing of Black-Letter type, something else had also gone out of broadside balladry at the opening of the eighteenth century. It did not die, by any means, but slackened perceptibly before gathering its resources for its second and last great period at the opening of the nineteenth century. The stage was being set for great social changes; when these reached their dramatic climax there came a staggering output of broadside printing, and a myriad voices lifted in popular song—perhaps for the last time in modern history.

E

WHITELETTER BALLADSHEETS

LONG SONG SELLER

"Two under fifty for a fardy!"

CHAPTER FOUR

WHITELETTER BALLADSHEETS

THE Whiteletter balladsheets at the opening of the eighteenth century were not substantially different in subject-matter from the seventeenth century sheets. There were love songs, bawdy songs of country wenches, songs of wars and especially of politicians. These sheets have always faithfully mirrored the range of human preoccupations between religion and politics. Old favourites were reprinted and new songs issued, although on the whole there seem to have been fewer sheets.

There were, however, some interesting developments in format, and a number of offshoots of the broadside form. The eighteenth century established the convention of the single column "slip" ballad, usually with the woodcut at the top and displayed title underneath it, and often with another decorative cut at the foot of the sheet. Many sheets did not bear the printer's imprint. The size of the single slips was usually about 4½ by 16 inches, roughly approximating to the earlier folio sheets slit lengthwise.

It must not be thought that the Black-Letter type continued uniformly up to 1700 before its disappearance. A great many of the seventeenth century sheets are in roman type; only the mystique of the bibliophile rates these lesser than the romantic Black-Letter.

The eighteenth century is the grand period of Chapbook activity. Links with a longpast tradition of folk balladry and storytelling had become weakened, and the folklore that mothers and nurses once carried in their memories could now be revived only by the chapman's booklets. These were the cheap libraries of ordinary folk, and indeed, forerunners of the cheap paperback novels of today. From our point of view they are simply broadsides folded into booklet form. The chapbooks had a wider range of material than the street ballads, although these were also to be found in their repertoire. Chapbooks have been classified as: Religious, Diabolical, Supernatural, Superstitious, Romantic, Humorous, Legendary, Historical, Biographical and Criminal, and they included ballads and songs (traditional and broadside), stories, jokes and almanacks.

Here are some typical titles:

"THE HISTORY OF DR. JOHN FAUSTUS"

"A FULL TRUE AND PARTICULAR ACCOUNT OF THE GHOST OR
   APPARITION OF THE LATE DUKE OF BUCKINGHAM'S FATHER"

"THE OLD EGYPTIAN FORTUNE TELLER'S LAST LEGACY"

"TOM THUMB"

"A TRUE TALE OF ROBIN HOOD"

"THE HISTORY OF MOTHER SHIPTON"

"MERRY FROLICKS"

"THE UNHAPPY BIRTH, WICKED LIFE, AND MISERABLE DEATH OF THAT
   VILE TRAYTOR AND APOSTLE JUDAS ISCARIOT"

"THE HISTORY OF THE MOST RENOWNED QUEEN ELIZABETH AND HER
   GREAT FAVOURITE THE EARL OF ESSEX"

"THE PLEASANT AND DELIGHTFUL HISTORY OF JACK AND THE GIANTS"

"JOE MILLER'S JESTS"

"BATEMAN'S TRAGEDY"

"PATIENT GRISSEL"

"THE DRUNKARD'S LEGACY"

"THE SURPRIZING LIFE AND MOST STRANGE ADVENTURES OF ROBINSON
   CRUSOE"

One of the most famous chapmen was Dougal Graham, born in Stirling in 1724, and famous in later life as the "skellat bellman" of Glasgow. He joined Bonnie Prince Charlie's army as a camp-follower in 1745 and later published a *Metrical History of the Rebellion*.

Perhaps the significant development during the chapbook periods is the disintegration of the oral tradition. Much of the material is still validly that of the broadside, but now the ordinary folk were reading prose rather than singing verses. Outside the towns, newspapers were virtually non-existent; those that circulated in polite society were brief and dull sheets of wars, foreign intelligence, political activity, and polished essays. For most ordinary folk, traditional and topical material were equally welcome subjects, but a desire had begun to set in for something more substantial than simple songs.

In cultured society, music had been undergoing many changes since the days of motets and madrigals. Classical instrumental compositions and professional composers were adding a new dimension to music. Broadside ballads were temporarily quietened by the new voices of Opera. This exciting vocal strain harmonized with the formation of glee clubs and concerts, and the elevation of the professional singer.

Italian opera was all the rage of polite society until John Gay wrote his famous "Beggars' Opera" in 1727. This remarkable production was an extraordinary mixture of folk tradition and polite sophistication, and had an enormous success. It opens with a dialogue between a ragged beggar and an actor. The beggar explains that he has written this piece "for celebrating the marriage of James Chanter and Moll Lay, two most excellent Ballad-Singers". There are over sixty songs in the "Beggars' Opera", all well-known street and folk airs set to new words.

Just as Bishop Percy's *Reliques* was to make balladry presentable for literature, so Gay's opera, less than forty years earlier, popularized folk airs for the world of refined and genteel music. Both innovations were ahead of their times. The literary ballads of Wordsworth and the German Romantic Revival led away from traditional balladry, while the songs of John Gay and the forty other ballad-operas which followed only diverted folk airs into sophisticated channels.

One important development of the age was the institution of Pleasure Gardens, like Vauxhall, Marylebone and Ranelagh, where music and song were a regular attraction. These were the cultured forerunners of the more vulgar Music Halls which became a feature of the nineteenth century. Both developments left their mark on broadside literature.

In the reign of Queen Anne and during the early Hanoverian period, there was a vogue for elaborately engraved sheets with the music and words of songs. These were called "Half-sheets", and are a somewhat sophisticated offshoot of the broadside. Dr. Blow's *Amphion Anglicus*, published in 1700, contains the following verses:

"Long have we been with balladry oppress'd;
Good sense lampoon'd, and harmony burlesqu'd:
Music of many parts hath now no force,
Whole reams of Single Songs become our curse,
With bases wondrous lewd, and trebles worse.
But still the *double entendre* takes the town.
They print the names of those who set and wrote 'em,
With Lords at top and blockheads at the bottom;
While at the shops we daily dangling view
False concords by Tom Cross[1] engraven true."

"Buy a bill of the play"

[1] A famous eighteenth century music engraver, proud of his skill.

There was an artificial and theatrical quality about the eighteenth-century songs which was to culminate in the robust burlesques of the Music Hall. Stereotyped fake-pastoral characters, shepherdesses and "Colins", with conventional references to the sun as "Fair Phoebus" had also featured at the start of the century, but they were usually animated by the robust and folk bawdry of Playford and D'Urfey. Now they were to become lay figures and posture side by side with Dibdin's Jolly Jack Tars. All through the century, concerts, operas and plays dignified popular song by removing it from the amateur field of the streets to the refined setting of the professional performance, with special harmonies and instrumental parts. Here is a group of late eighteenth-century street broadsides which shows the increased preoccupation with professional performers and shows:

"THE COUNTRYMAN'S RESOLUTION TO LEAVE LONDON, AND PARTAKE OF THE PLEASURES OF THE COUNTRY. A New Song."

"REASON: OR, THE UNWILLING MAID AND AMOROUS SQUIRE.
    A New Song."

"THE JOVIAL SAILORS.
    Sung by Mr. Beard. In the *Fair Quaker of Deal*."

"ADMIRAL KEPPEL TRIUMPHANT;
    Or Monsieurs in the Suds."

"A NEW SONG:
    Called the true blue on the defeat of the french fleet, by the honourable Augustus Keppel, Admirel of the blue, on the 27th of July. The words fir TIMOTHY WAGPOLE."
        (*this naval encounter was in 1778*).

"A NEW SONG.
    Sung by Mr. WILLSON. In the *Duenna*."
        (*Sheridan's "Duenna" was first performed in 1775*)

"A NEW SONG.
    Being a Dialogue on the S(t)ate of the Nation between two British Tars."
        (*mentions Charlestown and the American War*).

"WATER PARTED FROM THE SEA.
    A NEW SONG.
    Sung this SEASON. At all the Places of PUBLICK DIVERSION.
        (*the most popular song from Arne's "Artaxerxes", first performed in 1762*)

"THE MILLER AND MAID.

    A New Song. Sung by Miss FORMANTEL. At Vauxhall."

"I'D RATHER BE EXCUS'D.

    A New Song. Sung by Mrs. MARTYR. At Vauxhall."

"THE REFLECTING NYMPH.

    A New Song. Sung by Mrs. MATTOCKS. In the CHAPLET."

"MYRTILLA.

    A New Song. Sung in the Publick Gardens."

"THE LONDON DAMES.

    A New Song. Sung at Sadler's Wells."

"A NEW SONG.

    Sung by Mrs. MATTOCKS. In the Farmer."

        ("To hear a sweet goldfinch's song . . .")

"THE WARS ARE NOT OVER."

Just as a century earlier the broadside collector noted the change from Black-Letter to Whiteletter type, so he saw the movement from eighteenth century to nineteenth marked by the final disappearance of the long "s".

Behind the typographical variation there were significant social changes. The gilded life of the towns and cities could not conceal the parcelling out of the land and the dispossession of the countryman. The price of bread was rising and in 1800 there were food riots. The wars were certainly not over. After the troubles abroad with the French Revolution and the loss of the American Colonies there were new headlines on the broadsides, with the familiar names of Napoleon, Trafalgar, Waterloo, Pitt, Burke and Fox. An interesting offshoot of the broadside in the Hanoverian period was the rise of the political cartoons—those savage satires of Rowlandson and Gillray. These are, in effect, picture broadsides.

The Victorian period is one of startling contrasts. Under the cheerful philanthropic façade of the 1830s lay the underworld of the big cities—the gin-shops, penny gaffs, unemployment and grinding poverty; a world of paupers, murderers, criminals and baby-farmers, where little boys were put to climbing chimneys and women and children worked in the coalmines. It was also the age of progress—of railways, industrialization, social reformers, music-halls and pleasure gardens, Alfred Lord Tennyson, *Punch* magazine, and the Bloomer costume. . . . All these and many other themes are reflected in the street broadsides. The following headings show the range of subject-matter:

NEWS.   Politics, Wars, Murders and Executions. Curiosities of history—the Tichborne Trial, the "Boy Jones", the Franklin expedition, wife-sales, fashions (crinolines, bloomers, chignons, etc.).

RELIGION.   Moral stories on sheets and in chapbooks. (At the turn of the century John Evans & Sons had issued many of these, and later on printed for the Religious Tract Society.)

HARD TIMES.   Songs of poverty, transportation, conscription, and social injustice.

HUMOUR.   Frolics, *Countryman in London*, Music Hall, and the modern "minstrelsy" of the Ethiopian Serenaders: *Jump Jim Crow*, *Ole Dan Tucker* and other American pieces.

Here are a few titles:

"THE BELFAST MOUNTAINS"

"NEW SADLERS WELLS"

"THE STAGE STRUCK HERO"

"NAPOLEON TALKS OF WAR BOYS"

"THE ROVING BATCHELOR"

"ON ALMA'S HEIGHTS"

"THE STRIKE OF THE LONDON CABMEN"

"HERE'S A HEALTH TO THE HARD WORKING MAN"

"A NEW SONG OF THE BLOOMER COSTUME"

"PRETTY PEGGY OF DERBY"

"THE LIVERPOOL LANDLADY"

"WHAT'S OLD ENGLAND COME TO?"

"POOR OLD JOE"

"THE BLUE TAILED FLY"

"DANCE DE BOATMEN"

"THE BLESSINGS OF PEACE"

"COME INTO THE GARDEN MAUD"

"SOLDIER'S FAREWELL TO MANCHESTER"

"I'D CHOOSE TO BE A DAISY"

"PLEASE, GIVE ME A PENNY, SIR"

"THE NEW-FASHIONED CRINOLINE"

"I HAVE NO MOTHER NOW"

"CHEER, BOYS, CHEER!"

"A LIFE ON THE OCEAN WAVE"

"THE LAY OF THE LASH"

"OH! NO WE NEVER MENTION HER"

"AUSTRALIA IS OUR HOME"

"WOODMAN SPARE THAT TREE!"

"A COUNTRYMAN'S RAMBLE TO LONDON"

"THE IRISH BRIGADE IN AMERICA"

"LIFE OF AARON DAVIES, THE CHRISTIAN COLLIER"

"UNCLE TOM'S CABIN"

"THE MANIAC" . . .

The list could be an endless one. If there were fewer broadsides in the eighteenth century there was certainly a phenomenal output in the nineteenth. In the first half of their last hundred years, a flood of thousands upon thousands of sheets issued from an increasing number of printers.

One is astounded and sometimes overwhelmed by the sheer weight of material. The Baring-Gould Collection in the British Museum contains nearly twelve thousand broadsides, mostly from the nineteenth century, when one London printer alone advertised "upwards of five thousand different sorts of ballads".

All the social contrasts and kaleidoscopic changes of the period are faithfully mirrored in the broadside sheets. Now the broadside flowered in all its diverse forms. There were sellers of Theatre Playbills, street stationery, shorthand cards, Galleries of Comicalities, Conundrums, Topical and Magical Delusions (with Engravings), chapbooks and tracts. There were many separate varieties of song salesmen: chaunters, long-song sellers, song-book sellers, patterers (running or standing), statue-posers, pinners-up (who referred to "songs" not "ballads"), and many others. There are interesting factual details and firsthand accounts of popular street literature and its vendors in HENRY MAYHEW's magnificent nineteenth-century study *London Labour and the London Poor* (4 vols.). Although the original editions are long out of print, a slightly abridged version is currently available in three volumes.

It was during the nineteenth century that some of the last of traditional folk-song as we know it was being gathered by enlightened collectors. Many of the old country songs made their final appearance on the broadsides, things like:

"THE CRUEL SHIP'S CARPENTER"

"THE BOLD FISHERMAN"

"COLD BLOWS THE WIND"
"SIR JOHN BARLEYCORN"
"POLLY OLIVER'S RAMBLES"
"MY BONNY LAD IS YOUNG"
"THREE MAIDENS A MILKING WOULD GO"
"BLOW THE CANDLES OUT"
"THE GOLDEN GLOVE"
"THE SHEFFIELD APPRENTICE"
"DABBLING IN THE DEW"
"THE MANTLE SO GREEN"
"HIGH GERMANY"

Some of the real traditional ballads from olden times can also be found on these sheets:

"CAPTAIN WARD AND THE RAINBOW" (Child No. 287)
"THE BOLD PRISONER" (version of "ARCHIE O' CAWFIELD", Child No. 188)
"THE OUTLANDISH KNIGHT" (version of Child No. 4)
"BARBARA ALLEN" (Child No. 84)

It was common practice to print two or three items on the same sheet, and good traditional material was often balanced by topical and genteel songs, rather in the manner of the A and B sides of modern gramophone records.

Much has been said on the question of broadside versions of traditional songs and ballads. A few years ago it was fashionable to disparage the broadsides as "corrupt", "decadent" and "inferior" versions of the country tradition, just as in earlier times antiquaries had pontificated about country songs being a corrupt and imperfect recollection of written copies. Nowadays we are not so sure about some of the details of the intermarriage between the two streams of tradition—written and oral.

The original impulse in balladry belongs to an ancient past, but ever since the written tradition came into being it has helped to reinforce and stabilize oral tradition, and in some instances has given rise to new oral traditions. Many old ballads and most of the so-called traditional country songs are found on broadsides, and it is often difficult to decide which came first. There is occasional evidence of folk singers learning from printed sheets. In *English*

County Songs, Broadwood and Maitland state: "The spread of ballads in England was of course due to the pedlars, who sold ballad-sheets with their other wares ... only last year (1891), an old carter in Surrey, said he had one of his songs 'off a ballet' a long time since." Other writers have stated that nineteenth-century balladmongers rewrote the traditional material for broadside publishers who paid them a shilling apiece for such songs, but the easiest way to earn the money was surely to put down the words exactly as heard in travelling through the country. Indeed, most balladsheet versions seem nearly as accurately noted as those garnered by modern collectors. But when were they first written? By now it is very difficult to tell. Take a cheerful nineteenth century Anglo-Irish broadside piece like *Brian O Linn*:

> "Brian O Linn, his wife and wife's mother,
> Were all going home o'er the bridge together,
> The bridge it broke down, and they all tumbled in,
> 'We'll go home by the water,' says Brian O Linn."

"Thom Of Lin" is the name of a dance mentioned in the *Complaynt of Scotland* (1549), while a stage comedy by William Wager *circa* 1575 has a character quote lines from old songs, including:

> "Tom a Lin and his wife, and his wife's mother,
> They went over a bridge all three together,
> The bridge was broken and they fell in,
> The devil go with all, quoth Tom a Lin."

Again, some Anglo-American folk-songs often end with the couplet: "There's bread and cheese (*or* 'a bridle') upon the shelf, if you want any more you can sing it yourself." This sounds modern, but it is also in Wager's sixteenth century play:

> "I layde my bridle upon the shelfe,
> If you will any more sing it yourself."

Many of the nineteenth-century broadsides echo phrases and forms from a remote past, lost even to the oral tradition.

The dominant elements in balladry are those of poetic imagery, archetypal situation, and evocative sounds (apparently meaningless refrains or names of characters). These were shaped into different poetical and musical forms during the centuries. Around the

Middle Ages many were written down; in the sixteenth century they were printed. Circulation of printed sheets in the countryside gave rise to a whole new crop of variations. Many of the traditional country songs current today probably originated in seventeenth-century variation of broadside copies of earlier oral tradition, thus setting in movement two new streams of printed and oral tradition for the same songs. Today we can no longer be sure of the "purity" of an oral tradition, and must acknowledge the valuable function of the balladsheet in preserving and helping to form tradition. This was, however, largely an unconscious service performed by cheapjacks and tavern writers whose main aim was to make a little money in hard times.

The centre for broadside printing in nineteenth century London was Seven Dials, described by Charles Dickens in his early *Sketches by Boz*:

"Seven Dials! the region of song and poetry—first effusions, and last dying speeches: hallowed by the names of Catnach and of Pitts—names that will entwine themselves with costermongers and barrel-organs, when penny magazines shall have superseded penny yards of song, and capital punishment be unknown! ... Long rows of broken and patched windows expose plants that may have flourished when 'The Dials' were built, in vessels as dirty as 'The Dials' themselves; and shops for the purchase of rags, bones, old iron, and kitchen-stuff vie in cleanliness with the bird-fanciers and rabbit-dealers, which one might fancy so many arks, but for the irresistible conviction that no bird in its proper senses, who was permitted to leave one of them, would ever come back again. Brokers' shops, which would seem to have been established by humane individuals, as refuges for destitute bugs, interspersed with announcements of day-schools, penny theatres, petition-writers, mangles, and music for balls or routs, complete the 'still life' of the subject; and dirty men, filthy women, squalid children, fluttering shuttlecocks, noisy battle-dores, reeking pipes, bad fruit, more than doubtful oysters, attenuated cats, depressed dogs, and anatomical fowls, are its cheerful accompaniments."

Here, in these surroundings, pot-poets were hired to write doggerel on any topical events,[1] or to recall some country folk-

---

[1] Today the calypso singers of the West Indies improvise topical verses to order; these compositions are often published on gramophone records.

song, just as in the days of Queen Elizabeth nearly three centuries earlier. The price was a shilling a time with a quire of free copies, occasionally half a crown for an unusual ballad.

One of the most famous of the London broadside printers was James Catnach, who started his business at No. 2, Monmouth Court, Seven Dials, with an old wooden press which his father had used at Alnwick and Newcastle. Catnach's father had published a number of books with illustrations by the famous Thomas Bewick, whose beautiful cuts and engravings have become collector's items. "Jemmy" Catnach brought many of these blocks with him, and some of his most vulgar and sensational broadsides are dignified by the delicate and fascinating woodcuts of Bewick.

Catnach commenced printing in 1813, and in the following twenty-five years became the leading publisher of popular street literature. He printed any songs, old or new, but his most profitable broadsides were the Murder sheets, the "Last Dying Speeches and Confessions" that were the forerunners of the sensational Sunday newspapers. Some of the most famous murders of the time were those of Corder (Maria Marten of the Red Barn), Rush, the Mannings and Weare. It was common practice for some street poet to compose what was called "A Copy of Verses written by the Culprit", supposed to be found on the floor of the cell before the execution—a strange echo of the former dignity of speeches from the execution block in the sixteenth and seventeenth centuries. The price for the modern ghost-writer was the standard figure of one shilling.

One street author said: "I gets a shilling a copy for the verses written by the wretched culprit the night previous to his execution." Another comments: "I did the helegy on Rush. I didn't write it to horder; I knew that they would want a copy of verses from the wretched culprit. And when the publisher read it: 'That's the thing for the streets,' he says. But I only got a shilling for it." A gloomy comment from a third street author: "It's the same poet as does 'em all, and the same tip; no more nor a bob nor nothing."

No royalties in those days! Catnach sold 2,500,000 copies of the verses on Rush! Such circulation figures would have been the envy of early newspaper proprietors. As one street broadside seller of the period remarked: "There's nothing beats a stunning good murder . . ."

This "gallows-literature" is very valuable to the present-day collector, because it helps to date the period at which broadside printers were operating. It should be pointed out, however, that the dates specified so precisely on these sheets were often inaccurate by a day or two, as the printers rushed out their sheets without the facilities of the modern press. The Library of the Inner Temple, London, contains a collection of 128 of these sheets in two volumes. The specimens date from 1722 to the late nineteenth century and include examples of three consecutive sheets from the same printer, each giving a different or corrected date for a murder, arrest, or execution.

To Jemmy Catnach belongs the dubious distinction of creating a new category of broadside—the "catchpenny". Catnach cleared £500 on the sale of sheets of Weare's murder and the trial of Thurtell. After the execution he put out another sheet with big headlines: "WE ARE ALIVE AGAIN!" with so little space between the words "WE" and "ARE" that it looked as if the dead Mr. Weare had been miraculously revived. As it was only the headlines that the street sellers need show before purchase, thousands of these sheets were bought by an innocent public. Those who objected to this swindle aptly named it a "catch-penny"; many similar frauds were perpetrated. Another favourite trick was the printing of false news of murder or scandal at a time when genuine news was scarce. Such narratives were cleverly written up with convincing vague phrases like "a certain party", "Miss M——", "not far from this neighbourhood", and came to be called "cocks".

Catnach revived the popularity of the garlands—sheets and pamphlets of songs—and introduced the standard size of modern Crown quarto (about 10 by 7½ inches) for his broadsides. Single slips, price one halfpenny, were obtained by cutting the sheet into two. Some sheets had three or four songs on them.

Another Catnach innovation was the "Long song-sheet"— "Three yards a penny!" Actually the sheet was hardly one yard long, but in three columns; the street sellers would hint at incredible value for money by pinning up three long sheets together. . . .

F

Broadside publication had many of the problems of newspaper editorship. A contemporary of Catnach writes:

"I happened to call one day on an artist for the illustrated press, and found him busily engaged in sketching a funeral procession with some twenty coffins borne on the shoulders of men who were winding their way through an immense crowd. Upon inquiry, I was told that it was intended for the next week's issue, and was to represent the funeral of the victims of the late dreadful colliery explosions, for although the inquest was only just then sitting, and all the bodies had not yet been found, there was sure to be a funeral of that kind when it was all over, and as they did not know how many bodies were to be buried at one time, it was very cleverly arranged to commence the procession from the *corner of the block*, and so leave it to the imagination as to how many more coffins were coming in the rear . . ."

Careful inspection of broadside prints shows a surprising similarity between the alleged portraits of different murderers "drawn from life". In fact the same old block served for the ballad seller's flamboyant claim: "Here you have also an exact likeness of the murderer, taken at the bar of the Old Bailey by an eminent artist"!

There is a magnificent volume of Catnach prints in the Printing Library of St. Bride Foundation, London; these specimens were obtained by Mr. George F. Wilson from a descendant of Catnach. St. Bride houses Mr. Wilson's wonderful collection of street literature, as well as the Talbot Baines Reed collection of chapbooks.

Most of Jemmy Catnach's fortune was accumulated in coppers, so he used to take them to the Bank of England in large bags in a hackney coach. His neighbours would not change them for silver, dreading infection from the filthy coins collected by his broadside sellers. Eventually Catnach used to boil up the coppers in strong vinegar and potash to make them look like new coins. But all his workers were obliged to take their wages in copper, and at week-end would bring their wives or mothers to help them carry home anything from ten to forty shillings all in pennies and halfpennies.

Catnach naturally attracted more attention than other printers. He was the first and last great entrepreneur in the field, and was something of a "character". After his death, James Paul who had worked for him entered into partnership with Catnach's sister

Mrs. Anne Ryle. The business later passed to William S. Fortey, who reissued many of Catnach's sheets from stereos.

Catnach's great rival was John Pitts ("Toy and Marble Warehouse, No. 6 Great St. Andrew Street, London"). The Pitts family was well established at the time that Catnach started business; early sheets published for "J. Pitts" were first printed by C. Sheppard around 1787. Some of the first Pitts sheets bear a close resemblance to the large folio sheets of J. Evans, Long Lane, London. They are on paper tinted blue or green and without woodcuts, long prosy verse tales with "Garland" titles very much in a traditional idiom. The nineteenth century quarto-size sheets from Pitts are also on rough tinted paper, but with attractive woodcuts. The Pitts sheets are of very great interest, as they include many country songs, as well as town songs in the country style.

One Pitts sheet is worth special mention:

> "THE ROAST BEEF OF OLD ENGLAND,
> Cantata; by Young D'Urfey.
> Sold by J. Pitts, 14 Great St. Andrew Street, Seven Dials
> —price Three ha:fpence."

It is possible that the enhanced price was to attract buyers at one penny. . . . Little is known about the Pitts family. Frank Kidson in an essay on ballad printing writes:

> "It was about the beginning of the 19th century that *J. Pitts* first appeared. It is said that 'Johnny' Pitts was really a female who had been a bum-boat woman, serving the fleet with 'soft-tack' and a thousand and one other things, no doubt including ballad-sheets. . . Pitts probably disappeared from the ballad-printing world about 1815."[1]

As mentioned earlier, "J. Pitts" published in 1787. The other errors in this passage are probably due to a hasty reading of Hindley's *Life and Times of James Catnach* which states (p. 49):

> "At the time Jemmy Catnach commenced business in Seven Dials it took all the prudence and tact which he could command to maintain his position, as at that time 'Johnny' Pitts, of the Toy and Marble Warehouse, No. 6, Great St. Andrew Street, was the acknowledged and established printer of street literature for the 'Dials' district;

[1] *The Ballad Sheet & Garland* (Journal of the Folk-Song Society, No. 7, 1905).

therefore, as may be easily imagined, a powerful rivalry and vindictive
jealousy soon arose between these 'two of a trade'—most especially
on the part of 'Old Mother' Pitts, who is described as being a coarse
and vulgar-minded personage, and as having originally followed the
trade of a bumboat woman at Portsmouth . . ."

A footnote quoting George Daniel's *Democritus in London* makes
it clear that 'Johnny' Pitts and 'Old Mother' Pitts were two
separate persons. Hindley also says (p. 160): "During Catnach's
absence from London on the Alnwick election, his old rivals—the
Pitts family—were, as usual, concocting false reports, and exhibit-
ing lampoons . . ." This was the election of 1826, so it is unlikely
that "Pitts probably disappeared from the ballad-printing world
about 1815". Moreover in Robson's *London Directory* for 1820
(compiled 1819) I find an entry: "John Pitts, printer. 6, Gt. St.
Andrew's St. 7 Dials".

Two later printers claimed to take over the Pitts business:
Michelson of Clerkenwell Green, and Mrs. E. Hodges of Dudley
Street (and, later, Grafton Street), London. According to Mr.
Coote of the Folklore Society, lecturing in 1879, the business and
stock of "Mr. Pitt," was taken over about 1848 by Mr. W. S. Fortey
who, it will be remembered, also inherited the business of Jemmy
Catnach, Pitt's rival. However this may be, there is no doubt that
the Pitts family were publishing very interesting broadsides and
chapbooks for a great many years.

There is a fairy-tale atmosphere in Mr. Coote's description of
his search for a Pitts chapbook of the popular tale "Catskin",
known for so many centuries in many different countries under a
variety of names. This heroine was *Zuccaccia* in Italy, *Allerleirauh* in
Germany, *Afanassief* in Russia, *Peau d'Âne* in France, and *Rashie
Coat* in Scotland. She was known too in Spain, Lithuania, Greece,
Albania and, much earlier still, in ancient India. Mr. Coote says:

"Towards the end of last February a feeling of prevision took me to
Monmouth Court, Seven Dials, to the shop of Mr. W. S. Fortey,
printer and publisher of what literature still survives in that somewhat unsavoury locality, and there I learnt what follows:—

Thirty years ago his house took over from Mr. Pitt, a printer of the
neighbouring Little St. Andrew Street, his business, his copyrights,
and his unsold stock. Our re-discovered Catskin was amongst the

latter and the new purchasers continued to print and sell her story until about twenty years ago, when the public demand flickered and its re-production ceased. Old narrative poetry of this sort had been superseded by more appetizing pabulum. A similarly once popular ballad, called the *Fish and the King*, shared the same fate at the same time. Since that epoch Catskin has never been set up. She and her old-world sister, still unsold, were relegated to the obscurity of a garret in Monmouth Court, and there they are. 'It would take three or four whole days to look them through,' said Mr. Fortey, 'and without that looking through there would be no chance of finding Catskin.' Her ballad, I further learnt, was a little (penny) book, adorned with four woodcuts, perhaps one to each canto."

One of the earliest versions we know of the Catskin tale is the 18th hymn of the 8th book of the *Rig-Veda*, a pre-Brahmanic narrative of the young nymph Apata. This Cinderella heroine of a Vedic myth older than the Aryan migrations of ancient times travelled for thousands of years in many countries from the Himalayas to the British Isles, a royal princess destined to lie in captivity in the squalor of a Seven Dials garret.

There were other migrations. During the eighteenth and nine-teenth centuries, English ballad printers exported many broad-sides and chapbooks to America. At the same time, American printers had begun to issue their own sheets, some from the oral tradition of settlers, others copied from the English broadsides. From the seventeenth century onwards, English settlers in America had brought ballads and songs with them from both oral and broadside traditions, and by now it is very difficult to disentangle their interconnections. When a Kentucky folk singer recalls that he learnt a ballad "from his grandsire", we can roughly estimate a period when this piece became part of a family oral tradition, but how did his grandsire pick up the ballad? Was it part of the tradi-tion of his forebears in some quiet English village? Did some early relative learn it from a sheet sold by an itinerant ballad singer at an English country fair? These are complexities waiting to be unravelled and it is not yet too late. The rich oral tradition of ballads and folk-songs in America has been exhaustively collected and annotated. The printed tradition of broadside ballads is equally well represented by the collections in American public libraries, notably New York, Chicago, Boston and Providence, and in universities like Yale and Brown. As might be expected, the Houghton Library of Harvard University contains a magnificent collection of English and American broadsides and chapbooks; special mention should also be made of the Isaiah Thomas Collection of Ballads at the American Antiquarian Society, Worcester, Massachusetts. A recent major contribution to the analysis of the printed and oral traditions is the excellent study *American Balladry from British Broadsides* by G. Malcolm Laws (Philadelphia, The American Folklore Society, 1957).

Both the printed and oral traditions of nineteenth century America and England owe much to Irish emigration; hundreds of popular pieces carry echoes of Gaelic verse in their internal rhythms and stresses:

"On a *Monday* morning *early*, as my wandering steps did *lade* me
Down by a farmer's *station* and the meadows and green *lawns*,
I heard great *lamentation* the small birds they were *making*,
Saying, 'We'll have no more *engagements* with the boys of
Mullabaun.' "[1]

The Dublin printer P. Brereton deserves passing notice, as his sheets contain more inspired misprints to the square inch than any other at any time. His "AN ELEGY ON THE DEATH OF THE MUCH LAMENTED DOCTOR D M QBRIEN" opens: "Yon sous aad you dnuters of Frins bless'd natiou" . . .

During the nineteenth century there were more than fifty ballad printers in London, and many more in every large town and city. The business arrangements between publishers and printers, and the reissue of stocks, often involved a bewildering multiplicity of imprint on sheets. Here is an example:

"Bebbington, Printer, 26, Goulden-street, Oldham Road,
Manchester; sold by H. Andrews, 27, St. Peter-street,
and J. Beaumont, 176, York-street, Leeds.
Printed and Sold Wholesale & Retail by J. Wrigley,
3, Rochdale-road"

All this appears on one sheet!

It is difficult to realize, thumbing through old thin scraps of paper, that these thousands upon thousands of songs were printed

[1] Quoted from COLUM, Padraic. *Broad-Sheet Ballads*. Dublin, n.d.

to be *sung*. For more than fifty years the streets were filled with sound. There were songs to suit every taste and for every occasion. As well as traditional and topical ballads there were reprints of poems by Moore, Burns, Tennyson, Hood, Dickens, and many other authors. There is an anecdote told of Thomas Campbell, the poet, stopping to listen to a London street singer surrounded by an eager crowd. "I think I know that song," said Campbell. "Of course you do," said a friend. "It is your own 'Exile of Erin'." "Ah!" rejoined the author of "The Pleasures of Hope", "I have not heard it these twenty years; this is popularity indeed."[1]

It is perfectly true that many such compositions were in appallingly sentimental taste by modern standards, and some of the topical ballads are of an incredible crudity and naïvety—yet they were all *popular*. Part of the magic of the ballad, in all its disguises, is its strange power to move the heart rather than the intellect. Throughout the centuries educated men have stood among the eager crowds. In the seventeenth century, the worthy Richard Corbett, Doctor of Divinity, sang and sold ballads at Abingdon Cross, and in America the young Benjamin Franklin wrote and sold ballads. Forster tells of Oliver Goldsmith: "He would write sheet ballads to save himself from actually starving; sell them at the Reindeer Repository in Mountrath Court for five shillings apiece, and steal out of college to hear them sung. Happy night! to him worth all the dreary days." Charles Lever, when a student at Trinity College, Dublin, dressed as a ballad-singer and sang in the streets; he is said to have earned as much as thirty shillings a day.

A somewhat eccentric scholarly cachet is provided by Vincent Bourne's translation of *Black-eyed Susan* into Latin during the eighteenth century; this famous scholar also wrote a Latin poem which includes a picture of street singing in Seven Dials.

As the nineteenth century drew to a close, the broadside declined, just as unaccountably as it had burst into its final verses. In the latter period there was a fake-literary quality about many of the pieces, with lines like:

"The last golden beam kissed the brow of the mountain;
    The birds sung as softly in evening's ear;

[1] Quoted from "Street Songs and their Singers" (*The St. James Magazine*, vol. XIII, London, 1865).

When at the old tryst, by the silvery fountain,
Sat Annie, and Edwin the Brave Volunteer."

However, in that age of contrasts, there was also the cynical realism of *The Young Recruit, or Thirteen Pence A Day*, which opens:

"Come and be a soldier, lads, come lads come!
Hark! Don't you hear the fife and the drum,
Come to the battle field, march, march away;
Come and lose your eyes and limbs for thirteen pence
    a day."

One of the most charming examples of the pseudo-literary mythological style is provided by *The Colleen Rhue* (The Red-Headed Maid):

"Are you Aurora, or the goddess Flora,
Areana or Venus Bright,
Or Helen fair, that goddess rare,
That Paris stole from the Grecian sight?
Kind sir, be easy and don't tease me,
With your false praises so jestingly,
I'm not Aurora, or the goddess Flora,
But a rural female to all men's view
And my appellation is the 'Colleen Rhue'."

Nothing, however, excelled the sentimental excesses of Thomas Haynes Bayly, author of *I'd be a Butterfly*, whose compositions were aptly named "Boudoir Ballads" and had a great vogue amongst genteel young ladies. In contrast, the comedies of the Music Hall rested upon a high proportion of vulgarity, although it was the negative vitality of burlesque. The sad beauty and poetry of the old country folk-songs had left popular music. Costermongers were still delighted by songs like "All Around my Hat" ("I vears a Green Villow"), and "Lord Lovel", but these were the Cockney tongue-in-cheek versions of old favourites as served up by popular singers like Sam Cowell.

Broadsides died out in the first years of the twentieth century after more than three hundred years of vigorous prolific life. Throughout the nineteenth century the newspaper proper gained steady ground. After all, the prose newspaper is a more flexible form than the verse broadside. And it is not so great a step from such broadside titles as: "HORRIBLE AND BARBAROUS MURDER OF POOR JAEL DENNY", "SELF-DESTRUCTION OF FEMALE BY THROWING HERSELF OFF THE MONUMENT", to the more snappy headlines of the popular press. Many newspapers were elaborately illustrated, too, whereas the broadsides were decorated by any old woodcut, however inappropriate, often with surrealist effect. For example, the ballad of *The Poacher* is illustrated by a woodcut of the Royal Exchange; *The Sun that Lights the Roses* shows an oriental figure killing a wild boar; *The Death of Nelson* is headed by an archer pointing his bow and arrow at a frog!

The appearance of cheap, well-edited, illustrated newspapers in place of the old single-sheets found a ready-made public. In the early nineteenth century, when weekly newspapers were as high in price as sevenpence each, reading clubs were formed amongst working-class people, so that a dozen or more could share the news.

At the beginning of the twentieth century people had stopped singing songs for themselves, indeed, in many public-houses singing was discouraged or forbidden. In the cities, societies arose for the suppression of street noises, and local by-laws were passed to forbid music and cries in the streets.

Today the broadside tradition has virtually disappeared and the street singer has been moved on, or given a Ministry of Labour classification of trade that does not recognize the romance of the past. The cheap daily and evening newspapers have come into their own, and all that is left to recall their balladsheet origins is the Gothic style lettering of their title headings. This is not strictly a survival in the physical history of the newspaper, but a spontaneous reminiscence of style (as with the use of displayed headlines) when the balladsheet approach and technique passed into popular newspaper development. But today even the hint of Black-Letter type is vanishing before newer roman type faces and format. None the less, the newspaper contents and the journalistic style are still familiar material and would have served any street ballad singer for verse and music. The magic world of the minstrels has gone, but the broadside subjects have hardly changed in three hundred years since Middleton wrote in *World Tost at Tennis* (1620) that ballad writers were never without a "subject to write of; one hangs himself today, another drowns himself tomorrow, a sergeant stabbed next day; here a pettifogger in the pillory, a bawd in the cart's nose, and a pander in the tail; *hic mulier haec vir*, fashions, fictions, felonies, fooleries:—a hundred havens has the balladmonger to traffic at, and new ones still daily discovered."

"Songs, Penny a Sheet!"

BY-LAW
FOR
THE SUPPRESSION OF STREET CRIES.

- - - - - - - - - - - -

STREET SHOUTING

No person shall for the purpose of hawking, selling or advertising goods, call or shout in any street so as to cause annoyance to the inhabitants of the neighbourhood.

PENALTY.

Any person who shall so offend against the foregoing by-law shall be liable for every such offence to a fine not exceeding Forty Shillings.

The Common Seal of Mayor, Aldermen & Councillors of the Metropolitan Borough of Holborn, was thereto affixed this Twelfth day of October One Thousand Nine Hundred and Four.

L.S

CHAPTER FIVE

SURVIVALS AND REVIVALS

FROM time to time in the last few years there have been revivals of the broadside form, generally as a cultured artistic type of production. During the coronation of Queen Elizabeth II, there were a number of very pretty broadsides and loyal addresses, unusally made with loving care, in limited issue, on hand-presses. Most of these things lacked the crude vigour and vitality of the broadsides on the first Queen Elizabeth, but they were a very appropriate and nostalgic gesture. Much more in keeping with the sixteenth century was the anti-monarchist poster issued by the Scottish Nationalists—undoubtedly a genuine broadside. It reads:

"£2,000 REWARD FOR INFORMATION LEADING TO THE
IDENTIFICATION OF ELIZABETH 1ST OF SCOTLAND
DEAD OR ALIVE"

Historians will recollect that the "first" queen of Scotland has been a sore point for centuries. . . .

A very beautiful series of "Broadsides" was issued by the Cuala Press, in Ireland, edited by W. B. Yeats and F. R. Higgins, with illustrations by Jack Yeats. Many fine old songs were printed in the series, together with modern poetry. The folded sheets, with coloured illustrations and printed both sides of the page are, of course, technically broadsheets.

In 1953 the artist Feliks Topolski started his Broadsheet Chronicles. As these were a series of drawings they were nearer to the political broadsides of Gillray than to the street balladsheets. Topolski, however, was familiar with the broadside tradition and had his own collection of broadsides, which he exhibited in 1954. His Broadsheet Chronicle, now in its tenth year, still appears regularly.

In 1927, the Fuller Sisters issued *A Set of Six Folksongs and Ballads* in a limited edition of 500 copies. This was a folder of six broadsheets of songs and ballads collected by the Fullers, and decorated in bold folk-like style by Cynthia Fuller.

The various poetic broadsides issued around the 1930s by the Poetry Bookshop, *Flying Fame* and others, are charming collector's items, but really outside the broadside tradition. The same can be said for "Adrian Brunel's Broadsheets", a very interesting series of broadsides on statesmen and authors, published in 1953.

The best of the modern revivals come from Australia, where John Manifold and Ron Edwards have pioneered a lively folksong movement. They issued folders of *Bandicoot Ballads*, beautifully and simply printed broadsides entirely in a traditional idiom, equally suitable for teaching songs or for decorating a wall. The sheets are all old favourites like: *The Wild Colonial Boy*, *The Banks of the Condamine*, *Van Dieman's Land*, *Bold Jack Donahue*, and so on.

Some years ago, a bookshop in the East End of London issued broadsides of songs for Jewish immigrants. These were large folio sheets with text in English and Yiddish, with advertisements of other publications on the back. At the present time, the Youth and Education Department of the Jewish National Fund in London has issued a loose-leaf song book *Shiron*, built up from dozens of separate sheets with words in English and Hebrew script, and music in staff and tonic sol-fa. They are printed on both sides of an octavo sheet containing notes on the songs and the composers. One sheet even gives a series of illustrations of a Yemenite dance-song. The Zionist tradition of dance and song is, of course, still very much alive.

Another remarkable survival is the satirical broadside sheets still issued today during the Basle Fastnacht Carnival, Switzerland. These are long slips of coloured paper with little cartoons instead of woodcuts, the verses in a ribald carnival tradition.

When I visited Dublin about three years ago, I found one of the last of the Irish broadside sellers still at his pitch. The sheets were little more than small handbills, but a legitimate survival; some even had crude illustrations. Under oath of secrecy I was able to track down the printers. They were anxious to remain anonymous as they had once been threatened with prosecution for copyright on

a piece called *The Bard of Armagh*! Many songs which have legiti-
mately become folk property have sometimes passed to the copyright of music publishers. These few surviving broadsides, however,
were not the last of the living spirit of Irish balladry. Many of you
may remember the wonderful fuss in Baltinglass, County Wicklow,
in 1945, when the whole nation became inflamed over the case of
Miss Cooke and the post of sub-postmistress.

The siege by the police, and the pother in high quarters is now a
piece of local folklore, and a ballad singer named Sylvester Gaffney
wrote a popular ballad on it, from which I quote:

"The job of sub-postmaster or mistress, as might be,
   is not exactly one that leads to wealth and luxury;
But Korea was a picnic and Tobruk was just a pup
To the row the day the linesmen came to take the cable up.

     There were Bren guns and Sten guns and whippet tanks
       galore,
     The battle raging up and down from pub to gen'ral
       store;
     Between the Vintner and the Cook the pot was quite
       upset,
     And the Minister swore this Irish stew was the
       worst he ever 'et.

Now the case has gone to UNO, and we're waiting for the day
When Truman, Attlee, and McBride will come along and say,
'Get back behind your parallel, drop atom bombs and gas,
And respect the bound'ries and the laws of Sov'reign
    Baltinglass.' "

There is a printed songsheet of this epic, and only a purist will
complain that it is printed on *both* sides of the sheet. It is well in
the broadside tradition, even to its blatantly humorous exaggerations and inaccuracies! I think it was Frank Shay who first said:
"History is what actually happened: folklore is what people *think*
happened" . . .

The London counterpart of my Dublin broadside seller is Mr. J.
Smith, a disabled man of over 65 years. He is a familiar sight in
Oxford Street with his tray of original songs, printed on one side of
thin cards. When he was a young man he used to travel around the

country fairs. His songs are on topical political subjects, in the tradition of patter-songs, prose statements alternating with verse. On the other side of the road stands another old man selling "Old Moore's Almanack", the last of the modern chapbooks. Incidentally, the company that still prints one of the several "Original and Genuine" editions of Old Moore, used to print balladsheets in the nineteenth century. Meanwhile, Mr. Smith is the last of an English tradition. All honour to him. . . .

Is this the last of the popular broadside, then—some reprints, two old men and the evening newspaper? Far from it. Just as the newspaper absorbed the topical content of the broadside, so did the Tin Pan Alley songsheet exploit the musical side. The song broadside has not really died—rather it has been metamorphosed.

Tin Pan Alley is the modern Seven Dials, not many yards from the old haunts of Jemmy Catnach and Johnny Pitts, who would have smiled to see modern popular songs turned out like factory products. The reward is much in excess of the Catnach bards with their shilling a song, and the sheets are better printed. It is considered a little improper to sing in the streets today, but it is impossible to avoid hearing the latest hits on radio and television. After all, centuries of ballad and song have reached their logical conclusion in an age of mechanization—the Muse has become mechanized. It is a nostalgic thought that the modern song product is so often still called a "ballad" in the trade. . . .

Today the ancient Minstrel and his retinue are as alive as ever. The male and female crooner with their factory of electronic experts artfully augmenting the voice, and the army of songwriters, publishers and disc-jockeys, have a sweeter style than the old men of the streets with their cracked voices and strident melodies. But they are in the same tradition in the strange broadside marriage of art and commerce.

And, indeed!—here are some of the same names that were so popular centuries back. "Robin Hood"—a modern film hit song. The sheet music costs 1s. 6d. instead of a penny, but I suppose the cost of living has gone up. Strange that Robin Hood never died out. His name crops up in the early records of the thirteenth century, and "rymes of Robyn Hood" are mentioned in the fourteenth century "Piers the Plowman". We have no conclusive evidence as to whether this folk hero was a real person or a myth, but his popularity remains. There are innumerable garlands and stories about him even up to modern times. Here is a nineteenth-century chapbook for children: "Robin Hood and His Merry Men", and here is a twentieth century one on sale a few weeks ago: "Robin Hood, Told in Pictures".

If you look hard enough you will always find the past in the present. Here's "On Top of Old Smoky", a copyright new version from Tin Pan Alley—a song better known to collectors in America as a variant of the old English song "The Waggoner's Lad". In Dublin, Walton's have put out a whole set of modern songsheets of popular street pieces, very tastefully produced. And in London we should not forget McGlennon's Song Books—the modern survival of the Song Garland, still sold in the street markets.

The last few years have seen a great revival of interest in folk-songs and the allied form of Skiffle Music. Tin Pan Alley has tried to drive this bandwagon, but it is, in its nature, an amateur and not a professional movement. Part of its manifestation has gone into a revival of topical ballad-writing, and many modern street minstrels have sung and sold their broadsides on burning questions of the day, set to folk tunes and usually with a guitar accompaniment. Several magazines are devoted entirely to topical ballads of this kind, and at holiday time the guitars are out at the Aldermaston Marches. It is too early to say how this will work out. The ballads are often an uncomfortable blend of the fiercely partisan and the burlesque, but they have the vitality of young people in a bewildering modern world. Many of these pieces have been severely criticized for their uncompromisingly radical character, but this is absolutely in the tradition of political criticism that has distinguished broadside history and has always been its leading characteristic. After all, the field is wide open, and those who wish to popularize less controversial ballads are free to write them and sell them in the streets. A little variety and competition might actually be very welcome.

On a Sunday morning, in the Petticoat Lane, East London's great street market, you might find John Foreman with a sheaf of his own printed song slips and garlands. This young man has already produced a score of sheets quite in the tradition, and calls

G

himself with some justification "The Broadsheet King". His balladsheet on *The Smithfield Market Fire* was on sale within ten days of the event, not such quick work as old Jemmy Catnach's, but still topical. A note on the back of one sheet explains his viewpoint:

"A Word in your Ear! The Revival of English Folksong, legacy of the skiffle craze, has been lucky in being led by people not looking upon themselves as folk artists merely, but also as teachers. They have tried to diffuse the songs they sing, not to husband or exploit them. . . . If you are such a singer and have traditional or original material that you think should be more widely known, why not supplement your singing by giving away—or selling!—to your audience a copy of the words?"

It is a sincere view and one sympathizes with it. It will take more than one enthusiast to revive a whole tradition, but there must always be pioneers.

*   *   *

The mainstream of the broadside tradition is certainly over, at least, for the time being. The cinema and television have absorbed the popular arts of song, dance and drama that once found expression in the ballad. The one clear note of music has splintered into a million voices and a pandemonium of sound. The images of the poet have been drowned in the myriad sights and scenes that flicker on the television tube. The impresarios of Hollywood and the pundits of television have known the prestige and rich rewards that the crowd will give to the minstrel and the cheapjack; there are far costlier novelties than the toys of the market-place. Only these modern popular arts are *passive* ones so far as the crowds are concerned—in the old days people sang for themselves. The problem is inherently a metaphysical one. The present generation, rooted in mechanics and materialism, has developed the popular art forms most appropriate to its own times. Perhaps future antiquaries will collect our old gramophone records and tape recordings.

In every age there is a delicate balance between the trivial and the profound in human affairs. We may even now be on the edge of contacting once more the dark secret energies of balladry in some new form. Just now the crowds are silent, but we may be close to the magic moment of music that Siegfried Sassoon noted down in his poem *Every One Sang*:

> "Every one suddenly burst out singing;
> And I was filled with such delight
> As prisoned birds must find in freedom
> Winging wildly across the white
> Orchards and dark green fields; on; on;
>   and out of sight."

Until then, with the fading of old people's memories, the flimsy sheets of paper remain for our study in the great collections, and in the various books that have reprinted selections from Black-Letter and Whiteletter balladry. These ephemeral papers are of great importance to the social historian, the student of economics and politics, the antiquary, the song-lover, and the revivers of folk tradition. But we also need the living voices of song, in the folk traditional styles and the sounds of the market-places and streets; these can be studied on gramophone records as well as from life. If we sing a little ourselves and with our friends we can rediscover something of the power that kept the old songs alive.

There are some broadside ballads that may never die, but have rung down the centuries. Over three hundred years ago, in September 1580, in the reign of the first Queen Elizabeth, the Stationers' Company licensed to Richard Jones *A New Northern Dittye of the Lady Green Sleeves*. Jones reprinted this piece four years later in his Garland *A Handefull of pleasant delites*. It is highly probable that the tune is older than the reign of Henry, since songs and ballads invariably have an earlier life than their first appearance in print. Be that as it may, within twelve days from its first fourpenny entry, there was a solemn piece of piety called "Green Sleves Moralized to the Scripture, Declaring the Manifold Benefites and Blessings of God Bestowed on Sinful Man", and three days later there is a suggestion that there had been a vulgar version of the song in doubtful taste. The tune has always carried satires as well as any other songs of similar metre that called for a fine and well-loved air to catch the public fancy. Some people have heard versions of the tune to the words of "Christmas Comes But Once a Year" or "Which Nobody Can Deny"; it was in great favour by the Cavaliers who used it in the *Collection of Loyal Songs Written Against the Rump Parliament*; it was heard in that long and popular ballad *The Lord of Lorn and the False Steward*. A gypsy woman called Alice Boyce sang "Lady Green Sleeves" before Queen Elizabeth. At the height of its popularity five men and one woman knew it as the last music they heard on earth, because they were executed for conspiracy, at Tyburn 1588, and the crowd chanted "Green Sleeves" in place of the usual doleful lamentation of "Fortune My Foe" . . . Today, the song is known in the arrangement by Dr. Vaughan-Williams, or in the very beautiful singing of Richard Dyer-Bennett, the American folk-entertainer who might justly be called a Minstrel. He has revived the ancient and courtly role of the minstrel entertainer of centuries ago, singing all the old songs and ballads with the open "white" tone of the European tenor, but accompanying himself on guitar or lute in the old style. This, then, is one of the great broadside ballads. Some men lived off this song, some conspired and shaped a course of politics with it, and others died to it. It is of special interest to the social historian, for in its long version of nineteen verses it contains a full description of the wardrobe of an Elizabethan lady of fashion. . . .

Bonny Barbara Allen, another great broadside piece, is a genuine traditional ballad—Child No. 84. It is perhaps one of the most widely known and circulated ballads in current American oral tradition; in the state of Virginia alone, ninety-two variants were collected and a dozen different tunes. On January 2nd, 1666, Mr. Pepys wrote in his famous diary:

> "Up by candle-light again, and my business being done, to my Lord Brounckner's, and there find Sir J. Minnes and all his company, and Mr. Boreman and Mrs. Turner, but, above all, my dear Mrs. Knipp, with whom I sang, and in perfect pleasure I was to hear sing, and especially her little Scotch[1] song of Barbary Allen."

In 1765, Goldsmith writes in one of his essays:

> "The music of the finest singer is dissonance to what I felt when our old dairy-maid sung me into tears with 'Johnny Armstrong's Last Good-night' or 'The Cruelty of Barbara Allen.' "

[1] The terms "Scotch" and "Northern" were often used indiscriminately to indicate a country song.

You may remember that it was Mrs. Olive Dame Campbell who first drew the attention of Cecil Sharp to the untapped stores of English folk-song and ballad in the Southern Appalachian mountains of America, as a result of which Sharp spent nearly a year between 1916 and 1918 recovering some of our finest folk ballads and songs as a living tradition. Mrs. Campbell's interest started much earlier, and in a letter to Evelyn Kendrick Wells she describes how, at the Hindman School in Kentucky, she heard one of the girls sing "Barbara Allen":

"That was what started me off . . ." (she writes) "I was bewitched by the melody, so completely different from my childhood ones, and from that went on learning wherever I could find any singer."

In the nineteenth century, a street song seller told Mr. Henry Mayhew: " 'Barbara Allen's' selling yet!" . . .

One also remembers the political songs like "Lilli Burlero" which was so famous around 1688. Bishop Burnet wrote:

"The whole army, and at last the people, both in city and country, were singing it perpetually. And perhaps never had so slight a thing so great an effect."[1]

Many street songs did not achieve immortality, but the type and subject-matter have been recorded. In Shakespeare's *Winter's Tale* there is a typical little scene when Autolycus the pedlar offers his ballads to the Clown, who is in the company of two country wenches:

CLOWN. What hast here? Ballads?

MOPSA. Pray now, buy some. I love a ballad in print, a'-life: for then we are sure they are true.

AUT. Here's one to a very doleful tune, how a usurer's wife was brought to bed of twenty money-bags at a burden; and how she longed to eat adders' heads, and toads carbonadoed.

MOPSA. Is it true, think you?

AUT. Very true, and but a month old.

DORCAS. Bless me from marrying a usurer!

AUT. Here's the midwife's name to't, one Mistress Taleporter; and five or six honest wives that were present. Why should I carry lies abroad?

[1] BURNET, GILBERT. *Bishop Burnet's History of His Own Time* (reprint), Oxford, 1823.

MOPSA. Pray you now, buy it.

CLOWN. Come on, lay it by: and let's first see more ballads; we'll buy the other things anon.

AUT. Here's another ballad. Of a fish that appeared upon the coast on Wednesday the four score of April, forty thousand fathom above water, and sung this ballad against the hard hearts of maids; it was thought she was a woman, and was turned into a cold fish, for she would not exchange flesh with one that loved her. The ballad is very pitiful, and as true.

DORCAS. Is it true too, think you?

AUT. Five justices' hands at it; and witnesses, more than my pack will hold. . . .

Yet side by side with Shakespeare's sly humour, one remembers that in 1579 two Edinburgh poets were hanged for writing satirical ballads.

It was John Selden, first of the great broadside ballad collectors, who wrote:

"Though some make slight of libels, yet you may see by them how the wind sits. As take a straw and throw it up into the air, you shall see by that which way the wind is, which you shall not do by casting up a stone. More solid things do not show the complexion of the times so well as ballads and libels."

Through four centuries, such sheets have been eagerly bought and the songs sung by the common people. Broadsides have been pasted up on alehouse walls, and lovingly fixed in the albums of collectors. Many pieces were trivial and repetitive; some, like the modern newspaper, served only for the distraction of a day, others played a significant part in history. All possess a strange charm of their own, with their quaint woodcuts and exotic decorative types and borders.

How far removed from the cheapjack humours and tragedies of the street is the scholar and the collector of ballads? It has often seemed that the eighteenth century antiquary or the twentieth century librarian live in a more refined and dignified atmosphere than the lusty sweating crowds, yet they breath the same air. It is a strange and colourful past that has been bought and sold on old scraps of paper; even the pursuit and study of these flimsy relics is a fantastic affair. In his novel *The Antiquary*, Sir Walter Scott, one of the most famous ballad enthusiasts, has vividly characterized the excitement and fascination of broadside ballad collecting. He writes, more from his own enthusiasm than to help the story:

> "Not the least fascinating was the original broadside—the Dying Speech, Bloody Murder, or Wonderful Wonder of Wonders, in the primary tattered guise, as it was hawked through the streets and sold for the cheap and easy price of one penny, though now worth the weight of that penny in gold. On these the Antiquary dilated with transport, and read, with a rapturous voice, the elaborate titles, which bore the same proportion to the contents that the painted signs without a showman's booth do to the animals within.
>
> "Mr. Oldbuck, for example, piqued himself especially in possessing a *unique* broadside, entitled and called *Strange and Wonderful News from Chipping-Norton, in the County of Oxon, of certain dreadful apparitions which were seen in the air on the 26th of July, 1610, at half an hour after nine o'clock at noon, and continued till eleven, in which time was seen Appearances of Several Flaming Swords, Strange Motions of the Superior Orbs; with the Unusual Sparkling of the Stars, with their Dreadful Continuations; with the Account of the Opening of the Heavens, and Strange Appearances therein disclosing themselves, with several other prodigious circumstances not heard of in any age, to the great amazement of the beholders, as it was communicated in a letter to one Mr. Colley, living in West Smithfield, and attested by Thomas Brown, Elizabeth Greenaway, and Anne Gutheridge, who were spectators of the Dreadful Apparitions; and if any one would be further satisfied of the Truth of this Relation, let them repair to Mr. Nightingale's, at the Bear Inn, in West Smithfield, and they may be satisfied.*"

The Antiquary describes how his agent Davy Wilson tracked down such rare documents:

> "He had the scent of a slow-hound, sir, and the snap of a bull-dog. He would detect you an old black-letter ballad among the leaves of a law-paper. . . ."
>
> ". . . See this bundle of ballads" [he says] "not one of them later than 1700, and some of them a hundred years older. I wheedled an old woman out of these, who loved them better than her psalm-book."

Scott the antiquary, triumphs over Scott the novelist, when he cannot resist adding a footnote to the description of Mr. Oldbuck's *unique* broadside:

"Of this thrice and four times rare broadside the author possesses an examplar"!

"Antique Ballads, sung to crowds of old,
Now cheaply bought at thrice their weight in gold"

Even in the dignified Libraries in which the great broadside collections are housed, one senses echoes of a turbulent past and the manias of antiquaries. Professor F. J. Furnivall, co-editor of Percy's Folio MSS. says, in a passing reference: "Let any one contrast the contents of this Percy MS. with those of the other great Ballad-Book of our day, the volume of purloined Helmingham ballads, selected by Mr. Daniel, and bought (and rightly and generously printed) by Mr. Huth . . ."

Purloined ballads? In *The Ballad of Tradition*, Gordon Gerould writes:

"The only rival of Pepys as a collector in his own time was the Oxford antiquary, Anthony Wood, who died in 1695. Wood was less happy than Pepys, however, in the fate of what he garnered, for only 279 items remain in his collection. The evidence is fairly clear that one John Bagford, in the service of Robert Harley, first Earl of Oxford, stole on a grand scale from the Ashmolean Museum, to which

Wood had bequeathed his ballads. Harley's acquisitions, before his death in 1724, filled two volumes, while Bagford had three volumes of his own. Towards the end of the eighteenth century, the third Duke of Roxburghe, who at that time owned Harley's collection, added another great volume, largely made up of material likewise abstracted from Wood's papers. Who served the duke in this somewhat ignoble business has not been discovered. Presumably he did not soil his hands by stealing the broadsides for himself. . . ."[1]

This, then, is the last descent of balladry. An ancient and noble inspiration flowered with the seasons in the countryside, passed to beggar, rogue and mountebank, was sold for pennies in the streets, finally stolen and hoarded as dry leaves in the libraries of fanatical collectors. Yet it is the same impulse that runs through the whole of our great ballad story. The range of human emotions is the same, whether a man write a song or a thesis. One man earns an honest living, another cheats for pennies; one dies for a song, another sings for his supper. Life is a gigantic affair of many intricate and contradictory aspects, and if our elemental origins seem more heroic than the everyday passions and topics of civilization, they are none the less only part of the same picture.

The secret of the Universe may not be bought for a penny, but it is on these sheets and in the commerce that goes with them. The profound and the trivial in human affairs have always coexisted, and the real meaning of life lies in the truth that transcends both. All our affairs, large or small, are swept away in the great tide of history, and the passing pageant of life itself is as insubstantial as a dream. Everything that belongs to the everyday world of the senses is a moment only in our human consciousness, essentially ephemeral—like old scraps of paper or the words of a ballad half remembered.

There are as many ballads as pebbles on a beach, and they are of all sorts and shapes. Just as we collect new experiences and compare them with old ones, so we collect old and new songs to learn a little more about life. And collect we must, before these fragments pass away.

[1] My own collection has been acquired honestly, but I could tell many tales of the joys and sorrows of a collector, and of the half-world of booksellers' runners.

In 1892, the Rev. S. Baring-Gould, a great collector of folk-songs and broadside ballads, wrote:

"It is but a matter of a few years and the broadside will be as extinct as the Mammoth and the Dodo, only to be found in the libraries of collectors. Already sheets that fetched a ha'penny thirty years ago are cut down the middle, and each half fetches a shilling. The garlands are worth more than their weight in gold. Let him that is wise collect whilst he may."[1]

---

[1] BARING-GOULD, S. "Broadside Ballads" (in *Strange Survivals*, Methuen, 1892).

EPILOGUE

SONG'S ETERNITY

—John Clare (1793–1864)

What is song's eternity?
Come and see.
Can it noise and bustle be?
Come and see
Praises sung or praises said
Can it be?
Wait awhile and these are dead—
Sigh, sigh;
Be they high or lowly bred
They die.

What is song's eternity?
Come and see
Melodies of earth and sky,
Here they be.
Song once sung to Adam's ears
Can it be?
Ballads of six thousand years
Thrive, thrive;
Song awakens with the spheres
Alive.

Mighty songs that miss decay,
What are they?
Crowds and cities pass away
Like a day.
Books are out and books are read;
What are they?
Years will lay them with the dead—
Sigh, sigh;
Trifles unto nothing wed,
They die.

Dreamers, mark the honey bee;
Mark the tree
Where the blue cap "*tootle tee*"
Sings a glee
Sung to Adam and to Eve—
Here they be.
When floods covered every bough,
Noah's ark
Heard that ballad singing now;
Hark, hark,

"*Tootle tootle tootle tee*"—
Can it be
Pride and fame must shadows be?
Come and see—
Every season owns her own;
Bird and bee
Sing creation's music on;
Nature's glee
Is in every mood and tone
Eternity.

NOTES ON EXAMPLES

THE BROADSIDE AND THE BROADSHEET (pages 122–129)

Handbills, proclamations, advertisements, religious documents. . . .
Here are two addresses to the gentry of York: a Royal Proclamation
from Charles I just before the Civil War, and an Election Address of
1806 in which Wilberforce the liberator neatly claims that he "has been
the Slave of no Party".

Two election notices follow: a broadside *Few Words* against Tories,
and a handbill "One Last Word" from a Tory. There is little to choose
between the exuberant styles of 1802 and 1959 in a field where free
speech is expressed with traditional licence.

The Poster "£2,000 REWARD FOR INFORMATION LEADING TO THE
IDENTIFICATION OF ELIZABETH 1ST OF SCOTLAND" is a modern anti-monarchist piece by the Scottish Nationalists, actually pasted up during
the Coronation of 1953. It will be recalled that pillar-boxes and mail-
vans were redecorated "Elizabeth II", even in Scotland. A song in true
broadside style (by Thurso Berwick) amplified the Scottish Nationalist
view:

"Oh Scotland hasnae' got a king and she hasnae' got a queen.
How can ye hae the second Liz when the first yin's never been?
Nae Liz the yin, Nae Lillibet the twa, Nae Liz will ever dae.
We'll mak our land republican in a Scottish breakaway. . . ."

Hear Billy Graham speaking to London from Glasgow is a religious handbill
given in the streets, and shows an interesting excursion into the political
field of mass audiences and long distance relay. *He Had No Song* is a
religious broadsheet, being printed on both sides of a folded page. Many
such American and Canadian evangelical tracts are still distributed
throughout England.

J. Perren, Junr., Oil and Colorman, Varnish and Blacking Maker ingeniously
combines the broadside advertisement with the song sheet, giving a
shopping list in verse. Nineteenth-century blacking manufacturers often
retained a bard to hymn the praises of their product; in America at the

same period travelling salesmen put on minstrel shows for "Wizard Oil" and other patent preparations.

The advertisement printed on the back of the Canterbury Hall song sheet transforms a broadside into a broadsheet! *Those Bright Blue Eyes* is a routine sentimental ballad, but there are some interesting titles in *Sam Cowell's Song-Book*. *Billy Barlow* and *The Ratcatcher's Daughter* were two of Sam Cowell's most popular songs, *Lord Lovel* is a ballad in descent. Cowell's Cockney burlesque versions of folk-songs were very popular in England and America. As a boy, Cowell spent his early years in the Southern States of America, where he heard some of the Negro songs that were to sweep London—"Jim Along Josey", "Yaller Busha Belle" and "Old Zip Coon".

CHAPBOOKS, GARLANDS AND TRACTS (pages 130–134)

A broadside, folded into eight or more pages, becomes a Chapbook. These early "paperbacks" were sold uncut, and the purchaser would slit the pages and often stitch or pin them together. *Four Popular Songs* includes *Will the Weaver*, a folk-song that still lives in British and American oral tradition.

Chapbooks included folk-songs and ballads, as well as almanacks, religious subjects, and collections of jokes or nursery rhymes. Eight typical covers are illustrated. Both Sir Walter Scott and William Motherwell toyed with the idea of writing studies on the Scottish chapbook. Scotland was famous for these ephemeral productions and at the peak of their popularity published something like 200,000 a year. They were printed and reprinted until late nineteenth century, many with the legend "Printed for the Booksellers". It is interesting to see Bishop Percy's *Hermit of Warkworth* reprinted as a chapbook; this was an essay at the ballad form. *The History of Dr. Faustus* is a late survival of a popular subject; amusingly enough the woodcut is a portrait of Dougal Graham, the most famous of Scottish chapmen. The popularity of superstitious subjects in the nineteenth century is not surprising when we recall that as late as 1851, Andrew Dawson, a veterinary surgeon in practice in the Grampians, was arraigned by a Kirk Session on a charge of sorcery and excommunicated.

Three Garlands are illustrated—*The May Day Garland*, a chapbook *Garland of New Songs*, and *The Bristol Garland*. The latter is a narrative ballad of a pedestrian kind, and illustrates how the word "garland" came to be used for a single song.

Two Tracts are shown, *circa* 1694–5, concerned with the separate paths of religion and politics. The Quaker "Lament" complains of

"Ungodly Ballet-Singers", the "Inquiry into the Late Briberies and Corrupt Practices" deals with abuses of the East India Company. Note the Black-Letter type.

EARLY BROADSIDE BALLADS, BLACK-LETTER AND WHITE-LETTER (pages 135–138)

The Famous Battle between Robin Hood and the Curtal Fryar is a Black-Letter balladsheet of the sort that flourished between the early 1500s and 1700. The particular example shown is *circa* 1680, and the same cuts appear on ballads in the Roxburghe Collection. Note the alternation of Gothic and roman type in the verses, and the use of "VV" for "W", typical of the printing of the period.

The Suffolk Miracle is Child No. 272, a reluctant admission. Child writes: "This ballad is, in a blurred, enfeebled, and disfigured shape, the representative in England of one of the most remarkable tales and one of the most impressive and beautiful ballads of the European continent." Bürger's *Lenore* was composed from a German version of this tale, and Scott's translation of Bürger and similar pieces kindled an enthusiasm for Scottish balladry, later to find expression in the *Minstrelsy of the Scottish Border*. The broadside illustrated was printed about 1711.

The Just Judgment of God shew'd upon Dr. John Faustus was a very popular subject. The same woodcut was used earlier in *The Tragedy of Doctor Lambe* (1628) on a similar theme, and has also been copied in chapbooks.

The Lord of Lorn and the False Steward (Child No. 271) is a seventeenth century version of the old romance of *Roswall and Lillian*. The ballad was registered at the Stationers' Hall on October 6th, 1580, but both ballad and romance continued to circulate together. Sir Walter Scott comments (in *Tristem*): "Within the memory of man an old person used to perambulate the streets of Edinburgh, singing in a monotonous cadence the tale of Rosewal and Lilian." In the prologue to Cotton's *Burlesque upon Burlesque* in the seventeenth century are the lines:

"We in the country do not scorn
Our walls with ballads to adorn,
Of patient Grissel and the lord of Lorn."

This is a fine ballad with echoes of Grimm's *Goose Girl* in its situations and wistful melancholy. It was sung to the ever popular tune of "Greensleeves".

EIGHTEENTH-CENTURY SONG SHEETS WITH MUSIC
(pages 139–140)

D'Urfey's song is a typical bawdy piece of the period and is printed in *Wit and Mirth or Pills to Purge Melancholy*.

The Northern Lass is an example of the copperplate engraving of the eighteenth century "Half Sheets"; the artist is G. Bickham. Although both these song sheets are of a type bound into books, they are an off-shoot of the broadside form. The period is an interesting one in which extreme sophistication rubs shoulders with lusty bawdry.

EIGHTEENTH-CENTURY SINGLE SLIPS (pages 141–143)

A group of six slips in which the subjects vary from wars and battles to folk-song and polite opera. The *New Song* on Admiral Keppel uses the same woodcut as *Water parted from the Sea* (sung in Arne's "Artaxerxes"). The *Dialogue on the S(t)ate of the Nation* deals with the American War of Independence, while the last verse of *The Wars Are Not Over* echoes the theme of *The Devil and the Farmer's Wife*, a popular folk-song.

NINETEENTH-CENTURY SHEETS (pages 144–162)

The Chauntseller introduces a batch of ballads, old and new; the lines of the verses are made up from titles of popular songs of the time.

A Famous Sea Fight between Captain Ward and the Rainbow printed on one of the early large sheets of J. Pitts is Child Ballad No. 287, popular as a broadside from about 1680 onwards. One of Drake's four ships in the Cadiz expedition in 1587 was called *Rainbow*.

The Bold Prisoner on a later Pitts sheet is Child Ballad No. 188, a version of *Archie o' Cawfield*. A version is still sung by Harry Cox of Potter Heigham, Norfolk, one of the finest English traditional folk singers; he calls it *Bold Archer* and the sheriff is from "Honny Dundee". The ballad has been collected in American oral tradition as *John Webber* and *Billy and Johnny*. A copy of the Pitts broadside was cited by Professor F. E. Bryant in his *History of English Balladry*. This is an exceptionally interesting ballad with mysterious overtones. There is quite a hint of the style of the *Earl Brand* ballads in the disposition of the groups of ten bold fellows, and the pursuit in which Archie or Archer looks back and sees the sheriff and his men coming. There is also something odd about the iron fetters and the breaking of locks and bolts which recalls the group of Anglo-American folk-songs of the *Locks and Bolts*, *Locks and Bars* type. It is true that some versions of *Archie o' Cawfield* specify the fetters as "twenty pounds of good Spanish iron", but it may not be too fanciful to suppose that there is a remnant here of the old belief in the magical properties of iron with a spell being broken as well as the fetters.

Lord Bateman is a variant of Child No. 53, the ballad of *Young Beichan*. It was very popular with nineteenth-century costermongers, and even survived in American oral tradition. The version illustrated is substantially that immortalized by Cruikshank's illustrations in 1839, although he printed the song with exaggerated Cockney pronunciation. His *Loving Ballad of Lord Bateman* (with twelve most humorous engravings) was said to have been collected by Charles Dickens from a young criminal called "The Tripe-Skewer"; the solemn notes to the ballad (possibly contributed by Thackeray) are a most hilarious satire on pompous scholarship.

The True Ballad of Barbara Allen's Cruelty is Child No. 84, and the version printed here resembles Roxburghe II, 25. This is the ballad which so charmed Pepys, Goldsmith and others.

The Cruel Ship Carpenter (on the same sheet as *Death of Lord Nelson*) is a folk-song which survives in American oral tradition as *Pretty Polly* (a version of this is recorded on Disc AAFS.3 of the Library of Congress Folk Music Series).

Two more folk-songs are printed on the Williamson sheet: *Three Maids A-Milking Would Go* and *The Butcher and the Taylor's Wife*; the first piece is a fine example of poetic folk bawdry. A less outspoken version is sung by Richard Dyer-Bennett as *Two Maidens Went Milking One Day* on an American disc—Stinson SLP.2 (Long Play). The printer Williamson appears to have had a working arrangement with Walker of Durham, as they shared a long series of broadsides between them.

The Pretty Plough Boy is on a sheet printed by the famous Jemmy Catnach. This particular folk-song is still sung by Harry Cox of Potter Heigham, from oral tradition; his version, learnt from his grandfather is very similar to the sheet in essentials.

The Ratcatcher's Daughter, in humorous Cockney dialect, is another of the songs popularized by the singer Sam Cowell.

The next group of sheets show topical subjects, very much in a popular newspaper style although somewhat more outspoken than present-day journalism. *The Wants of Princess Alice* stirs up good-humoured indignation at the dowry of the Princess Royal in 1859. *Downfall of Old Roger* is one of many broadside songs on the famous Tichborne Trial of 1874. *Nightingale in the East* presents a popular heroine of the 1850s, the outspoken self-sacrificing Florence Nightingale. In contrast, *Sir J. Franklin and His Crews* tells the unhappy story of the ill-fated Franklin expedition when extreme privations reduced the survivors to

H

cannibalism. *Long Life to Captain Webb!* celebrates the remarkable achievement of Captain Matthew Webb on August 24th, 1875. This was Webb's second attempt and his success against an American rival is extolled in good-natured jingoistic style. Eight years later Webb lost his life attempting to swim the rapids at Niagara Falls. *The Present Times, or Eight Shillings a Week* is a sheet on the theme of Hard Times; it dates from the 1830s but was often reprinted with topical variations. The decay of the times is a perennial theme. . . .

The Vocal Grove; A Variety of Songs is one of the famous "Long Song Sheets" started by Catnach. One of the songs (*The Forsaken Shepherdess*) is marked "Quod J. C. Jan. 3, 1823" and is probably the work of Catnach himself. Some of the woodcuts are by Bewick.

Sale of a Wife was a popular recitation or song, and although the present example is a standard version, many actual instances of wifesales are recorded as late as the nineteenth century. It was a folk belief that it was legal for a man to sell his wife when tired of her provided that he took her to a market-place with a rope round her neck, thus putting her in the category of cattle! Here are newspaper entries of the time:

Morning Herald, March 11th, 1802: "On the 11th of last month, a person sold, at the market cross, in Chapel en le Frith, a wife, a child, and as much furniture as would set up a beggar, for eleven shillings."

Morning Post, October 10th, 1807: "One of those disgraceful scenes, which have, of late, become too common, took place on Friday se'nnight at Knaresborough. Owing to some jealousy, or other family difference, a man brought his wife, equipped in *the usual style*, and sold her at the market cross for 6d. and a quid of tobacco."

JOHN ASHTON's *The Dawn of the XIXth Century in England* which quotes these extracts, also mentions incidents as late as 1882, when one woman was sold by her husband in a public-house for a glass of ale, and another husband disposed of his spouse for the bargain price of one penny and a dinner.

The Wild Irishman in London is a cross between the stage-Irish "Poor Paddy" subject and the ever-popular *"Countryman in London"* theme. *A New Song of the American War* attempts to enlist Irish sentiment on the English side.

The Dying Soldier to his Mother, an American broadside, is a popular sentimental song of the Civil War. This is a lithographed sheet and the printer, Charles Magnus of New York, advertises "500 Illustrated Ballads". The illustration is coloured, probably by hand, but I do not know whether it was issued in this state. A number of English nineteenth-century balladsheets were coloured by the purchaser, and some modern dealers tastefully colour sheets in order to enhance their value.

EVOLUTION OF THE POPULAR NEWSPAPER (pages 163–169)

The Downfall of the Tyrant Bonaparte is a broadside news item posted up in the street at an exciting period in history. Presumably from patriotic reasons, sheets were even available gratis from the publisher J. Aston of Coventry.

An Account of the Terrible Storm on Land and at Sea and *Sea Storm Terror* show how closely the news broadsides resemble modern evening newspapers, although some one hundred and twenty years separate them. It will be noted that the early nineteenth century news-sheet often copied its particulars from the scarcer and more expensive "Courants" or newspapers, which at that time were beyond the purse of the common people.

The Post Boy was an early newspaper that started life as "An Account of the Publick Transactions in Christendom in a Letter to a Friend in the Country" in 1694. The issue illustrated (No. 178, March 24th–26th, 1696) reports the trial of Sir William Perkins, who plotted with Sir John Friend and other conspirators to assassinate William III. Newspapers like these were for the more cultured public; the crowds that thronged to Tyburn the following month for the executions sang the street ballads on the event which were printed as broadsides.

Prince of Wales' Marriage is a nineteenth-century example of the news in verse, with all the good-humoured outspoken criticism of royalty typical of the period. The Royal Arms was a favourite woodcut on many sheets, and is curiously reminiscent of the similar convention in twentieth-century popular newspapers where some such device was printed with the Gothic type headings.

A group of three nineteenth-century "Murder Sheets" demonstrates sensational subjects of a type still common in modern evening papers and Sunday press. There is little to choose between the horrors of *The Outrage and Murder on a Little Child at Purfleet* and *He Raped Barbara, Murdered Brenda* a century later in our own times.

SURVIVALS AND REVIVALS (pages 170–183)

Here are some interesting comparisons of old and new.

An eighteenth-century Garland of Robin Hood stories and ballads can be compared with a modern paperback of 1959, a true descendant of the chapbook. A nineteenth-century chapbook on Robin Hood is seen with a modern song sheet of a popular film hit, both in the same genre.

The London Singer's Magazine is a weekly broadsheet songster *circa* 1838, edited, at different periods, by Thomas Prest (who immortalized "Sweeney Tod") and John Labern. "Catalani Joe" on the cover of the issue shown introduces the titles of popular broadside songs of the period. A modern counterpart of *The London Singer's Magazine* is *Sing* Magazine, published in London, which prints songs in the broadside tradition. The cover of the December 1961 issue shows a very topical "Carol for the Space Age".

A very old and ever-popular song is the *Frog and Mouse* and many different versions are current of this odd marriage. In 1580 the Stationers' Company licensed a ballad entitled *A Moste Strange Weddinge of the Frogge and the Mouse. A New Ditty on a High Amour at St. Jamese's* is a satirical ballad by D'Urfey. *The Frog and Mouse* is an eighteenth-century version with verses reminiscent of the *Mr. Froggie* of Burl Ives, present-day popular folk singer. A version of *Mr. Froggie Went A-Courtin'*, with music arrangement and folk-song lyric revision by Burl Ives, is published by Leeds Music Limited. The whole complex of Frog Wedding tales and songs may well be a diffuse survival of the earliest singing of the Mysteries, best typified in the symbolism of Grimm's "Frog Prince".

The Battle of Baltinglass is one of the popular ballads still composed and sung on topical subjects in present-day Eire.

A fascinating old and new parallel is provided by two "Great Exhibition" Songsters—one from 1851 with an illustration of the Crystal Palace, the second from 1951 illustrating the South Bank Exhibition. Both were sold in the streets.

The Broadsheet No. 1 featured the graphic "Chronicle" of the artist Feliks Topolski and synchronized with the opening of his exhibition of "Historical and Contemporary Broadsheets" in October 1954.

The Wild Colonial Boy is a beautifully produced modern broadside from Australia.

Go Down, You Murderers! is a very fine revival of broadside balladry, one of the sheets printed and sold in the streets by John Foreman of London. The song, by Ewan MacColl, refers to a famous criminal case of 1953; many people believe that Timothy Evans was wrongly condemned.

The Women are Worse than the Men! and *The Wild Colonial Boy* are two of the last of the Dublin sheets in broadside format. The copyright fuss on *The Bard of Armagh* prompted the cautious sub-title "Original Version—First Printed 1880" on the ever-popular *Wild Colonial Boy* sheet.

The Silly Sentry and *Army Life* are two typical anti-militarist pieces, the first from Mr. J. Smith, the old broadside seller of Oxford Street, London, the second from Mr. John Foreman who has revived the form and calls himself with some justification "The Broadsheet King". These two pieces represent the last of a tradition and the first of a revival.

The final two pieces are also modern, and show the everlasting conflict of interest between Church and State. At one time or another, organized religion has tended to move into the field of politics; sometimes political decree has encroached upon the territory of religion. Often religion has recognized that its valid sphere is outside and beyond politics and its real message eternal and not ephemeral. In every age, however, optimistic reformers have believed that the passing contemporary scene may be redeemed by appropriate political consciousness and action. Both religion and politics, eternal themes of the broadside, are as old as mankind.

Songs for the March for Life are printed in a broadsheet songster and are completely in the balladsheet idiom. The Wayside Pulpit *Thought for the Week* is a broadside for pasting up in the street, a true ancestor of the broadside ballad.

EXAMPLES

Treasure for Autolycus

"My father named me Autolycus; who being, as I am, lettered under Mercury, was likewise a snapper-up of unconsidered trifles."

A WINTER'S TALE, iv, iii, 25.

A Gathering of Books, Pamphlets, Broadsides, Proclamations, Ballads, Songs, Newspapers and Periodicals illustrative of the literature and life of bygone days.

To Wit—

	NOS.		NOS.
Old Broadside Ballads	... 15-20	Medical Quacks, etc....	... 267-276
Broadsides in Verse ...	... 34-46	Mohun and Hamilton Duel ...	287
Old Chap Books	... 58-69	The Duke of Monmouth	... 288-291
Old Books for Children	... 78-131	Thomas Moore	... 292-299
Books on Conjuring ...	... 137	Newspapers & Periodicals	... 311-375
Books on the Drama...	... 152-165	Old Quarto Plays	... 414-441
Drydeniana ...	... 167-181	Anonymous Poems ...	... 446-451
Books on Freemasonry	... 196-199	Popular Tracts	... 458-479
Hair-dressing ...	... 213-214	Proclamations...	... 484-502
Tracts on Highwaymen	... 219-222	Shakespearean Pamphlets	... 537-551
Tracts on King James II.	... 234-241	Sir Henry Vane	... 585-592
Pamphlets on the Jews	... 244-249	Books on Witchcraft...	... 604-611

Offered for sale at very moderate prices by

P. J. & A. E. DOBELL,

8, BRUTON STREET, NEW BOND STREET, LONDON, W. I.

And at 77, Charing Cross Road, W.C. 2.

Telephone: MAYFAIR 5711.

Telegraphic and Cable Address: "BIBLIA, LESQUARE, LONDON."

$(8\frac{3}{8}'' \times 5\frac{1}{2}'')$

HIS MAJESTIES SPEECH TO THE

Gentry of the County of YORKE,

Attending his Majestie at the City of *Yorke*, on
Thursday the 12th of *May*, 1 6 4 2.

Gentlemen,

I Have cause of adding not altering, what I meant to say when I gave out the summons for this dayes appearance, I little thought of these Messengers, or of such a Message as they brought, the which, because it confirmes mee in what I intend to speake, and that I desire you should be truly informed of all passages between me and the Parliament, you shall here read, First, my answer to the Declaration of both Houses concerning *Hull*, the answer of the Parliament to my two Messages concerning *Hull*, together with my Reply to the same, and my Message to both Houses declaring the Reasons why I refused to passe the Bill concerning the *Militia*.

All which being read his Majesty proceeded.

I Will make no paraphrases upon what yee have heard, it more besiting a Lawyer then a King, onely this observation, since Treason is countenanced so neere me, it is time to looke to my safety : I avow it was part of my wonder, that men (whom I thought heretofore discreet, and moderate) should have undertaken this imployment, and that since they came (I having delivered them the Answer: you have heard, and commanded them to returne personally with it to the Parliament) should have flatly disobeyed me upon pretence of the Parliaments command. My end in telling you this, is to warne you of them, for since these men have brought me such a Message, and disobeyed so lawfull a Command. I will not say what their intent of staying here is, onely I bid you take heed, not knowing what doctrine of disobedience they may preach to you, under colour of obeying the Parliament. Hitherto I have found and kept you quiet, the enjoying of which was a chiefe cause of my comming hither (Tumults and disorders having made mee leave the South) and not to make this a seat of Warre, as malice would (but I hope in vaine) make you beleeve; Now if disturbances doe come, I know whom I have reason to suspect.

To be short, you see that my Magazine is going to be taken from me (being my owne proper goods) directly against my will; The Militia (against Law and my consent) is going to be put in Execution: And lastly, Sir *Iohn Hothams* Treason is countenanced; All this considered none can blame me to Apprehend dangers. Therefore I have thought fit (upon these reall Grounds) to tell you, That I am resolved to have a Guard (the Parliament having had one all this while upon imaginary Iealousies, (onely to secure my person. In which I desire your concurrence and assistance, and that I may be able to protect you, the Lawes, and the true Protestant profession from any Affront or Injury that may be offered, which I meane to maintaine my selfe without charge to the Countrey, intending no longer to keepe them on foote, then I shall be secured of my just Apprehensions by having satisfaction in the particulars before mentioned.

Printed at Yorke, *and now reprinted at* London *by* Alice Norton, *for* Humphrey Tuckey, *at the Blacke spread Eagle in Fleet-street.* 1 6 4 2.

(15" × 11¼")

TO THE
GENTLEMEN,
CLERGY and FREEHOLDERS,
OF THE COUNTY OF YORK.

GENTLEMEN,

THE very unexpected Tidings of an intended Diffolution of Parliament found me in the oppofite Extremity of the Kingdom, where I was refiding with a View to the Reftoration of the Health of a Part of my Family. Having learnt from Letters received on the Road, that an active Canvafs has been carrying on during my Abfence, I have haftened to you with the utmoft Expedition, and to as many of you as the Time will allow, it is my earneft Wifh to pay my Perfonal Refpects. But may I not be permitted, without Prefumption, to exprefs a Hope, that a faithful Service of Two and Twenty Years, may have prevented your Minds from being found fo utterly unoccupied, as that the mere Circumftance of your being previoufly canvaffed by another Candidate, fhould have been fufficient to pre-engage You?

I am aware of the Unfeemlinefs of fpeaking of myfelf: but being now called to account to you for my Execution of the important Office, which you have Four Times committed to me, I muft unavoidably become an Egotift. Confcious then, that a Member for Yorkfhire is honoured with one of the moft dignified Trufts, which a British Subject can receive at the Hands of his Countrymen, I have endeavoured, it is not for me to fay with what Succefs, to maintain unimpaired the Credit of that high Station, by an independent and diligent Difcharge of its various Duties.

To your local Concerns, fome of them, both from their Importance, and from the Numbers they affect, juftly claiming the larger Appellation of National Interefts, I have attended affiduoufly. But I have felt it my Duty to allot as large a Share as poffible of my Time and Thoughts to public and general Queftions; and in no preceding Period of Englifh Hiftory, have fo many of thefe, and of fuch extreme Importance, come before the Houfe of Commons in an equal Space of Time. In performing this moft important Part of my Parliamentary Service, I have had no perfonal Object either of Intereft or Ambition. I have looked neither to Emolument nor to Aggrandifement; remembering that I was the Reprefentative of Yorkfhire, and that, efpecially in thefe Days, and with my peculiar Connections, it became me to be *ftrictly Independent*. I have been the Slave of no Party; and if for the moft Part I have fupported the Meafures of a diftinguifhed Statefman and Patriot, now no more, it has been becaufe I have judged them beft calculated to promote the Welfare of my Country.

When I have thought otherwife of any of them, I have publickly and actively oppofed them, at no fmall Coft of perfonal Feeling, from appearing for the Time to be numbered among the Political Opponents of a MAN, whofe Friendfhip conftituted one of the higheft Honours of my Private Life.

Such, I can truly affirm, has been the general Courfe of my Parliamentary Conduct for Two and Twenty Years; and after having thus fpent the beft Part of my Life in your Service, I truft, that you will not lightly caft me off.

Is it too much to fay that this would be to teach the Members for great Counties, and efpecially thofe who may hereafter reprefent our own, which from the high Place it occupies in the Scale of National Importance, fhould hold out an Example to all the Reft, that he who would fecure the Continuance of your Support, muft refort to other Expedients, and reft his hopes on other Ground, than that of an upright, diligent, and independent Difcharge of the Duties of his Station.

On that Bafis I have hitherto built, and hitherto not in Vain. I truft you will not at Length inculcate on me a different Leffon, a Leffon, which, however, I frankly own to you, I can never learn. Grateful for all your liberal and difinterefted Kindnefs, which, let the Event be what it may, will never be erafed from my HEART!

I remain, GENTLEMEN,

Your devoted Servant,

W. Wilberforce.

York, October 25th, 1806.

$(11\frac{3}{8}'' \times 7\frac{1}{8}'')$

A FEW

WORDS

TO

A FREEMAN, and TRUE BLUE.

Mr. Brazen Face,

THE moment I saw your address this morn-
ing, it brought to my mind the old saying, " Great words
often come from a weak Stomach." What a clever, penetrating
fellow you must be, to assert, that " no one blue has deserted
his colours," &c. This is *True Blue assurance*, with a
witness. I suppose you are some compound creature, made
up of the *Hawk* and *Owl*; the one would destroy its own
species, and the other chuses the dark to seek its prey: yet I
am much mistaken if the *Crocodile* does not make a part of
your composition.

It is true, that the *Independent Freemen of Coventry* are
now struggling against " *undue influence, threats, and tamper-
ing of the common enemy.*" They are not tame enough yet, to be
sold like cattle at Smithfield Market. It is in character for an
Indian Nabob to say the people may do *without a King*, and wish
to govern *us* himself. Let him purchase *slaves*, and sell them
again; but FREEMEN value their liberty, and will stedfastly
resist every mean attempt to enslave them. Support

JEFFERYS AND BARLOW,

the true sons of freedom; and tyranny will never again attempt
to raise its hydra head in this City. It is NOW, or NEVER. The
Issue of the present contest will determine, whether Coventry
is to continue a *free City* or an *enslaved borough*. It is not the
downfal of *Corporation Tyranny*, but *Independence* you are
attempting to destroy. Freemen, rally round the standard of
those who are the defenders of your privileges, and victory will
be yours.---JEFFERYS and BARLOW for ever !

JULY 14, 1802.   A real Independent Freeman.

MERRIDEW's Office, Coventry.

(12½″ × 7½″)   124

One Last Word

from GEOFFREY JOHNSON SMITH

Time and time again I have publicly asked the Socialist Candidate, Mrs. Jeger :

> *"Where do you stand on the Red Flag issue in St. Pancras?"*
> *Can I get a straight answer?*   No.

I MUST THEN ACCEPT THAT SHE SUPPORTS THE FLYING OF THE RED FLAG AND <u>ALL IT IMPLIES</u>.

To be fair, Mrs. Jeger has stated she "never made a statement injurious to the Labour Group".

What kind of double talk is this? She speaks against the Party Line on Nuclear Disarmament. Why then did she refuse to condemn her former Socialist Leader, ex-Councillor John Lawrence?

*   *   *

However, let's pay tribute to her foresight. On the front of her Election Address Mrs. Jeger is seen <u>WALKING AWAY</u> from the House of Commons.

Let's not hinder or detain her—let's keep her walking

THIS TIME VOTE CONSERVATIVE

for

Geoffrey JOHNSON SMITH

Published by Miss. P. Blakemore, 5, Guilford Place, W.C.I. and Printed by Lakeman & Co., W.C.I.

$(8\frac{1}{2}" \times 5\frac{1}{2}")$

£2,000 REWARD

FOR

INFORMATION LEADING TO THE IDENTIFICATION OF

ELIZABETH 1st OF SCOTLAND

DEAD OR ALIVE

$(14\frac{1}{4}'' \times 17\frac{3}{4}'')$

He Had No Song

OR

Trying to get to heaven without a Saviour

SEVERAL years ago, while passing out of the meeting one evening, a lady asked me to go with her and see her husband, who was quite sick. On her way, she told me he was anxious about his soul, knowing he would soon have to die. When I entered the room, I found him sitting in an easy chair, as he could not lie down without coughing. After a few words about his bodily sufferings, I asked him about his soul—did he think his sufferings would end when his body yielded and death came.

"Well," he said, "I think my chances for getting to heaven are pretty good."

"Do you believe heaven is a reality?" I asked.

He said, "Yes."

"Is it true there is a hell?"

He replied, "Yes, I believe it."

"And you have an immortal soul that will soon be in one or other of these places forever."

"Yes," he said earnestly.

"You just now said you thought your chances for heaven were pretty good; you believe heaven is a reality, and hell is a reality, and your precious, immortal soul will soon be happy in heaven forever. You must have some reason for it. Would you tell me what it is?"

His voice was weak, and I waited for his answer as it came slowly; "Well, I've always been kind to my wife and children and I have not intentionally did an injus-

Scripture (I Tim. 1:15). "This is a faithful saying and worthy of all acceptation, that Christ Jesus came into the world to SAVE sinners." He repeated, "To save — sinners!

"Yes," I said, "to SAVE sinners—not to HELP sinners to be saved, but to SAVE sinners. He is not a helper, but a SAVIOUR, and God's Word is, To him that WORKETH NOT, but believeth on Him that justifieth the ungodly, his faith is counted for righteousness.' And again 'Believe on the Lord Jesus Christ, and thou shalt be saved'." He did believe. I left him that night, after reading other Scriptures to him, with a new hope—not based on what he had done, but believing what God says about what Christ had done.

I called the next morning to see him. As I entered he looked up with joy in his face, and said, "Oh, I'll have a song now! It will be, "Unto Him that loved us, and washed us from our sins in His own blood."

He was with us about a week more, and fell asleep happy in the Lord.

Reader, will you be able to sing that song, or will you have to say, "I am tormented in this flame?" It will be one or the other. "He that believeth and is baptized shall be saved, but he that believeth not shall be damned." (Mark 16:16). And again, "He that believeth on the Son hath everlasting life; and he that believeth not the Son shall not see life, but the wrath of God abideth on him." (John 3:36).

—J.H.W.

Evangelical Tract Distributors, Inc.
P. O. Box 146,   Edmonton, Alta., Can.

(Folded to 5¾" × 3")

HEAR **BILLY GRAHAM**

SPEAKING TO LONDON FROM GLASGOW

By direct long distance relay to 37 London centres

From MONDAY, APRIL 18

EVERY EVENING (Sunday Excepted) **AT 7-30 P.M.**

Doors open at 7-0 p.m.

COME AND HEAR **BILLY GRAHAM** AT

VERNON BAPTIST CHURCH

KING'S CROSS ROAD, W.C.1

(Where Penton Rise and Vernon Rise and Weston Rise all meet)

ACCESS: Buses and Trolley Buses pass the door
Bus 63.   From King's Cross—
Trolley Buses: 613, 617, 621, 659
(alight at bottom of Swinton Street)
From the City—Trolley Buses: 513, 517, 521
(alight at Swinton Street)

BRING YOUR FRIEND

W. A. Hitchcock (Printers) Ltd., 30, Homefield Road, Wimbledon, S.W.19

(Bottom: 7½" × 5")

J. PERREN, JUNR,
OIL AND COLORMAN, VARNISH
And Blacking Maker,

SHOP LIST,

This is the age in which Cheap things go down,
For all o'er England "prices low" have much renown ;
But here I think you will with me agree,
That cheapness should be join'd with Quality ;
When cheapness is with quality combin'd,
Then are your bargains such as suit your mind.
With introductions I'll not waste your time,
But come unto the subject of my rhyme ;
Which is, in as few words as I can tell,
To give you a list of articles I sell ;
Brushes and Brooms, with which you sweep things clean,
All sorts and sizes, these shall be my theme ;
Come forth Hair Brooms, not short but long,
And help to form the subject of my song ;
Black Lead, Round Oil, and Scrubbing Brush-s too,
'Sides those with which you clean your shoe.
Next Candles for good quality renown'd
And Pepper which we sell both Whole and Ground ;
But Soaps to mention I must not forget,
The Mottled's hard, the Yellow not too wet.
Next Starch and Blue of quality first rate,
Come try, and you will say a truth I state
Also Soda, used the Soap to save,
About its quality I am not going to rave :
Step in and buy a pound, or two, or three ;
And then you'll want no eulogy from me.
Next comes Salt, Fine Mustard and Good Pepper,
Search Walworth o'er I known you'll find no better ;
'sides these we've Pickles, and those very fine,
Which makes Cold Beef eat nice in Summer time ;
Or when you've Fish, you can without remorse,
Purchase some excellent Anchovy Sauce.
Fine Cloves, Best White Ginger, and other spice,
First of which makes Apple Pies eat nice ;
The Best Green Treacle, likewise fine Honey,
May here be bought with very little money.
Best Shag Tobacco, Rappee and Scoth Snuff,
For quality 'tis out and out good stuff ;
The latter Snuff so strong it really is,
Warms old one's noses, and makes the young ones sniz, (sneeze)
Next to the Economist I have to say,
A word about the night tho', not the day ;
It is just this, that if you have a wife,
Who is petickler careful of her life,
And who can never sleep within the dark,
For fear that some unruly rat should lark ;
Or who is 'fraid, of waking in a dreadfull fright
From the visit of a Ghost or Spright;
I have a Charm to drive these tears away.
And makes the room appear almost like day ;
It is a Box of " Star Lights " for three pence,
To last three months, likewise your costs condense ;
One trial I am sure will do no harm,
T will save your pockets, also much alarm.
Next I'll whisper to each damsel fair,
I've Paper White and Brown, for curling hair ;
And as sometimes she does her fingers soil,
I'll just inform her I've some Scented Oil ;
These things combined with Looking Glasses,
Will we I assist our Charming lasses.
And should your Shoes, or Boots, a clean be lacking,
Pray dont forget to ask for **PERREN'S BLACKING !**
With very little labour it will shine,
And as for price, no fault with that you'll find ;

For a small Bottle, Threepence is the charge,
And Ninepence only, for a Bottle large;
The middle size we only charge Sixpence,
At this, I'm sure you cannot take offence :
If this dont suit, we have the Paste in Pots ,
At just Three-half-pence, or we've Penny lots.
Dear Blacking may now be dispensed with,
And no longer thought to be expensive,
And as our Blacking is both Cheap and Good,
That you will call, I hope 'tis understood.
Next Black Lead ; but to puff I don't pretend,
Yet 'tis rightly nam'd " The Servant's Friend";
And if you have a mind this Friend to try,
I hope you will call in as you pass by.
Hearth Stones, and Flander's Brick I here must name,
As they to usefulness must have some claim ;
Glass-paper, Emry, Rope and Croydon Sand,
Tho' altogether, they make a motley band.
Best Laid Cord, Ran Thread, Pack Tread, and Dutch Twine,
With Clothes Lines, Silver Sand, and good Sash Line ;
Pipes, and Pipe Clay, I to your notice bring.
Mason's Dust, Fuller's Earth and Fine Whiting ;
Rottenstone, and Droppings of Sweet Oil,
Without which undoubtedly you'd have more toil.
Old man's Plasters, do not say I'm bold,
There very excellent in case of cold :
Or at least, when pains one's back do rack,
And when we wish for ease and comfort back ;
Or if for an aperient constitution halts,
I strongly urge the use of " Epsom Salts ";
This article by taste is seldom recommended :
But by utility, 'tis oft befriended.
Next comes something which you must well rub in,
Tis no other than the far fam'd Dubbin :
A bit of this I'd say (yet will not bet,)
Will make your shoes impervious to the wet.
Next comes Cart Grease, Ink, and Orchil Dye,
Last of which makes chairs to suit the eye :
And should I not your patience harrass,
I would just say I have some Plaster of Paris
Just thought of it I a word to Sporting Lads,
I have some excellent Percussion Caps :
Gunpowder too, the Fine as well as Coarse.
And Shots - dear me I'm getting very hoarse,
And as I've gone my stock all o'er,
I really cannot say much more.
Yet by the by I have not said enough,
There is one thing, and that is Kitchen Stuff ;
This article upon such terms we buy,
As competition's terrors to defy.
And now to make my ryhming more prolific ;
I'll say a word unto the scientific.
I think I hear them me a poetaster call,
Denouncing this a stupid, senseless scrawl ;
Or try me by a paying Critic's Rule,
And call me a consummate, arrant fool.
But yet their criticism they may spare,
As I of Pots fame expect no share.
The faults they see, I hope they will forgive,
Living themselves, yet letting others live ;
And now I've said thus much I here end my lay,
With a good night, or if it be day—Good day.

40, GEORGE STREET, RICHMOND ST.
WALWORTH.

LEE, Printer, Rose Court,   High-street, Newington att.

(9⅞″ × 7½″)

(7½″ × 3½″)

(7½″ × 3½″)

See gang awa' get out the mare,
  We'll baith slip ob the back o't:
For gin I wait my fathers time,
  I'll wait till I be fifty—
But na, I'll marry when I am young
  An' mak' a wife fu' thrifty.

Wow? Robin was an angry man,
  At losing o' his dochter;
Thro' a' the kintra side he ran,
  An' far an' near he sought her;
But when he cam' to our fire-end,
  An' fand us baith thegither,
Quo' I gudeman, I vea'en your bairn
  An' ye may tak' my mither.

Auld Robin gird'd an' sheuk his pow,
  Guid faith? quo he you're merry;
But I'll just tak' you at your word,
  An' end this hurry burry.
So Robin an' our auld guidwife
  Agreed to creep thegither;
Now I hae Robin Tamson's pet,
  And Robin has my mither.

Will the Weaver.

Mother dear now I'm married,
  I wish I had longer tarried

For my wife she does declare,
  That the breeches she will wear.
Is she bold or is she quiet?
  Is she costly in her diet?
Loving son give her her due,
  Let me hear no more from you.

Going one night to my treasure,
  Their I met an honest neighbour;
Says, kind sir, I'll tell you who
  I saw with your wife just now.
I saw her and Will the weaver;
  They were unco close the-gither,
At the threshold of the door,
  They went in I saw no more.

Thank you kindly honest neighbour,
  I'll reward you for your labour;
If I catch him at my corn,
  Better had he ne'er been born.
He went home in a great wonder,
  Knocking at the door like thunder,
Who is that? Will the weaver cries,
  'Tis my husband, you must rise

My cave would be a lover's bower,
  Tho' raging winter rent the air,
And she a lovely little flower,
  That I would tent and shelter there.

O sweet is she in yon town,
  The setting sun's gaun down upon;
The dearest maid's in yon town,
  His setting beam e'er shone upon,
If angry fate be sworn my foe,
  And suffering I am doomed to bear,
I'll careless quit aught else below;
  But spare, Oh! spare my Jeanie dear.

For while life's dearest blood is warm,
  My thoughts frae her shall ne'er depart;
For as most lovely is her form,
  She has the truest kindest heart.

FINIS.

FOUR
POPULAR
SONGS,

viz.

ALICE GRAY.

My Mither men't my auld breeks.

WILL THE WEAVER,

AND

O WAT YE WHA'S IN YON TOWN.

STIRLING:
PRINTED BY E. JOHNSTONE, BOOKSELLER.

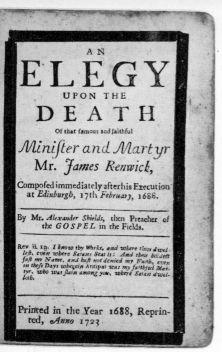

AN
ELEGY
UPON THE
DEATH
Of that famous and faithful

Minister and Martyr
Mr. *James Renwick*,

Compofed immediately after his Execution
at *Edinburgh*, 17th *February*, 1688.

By Mr. *Alexander Shields*, then Preacher of
the *GOSPEL* in the Fields.

*Rev ii. 13. I know thy Works, and where thou dwel-
left, even where Satans Seat is: And thou holdeft
faft my Name, and haft not denied my Faith, even
in thofe Days wherein Antipas was my faithful Martyr, who was flain among you, where Satan dwel-
leth.*

Printed in the Year 1688, Reprinted, *Anno* 1723

THE
SCOTCH HAGGIS;
A SELECTION OF
CHOICE BON MOTS,
IRISH BLUNDERS, REPARTEES, ANECDOTES, &c.

Care to our coffin adds a nail no doubt,
While every laugh so merry draws one out.

GLASGOW:
PRINTED FOR THE BOOKSELLERS.
37

THE
BATTLE OF
BOTHWELL BRIGG;
AN
OLD SCOTCH BALLAD.

GLASGOW:
PRINTED FOR THE BOOKSELLERS.
73.

Two Excellent
NEW SONGS:

I. In allufion to a game at Cards called Whisk;
or, all the advantages gained over the French
to the end of the year 1759.

II. A dialogue between a highland Gentleman
and his Lady on his being made a Captain.

Compofed in Pollock Shaws by I. H.

Printed at Glafgow for the year 1760. and fold
fecond Shop below Gibfons Wynd.

(*Top:* 6″ × 3⅞″)

(*Bottom:* 6″ × 3¾″)

(*Top:* 6″ × 3⅞″)

(*Bottom:* 7″ × 4¼″)

THE

TRAGICAL BALLAD OF

LORD JOHN'S MURDER;

TOGETHER WITH

THE CRUEL BROTHER.

GLASGOW
PRINTED FOR THE BOOKSELLERS.
79.

THE

WAY TO WEALTH,

Written by the late

DR. FRANKLIN.

Extracted from his Political Works.

" For age and want save while you may
" No morning sun lasts a whole day."
POOR RICHARD.

NOTTINGHAM:
PRINTED BY C. SUTTON, BRIDLESMITH-GATE.

[Price One Penny.]

THE

HERMIT

OF

WARKWORTH:

A

NORTHUMBERLAND TALE.

IN THREE PARTS.

BY DR. THOMAS PERCY, BISHOP OF DROMORE.

GLASGOW:
PRINTED FOR THE BOOKSELLERS.

HISTORY OF

Dr. FAUSTUS

SHEWING

His wicked Life and horrid Death, and how he
sold himself to the devil, to have power for 24
years to do what he pleased, also many strange
things done by him with the assistance of

MEPHOSTOPHILES.

With an account how the devil came for him at
the end of 24 years, and tore him to pieces.

GLASGOW:
PRINTED FOR THE BOOKSELLERS.
119

(*Top:* 6″ × 3⅞″)

(*Bottom:* 6″ × 3¾″)

(*Top:* 6¼″ × 4″)

(*Bottom:* 6″ × 3¾″)

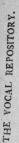

THE VOCAL REPOSITORY.

SECOND SERIES.

THE MAY DAY GARLAND.

Being a Choice Collection of
POETICAL FLOWERS, or SONGS.
Suited to that Day and Season

MAY.

10. ...
11. THE HERD.
12. THE RISING DAY.
13. ADVICE TO THE FAIR.
14. MORNING.
15. SPRING.
16. THE VIOLET.
17. A RURAL LIFE.
18. THE GENEROUS MAID.

...OF GRACE
...S CALL.
...R SONG.
...TH OF MAY.

...and Toy Warehouse, 6, Great st, andrew street. 7 Dials,

Printed by D. Wrighton, No. 86, Snow Hill, ...mingham

THE BRISTOL GARLAND.

PART I.

A Merchant's Son of worthy Fame,
From the Town of Bristol came,
Two a sweet & pleasant Green,
Where little Girls are to be seen.

Who ...ed in the Month of May,
With flow'ry Garland, fresh & gay,
With Music for to entertain,
The youthful charming rural plain.

Amongst these youthful Ladies bright,
None did excel for Red or White,
Lucy a Shepherd's daughter fair,
She like an Angel did appear.

The Merchants Son, who never knew,
Before that time what Love could do,
Began to feel an inward flame,
So with these words to she, he came.

Thou charming beauty of the day;
Who far exceeds the month of May,
And all the Beauties of the Plain,
Do not my humble suit disdain.

She answer'd with a modest voice,
Sir, you're mistaken, in your choice,
Don't set your heart & Love on me,
Who am one of mean degree.

But a poor Shepherd's daughter, ...
With that the small school ...
He did these words to her express,
Mydear, I love you ne'er the less.

How many Men of worthy Fame,
In former days that I could name,
Who made it their easy way to keep,
Their mighty Flocks, to Lambs & sheep.

Then let us try father joy,
And if he's willing to be our,
His daughter's on me I'll rejoice,
And be well pleased with the choice

Accordingly she gave consent,
And to her Father straitway he went,
Here be then treated love of Love,
And that he would right constant...

Said he...
That in the...
You'll not...
So now faint...
Returning...
With bitter...
I'an grieve...
That, I was...
let me...
Nor sighs...
I'll set my...
And by c...
Be than...
We'll wit...

A GARLAND OF NEW SONGS.

Sweet Willy o' the Green.
The Yorkshire Concert.
The Yorkshire Irishman.
The Woodland Maid.

Newcastle upon Tyne:
Printed by J. Marshall, in the Old Flesh-Market.
Where may also be had, a large, and interesting Collection
of Songs, Ballads, Tales, Histories, &c.

If tears... you on...
God gave it me thus to serve you,
Thus was he dutiful & kind,
New Sons & Daughters bear in mind,
How tender he was to his Friends,
And thus my resolved duty ends.

...substain,
...the main.

Pounds & more,
...fore,
...I then seiz'd,
we ne'er plac'd.

(*Top:* 7½″ × 5⅛″)   (*Centre:* 6″ × 4″)   (*Bottom:* 9¼″ × 10½″)

A
SUPPLEMENT
TO THE
COLLECTION
OF THE
Debates and Proceedings
IN
PARLIAMENT,
In 1694, and 1695.
Upon the INQUIRY into the
Late Briberies
AND
Corrupt Practices.

Venális Populus, venális Curia Patrum.
Est favor in pretio.
Ipsáq; Majestas Auro corrupta jacebat.   Petron. Satyr.

LONDON, Printed in the Year MDCXCV.

A
LAMENTATION
OVER THE
CITY
OF
GRONINGHEN.
CONTAINING

An Answer to Four Papers written against
the People called *Quakers*, Two by the Magistrates,
and Two Lies sung in the Street, by the Wild and
Ungodly Ballet-Singers, which shews that the Spirit of Persecution and Mockery comes all from one
Ground.

Amos 5.1. *Hear ye this Word which I take up against you, even a Lamentation,*
O House of Israel.
Amos 8.10. *And I will turn your Feasts into Mourning, and all your Songs*
into Lamentation, and I will bring up Sackcloath upon all Loyns, and Baldness
upon every Head: And I will make it as the Mourning of an only Son, and
the end thereof as a bitter Day.

LONDON, Printed by T. Sowle, 1694.

(Top: 8½″ × 6½″)

(Bottom: 7⅛″ × 5½″)

The Famous Battle between ROBIN HOOD, and the *Curtal Fryar*.
To a New Northern Tune.

Robin Hood.   The Curtal Fryar.

IN summer time when leaves grow green,
  and flowers are fresh and gay,
Robin Hood and his merry men,
  were disposed to play:
Then some would leap and some would run,
  and some would use Artillery,
Which of you can a good bow draw,
  a good archer to be?
Which of you can kill a Buck?
  or who can kill a Doe?
Or who can kill a Hart of Greece,
  five hundred foot him fro?
Will. Scadlock he kill'd a buck,
  and Midge he kill'd a Doe;
And little John kill'd a Hart of Greece,
  five hundred foot him fro:
Gods blessing on thy heart, said Robin Hood
  that shot such a shot to me,
I would ride my horse an hundred miles,
  to find one could match thee.
That caused Will Scadlock to laugh,
  he laught full heartily,

There lives a curtal Fryar in Fountain-Abby,
  will beat both him and thee.
Robin Hood put on his harness good,
  and on his head a Cap of steel,
Broad sword and buckler by his side,
  and they became him weel.
He took his bow into his hand,
  it was of a trusty tree,
With a sheaf of arrows at his belt,
  to the Fountains Dale went he.
And coming unto Fountains Dale,
  no farther would he ride,
There was he ware of a Curtal Fryar
  walking by the water side.
The Fryar had a harness good,
  and on his head a cap of steel,
Broad sword and buckler by his side,
  and they became him weel.
Robin Hood lighted off his horse,
  and tyed him to a thorn,
Carry me over the water thou Curtal Fryar,
  or else thy life's forlorn.
The Fryar took Robin Hood on his back,
  deep water he did bestride,
And speak neither good word nor bad,
  till he came at the other side.
Lightly stept Ro. Hood off the Fryars back,
  the Fryar said to him again,
Carry me over the water thou fine fellow,
  or it shall breed thy pain.
Robin Hood took the Fryar on his back,
  deep water he did bestride,
And speak neither good word nor bad,
  till he came at the other side.
Lightly leapt the Fryar off Robin Hoods back
  Robin Hood said to him again,
Carry me over the water thou Curtel Fryar,
  or it shall breed thy pain.
The Fryar took Robin Hood on's back again,
  and stept up to the knee,
Till he came at the middle stream,
  neither good nor bad spake he.
And coming to the middle stream,
  there he threw Robin in,
And chuse thee, chuse thee, fine fellow,
  whether thou wilt sink or swim.

(9¼″ × 7¾″)

135

THE
SUFFOLK MIRACLE;

BEING

The Relation of a young Man, who after his Death
appeared to his Sweetheart, and carried her behind him Forty Miles
in two Hour's Time, and was never seen after, but in the Grave.

Tune of, *My Bleeding Heart*, &c.

A Wonder strange as e'er was known,
Then what I now shall treat upon,
In *Suffolk* there did lately dwell,
A Farmer Rich, and known full well.

He had a Daughter fair and bright,
On whom he plac'd his chief Delight,
Her Beauty was beyond compare,
She was both virtuous and fair.

A young Man there was living by,
Who was so charmed with her Eye,
That he could never be at Rest,
He was with Love so much possest.

He made Address to her, and she
Did grant him Love immediately,
But when her Father came to hear,
He parted her, and her poor Dear.

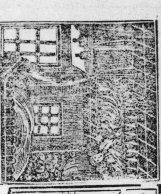

Forty Miles distant was the sun,
Unto her Uncle's, with Intent,
That she should there so long remain,
Till she had chang'd her Mind again.

Hereat this young Man sadly griev'd,
But knew not how to be reliev'd;
He sigh'd and sobb'd continually,
That his true Love he could not see.

She by no Means could to him send,
Who was her Heart's espoused Friend;
He sigh'd, he griev'd, but all in Vain,
For the confin'd must still remain.

He mourn'd so much that Doctor's Art
Could give no Ease unto his Heart,
Who was so strangely terrify'd,
That in short time for Love he dy'd.

She that from him was sent away,
Knew nothing of his dying Day,
But constant still she did remain,
To Love the Dead was then in vain.

After he had in Grave been laid,
A Month or more, unto this Maid,
He came about Middle of the Night,
Who joy'd to see her Heart's Delight.

Her Father's Horse which well she knew,
Her Mother's Hood and Safeguard too,
He brought with him to testify,
Her Parents Order he came by.

Which when her Uncle understood,
He hop'd it might be for her Good,
And gave consent to her straight way,
That with him she should come away.

When she was got her Love behind,
They pass'd as swift as any Wind,
That in two Hours, or little more,
He brought her to her Father's Door.

But as they did this great Haste make,
He did complain his Head did ake;
Her Handkerchief he then took out,
And ty'd the same his Head about.

And unto him she thus did say,
Thou art as cold as any Clay,
When we come home a Fire we'll have,
But little dream't he went to Grave.

Soon were they at her Father's Door,
And after she ne'er see him more;
I'll let the Horse up then, he said,
And there he left this harmless Maid.

She knock'd, and straight amain, he cry'd,
Who's there? 'tis I, the then reply'd:
Who wonder'd much her Voice to hear,
And was possest with Dread and Fear.

Her Father he did tell, and then,
He star'd like an affrighted Man.
Down Stairs he ran, and when he see her,
Cry'd out, My Child, how can it thou here?

Pray Sir, did you not send for me,
By such a Messenger, said she,
Which made his Hair stand on his Head,
As knowing well that he was dead.

Where is he then, to her he said,
He's in the Stable, quoth the Maid,
Go in said he, and go to Bed,
I'll see the Horse well littered.

He star'd about, and there could he
No Shape of any Man find see,
But found his Horse all in a Sweat,
Which put him in a deadly fright.

His Daughter he said nothing to,
Nor no one else, though well they knew
That he was dead a Month before,
For fear of grieving her full sore.

Her Father to his Father went,
(Who was decay'd) with this Intent,
To tell him what his Daughter said,
So both came back unto this Maid.

They asked her, and she still did say,
'Twas him that then brought her away;
Which when they heard they were amaz'd
And on each other strangely gaz'd.

A Handkerchief, she said, she ty'd
About his Head, and that they try'd;
The Saxton they did speak unto,
That he the Grave would then undo.

Affrighted then they did behold
His Body turning into Mould;
And tho' he had a Month been dead,
This Handkerchief was about his Head.

This thing unto her then they told,
And the whole Truth they did unfold,
She was thereat so terrified
And griev'd, she quickly after died.

Part not true Love, you rich Men can,
But if they be right honest Men,
Your Daughter's Love give them their own,
For Force oft breeds their Life's decay.

Newcastle upon Tyne: Printed and Sold *JOHN WHITE.*

(*Trimmed to* 8½″ × 13″)

136

THE
Just Judgment of GOD shew'd upon Dr. *John Faustus*.

To the Tune of, *Fortune my Foe*, &c.

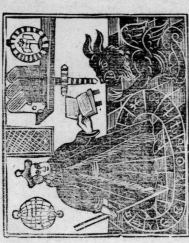

ALL Christian Men give Ear a while to me,
How I am plung'd in Pain, but cannot see:
I liv'd a Life, the like did none before,
Forsaking Christ, and I am damn'd therefore.

At *Wertenburgh*, a Town in *Germany*,
There was I born and bred of good Degree,
Of honest Stock, which afterwards I sham'd,
Accurst therefore, for *Faustus* was I nam'd.

In learning high, my Uncle brought up me,
And made me Doctor of Divinity:
And when he dy'd he left me all his Wealth,
Which curfed Gold did hinder my Soul's Health.

Then did I shun the Holy Bible Book,
Nor on God's Word would never after look;
But studied the accursed Conjuration,
Which was the Cause of my utter Damnation.

The Devil in Fryers Weeds appeared to me,
And straight to my Request he did agree,
That I might have all Things at my Desire,
I gave him Soul and Body for his Hire.

Twice did I make my tender Flesh to bleed,
Twice with my Blood I wrote the Devil's Deed,
Twice wretchedly I Soul and Body fold,
To live in Pleasure, and do what Things I would.

For four and twenty Years this Bond was made,
And then at length my Soul for it was paid;
Time ran away, and yet I never thought,
How dear my Soul our Saviour Christ had bought.

Would I at first been made a Beast by Kind,
Then had not I so vainly set my Mind;
Or would not when Reason began to bloom,
Some darksome Den had been my deadly Tomb.

Wo to the Day of my Nativity!
Wo to the Time that once did foster me!
And wo unto the Hand that sealed the Bill——
Wo to myself the Cause of all my Ill!

The Time I pass'd away with much Delight,
'Mongst Princes, Peers, and many a worthy Knight,
I wrought such Wonders by my Magick Skill,
That all the World may talk of *Faustus* still.

The Devil carried me up in the Skie,
Where I did see how all the World did lie:
I went about the World in eight Days Space,
And then return'd into my native Place.

What Pleasure I did wish to please my Mind,
He did perform, as Bond and Seal did bind:
The Secrets of the Stars and Planets told,
Of Earth and Sea, with Wonders manifold.

When four and twenty Years was almost run,
I thought on Things that then was past and done;
How that the Devil will soon claim his Right,
And carry me to everlasting Night.

Then all too late I curst my wicked Deed,
The Dread thereof does make my Heart to bleed:
All Days and Hours I mourned wond'rous sore,
Repenting then of all Things done before.

I then did wish both Sun and Moon to stay,
All Times and Seasons never to decay:
Then had my Time ne'er come to dated End,
Nor Soul and Body down to Hell descend.

At last when I had but one Hour to come,
I turn'd the Glass for my last Hour to run:
And call'd in learned Men to comfort me,
But Faith was gone, and none could succour me.

By Twelve o'Clock my Glass was almost out,
My grieved Conscience then began to doubt:
I pray'd the Studious to stay in Chamber by,
But as they staid they heard a doleful cry.

Then presently they came into the Hall,
Whereas my Brains were cast against the Wall;
Both Arms and Legs in Pieces they did see,
My Bowels gone, there was an End of me.

You Conjurors and damned Witches all,
Example take by my unhappy Fall:
Give not your Souls and Bodies unto Hell,
See that the smallest Hair you do not sell.

But hope in Christ his Kingdom you may gain,
Where you shall never fear such mortal Pain;
Forsake the Devil and all his crafty Ways,
Embrace true Faith that never more decays.

F I N I S.

137

A pretty Ballad of the Lord of LORN, and the false Steward.

To the Tune of Green Sleeves.

Licen'd according to Order.

IT was a worthy Lord of Lorn,
he was a Lord of high degree,
He sent his Son unto the School,
to learn some civility.

He learned more in one day,
than other Children did in three,
And thus bespake the School-master,
to him most tenderly:

In faith thou art the bonniest boy,
as e're I blickt on with my Eye,
I hope thou art some Easterling born,
the Holy Ghost is with thee:

He said he was no Easterling born,
the Child thus answer'd courteously,
My Father is the Lord of Lorn,
and I his Son perdye.

The Schoolmaster turn'd round about
his angry mood he could not swage,
He bring of to render Age,

He girt the Saddle to the Steed,
the Bridle of the best Gold shown,
He took his leave of his fellows all,
and quickly he was gone.

And when he came to his Father dear,
he kneeled down at his knee,
I am come to you Father he said,
God's blessing to me give:

Thou art welcome, my Son, he said,
God's blessing I thee give:
What rydings that thou brought, my
being come to hastily: (Son
I have brought rydings, Father, he said
and so bleed it may be,
There's neer a Doctor in all the realm
for all he goes in rich array,
I can write him at ten for one,
to learn in seven Years Day.

That is good rydings, said the Lord,
all in the Place where I do stand,
My Son thou hast into France go,
to learn the Speeches of each land,
Who shall go with him I faithful lady
Husband, we have none but he,

Madam, he said, my head Steward,
he hath been true to me.
She call'd the Steward to an account,
a thousand pound the gave him anon
Says, Good Sr Steward, I good to me
while he is far from home.   (Child,
If't be false to my young Lord,
may God justly punish me indeed.
And now to France thy lov't are gone
and God be their good speed.
They had not been in France Land,
not three weeks to an end,   (none
But Meat and drink the Child got
nor Money in purse to spend.
The Child run to the River side,

As the told the Steward let me have my Life,
to put the Child therein.
But nay, marry, said the Child,
he ask'd Mercy pitifully:
Good Steward let me have my Life,
what e're to me come.
Now pull off thy fair cloathing,
and give it me to my Body:
So pull off thy likling Shirt,
with many a golden Seam.
But when the Child was stript naked,
his body as white as a Lilly-flower,
He might have been seen for is body
a Princes Paramount.
He put him on an old Kelter Coat,
and hose of the same above the knee,
He bid him go to the Shepherd's house
to keep Sheep on a love lovely.
The Child said, what shall be thy name
good Steward tell to me:
Thy name shall be Poor, dust thou wear
that thy Name shall be,   (choule
The Child came to the Shepherd's
and asked mercy pitifully:
Say, Good Shepherd take me in,
to keep Sheep as a love lovely:
But when the Shepherd saw the child
he was so pleasant in his eye,

I have no Child, I'll make thee my Heir
thou shalt have my Goods perdye.
And then bespoke the Shepherd's wife
unto the Child so tenderly,   (said
Thou must take the Sheep, and go to the
and keep them on a love lovely.
Now let us leave talking of the child,
that is keeping Sheep on love lovely
And we'll make more of the false Ste-
that a Lord might we come to worn, (ward
He brought himself's Suns of apparel,
and call'd himself the Lord of Lorn.
The Duke he welcomd the Lord,
with three bac'd Stags anon.
If he had wist him the false Steward,
to the Devil he should have gone,
But when they were at Supper se,
with dainty delicate, that were there
theDuke said, if you'll dest my daughter
I'll give thee a thousand pound a Year
the Lady would see the red buckram,
and also for to hunt the Doe,
And with a hundred lusty Men,
the Lady did a hunting go,
The Lady did a hunting gone,
over Feantor that is so high,
There was the aware of a Shepherds
with Sheep on a love lovely,   (boy
And e're he sighed and make moan,
and cryed out pitifully:
My Father is the Lord of Lorn,
and I know not what becomes of me,
And then bespake the Lady gay,
unto her Maid anon,
Go fetch my bitter the Shepherd's boy
why maketh he all this mean?
But when she came before the Lady,
with Sheep on a love lovely,
where wast thou born my bonny child?
for whose sike make you all this mean
My dearest friend, Lord, he said,
is dead many Years agone,

Tell thou me, thou lovely Child,
tell me the truth, and do not lie,
I wou'd thou wert not the young Lord Lorn,
Is it come a wrong unto me.
Ye perforce, faith the Child,
I know the Lord I born verily,
The young Lord is a valiant Lord,
at home in his own Country,
Wilt leave thy Sheep, thou bonny child
and come in service unto me,
Yea, forsooth then faith the Lord,
at your bidding will I be.
When the Steward lookt on the child
he bewailed him villianously,
Where was thou born thou Vagabond?
or where is thy Country?
He down, he down, said the Lady,
the call'd the Steward then perf only
Without you hear him more good will,
you get no love of me.
Then bespake the false Steward
unto the Lady hastily,
At Aberden behind the Seas,
his Father robbed thousand three.
But then bespake the Lady gay,
unto her Father courteously,
Saying, I have found a bonny child,
my chamberlain to be,
Not so, not so, then said the Duke,
for so it may not be,
For the Lord of Lorn that comes a
will think no good of the. nor me,
When the Duke lookt upon the Child
he seemed so pleasant in the Eye,
Child, because thou lovest Horses well
my Groom of Stable thou shalt be,
The Child ply'd the Horses well,
a twelve Month to an end,
He was so courteous and so true,
every Man became his Friend:
He le'd a fair Gelding to the Water,
where he might drink verily,
The gelding up with his heel,
and hit the Child above the eye,
Wo worth the boy, fetion say the child
that ever Mare foaled thee,
thou little knowst what thou hast done
thou hast a stricken a Lord's degree,
The Duke's daughter in a garden green
the heard the child make great moan
She ran to the Child all weeping,
and let her Maiden all alone
Sing on thy Song: thou bonny child,
I will release thee of thy pain,
I have made an oath, Lady, he said,
I dare not tell my tale again,
tell the bonisty tale thou bonny child
and so by Oath that I'swed be,
But when he told the Horse his tale,
the Lady wept most tenderly,
I'll do for thee, my bonny Child,
in faith I will do more for thee,

And for thy sake, my bonny child,
I'll make my wedding of Monto three
The Lady did write a Letter then,
full privily with her own hand,
She sent it to the Lord of Lorn
wheres he dwelt in fair Scotland.
But when the Lord had read the letter,
his Lady wept most tenderly.
I knew wo it would be wore of my child
in such a far Country.
The old Lord call'd up his merry men,
and all that he gave Cloath and Fee,
With Seven Lords by his side,
and into France rides he.
The Windserv'd and they did fail:
so far into France Land,
They were aware of the Lord of Lorn
with a Porter's staff in his hand,
The Lords they moved hat and hand,
the serving Men fell on their knee,
What folks be yonder, said the Steward
that make the Porter Courtesie. (Lorn
Thou art false thief, quoth the lord of
no longer might I bear with thee,
By the Law of France thou shalt be
whether it be to love or dye, I judg'd
A Quest of Lords there chosen was,
to fetch they come hastily,
But when the quest was ended,
the false Steward must dye.
First they did him half hing,
and then put him in boyling lead,
And then was fodden breast and bone
And then bespoke the Lord of Lorn,
with many other Dukes more,
Sir Duke if you be as willing as we,
we'll have a Marriage before we go,
These Children both they did rejoyce
to hear the Lord say all so ended,
they had rather to day then to morrow
so he would not be offended.
But when the wedding ended was,
there was delicate dainty cheer,
I'll tell you how long the wedding did
full three quarters of a Year, [last
Such a banquet there was wrought,
the like was never seen,   [then,
The King of France brought with him
a hundred tun of good wine,
Five fets of Musitians were to be seen
that never refted night or day,
Also Italians there did sing,
full pleasantly with great joy,
Thus have you heard how troubles
unto succesive joys did turn, [great
And happy news among the rest,
unto the worthy Lord of Lorn,
Let Rebels therefore warned be,
how mischief once they do pretend,
For God may suffer for a time,
but will disclose it in the end.

THE
Northern Lass.

G.Bickham jun. sculp.   The Musick by Mr. W.m Fisher, at Hereford.

Come take your Glass ye Northern Lass so prettily advis'd, I drank her

Health, & realy was Agree-a-bly Surpriz'd, Her Shape so neat, her Voice so sweet, her

Air and Mein so free, The Syren charm'd me from my Meat, but take your Drink said she.

If from the North such Beauty comes,
    How is it that I feel;
Within my Breast ye glowing Flame,
    No Tongue can e'er reveal:
Tho cold & raw ye North Wind blows,
    All Summer's on her Breast,
Her Skin was like the driven Snow,
    But Sun-shine all ye rest.

Her Heart may southern Climates melt,
    Tho Frozen now it seems;
That Joy with Pain be equal felt,
    And ballanc'd in Extreams;
Then like our genial Wine shall charm,
    With Love my panting Breast;
Me, like our Sun her Heart shall warm,
    Be Ice to all the rest.

FLUTE.

A NEW SONG:

Called the true blue on the defeat
of the french fleet, by the honou-
-able Augustus Keppel, Admirel
of the blue, on the 27th of
July. The words fir Timothy

WAGPOLE

Once more von bold Brittons like lyons be roufed,
  Show Monfieurs your courag your caufe to
And bid a defiance to all daring foes, fefpoufe,
Who dare to to engage with old England,
And its oh fae old Englifh true blues.

It is thought an invafion is furely at hand,
For war they have declared & were comming to land
But now their are afraid that they'll furly get hang'd,
All by the true blues of old England,
  And its oh the Englifh, &c.

No fooner brave Keppel with his fleet had fet out,
But Monfieurs he met and put them to the rout,
And the brave Britifh heroes he made them to fhout
So ftanch is the tars of old England.
  And its oh the old Englifh, &c.

We fought yard arm to yard arm half hour or more,
While many bolb Britton did lay in his gour,
But we foon made them glad to run on their fhore
So ftanch was the tars of old England.
  And its oh the old Englifh bold tars. fcur,

And when the French Admiral was beat then Mon-
With his fleet in Weft harbour well fhatterd did fleer
Which difmay'd the French King whom be come for
  How that he was beat by old England,
  And its oh the old Englifh true blues.

So now my brave boys let us pufh round the can,
May we beat off the forces they are able to fend,
For to fight againft Brittons they never can ftand,
for which the bold tars of old England,
  And its oh the old Englifh, &c.

WATER PARTED
FROM THE SEA.

A NEW SONG

Sung this Season,

At all the Places of Publick

DIVERSION,

Water parted from the sea,
  May increafe the River's Tide
To the bubbling fount may flee,
  or tho' the fertile vallies glide,

Water parted from the Sea
  May increafe the Rever's Tide,
To the bubbling fount may flee,
  Or thro' the fertile vallies glide,

Tho' in fearch of foft repofe,
  Tho' the land it,s free to roam,
Still it murmurs as it flows,
  Panting for its native home,

Tho' in fearch of foft repofe,
  Thro' the Land its free to roam,
Still it murmurs as it flows,
Panting for its native home,   T W

(13⅛″ × 3⅞″)

(11⅛″ × 3⅞″)

141

A NEW SONG,

Being a Dialogue on the Sate of the Nation between two Britiſh Tars,

WELL met, brother John, I am juſt come from
    Charles-Town,
So pray tell me what news you're in fair London town,
Why my dear brother James, the news it runs common
You've the Americans beat, and burnt moſt of their towns,
Yet here we are told, that they mean to invade us,
And bid all the nation in defiance to ſtand,
That the French and Spaniards join them in all alliaur,
So they threaten Old England they'll take ſword in hand,

Too true, by my ſoul, I'm afraid is the Story,
All hands ſay, The Frenchmen we'll ſoon declare War,
Let them think of the laſt,—they were cropt in their glory
For to ſtand againſt Britons, You know they'll ne'er dare
Our men brave and outragious, like lions ſo bold,
Never fear thoſe two Nations, but we'll make them tremble
We'll ſoon change our lean into Silver or Gold,

Come, come, this is boaſting, no more of ſuch poher,
As good as three nations againſt us will ſtand,
Tho' American parties our ſea-coaſts will bother,
Our Navy diſpers'd, and our troops from the land,
For all that's Hearty Cock, we will give them their beating
Each Country'd regiment is raſing out of hand,
With my glittering broad ſword I am miſtaken,
No French, Spaniard, or Yankee before me deſire to ſtand

The Game-act hath diſarm'd all Your Yeomen ſo bold,
All around the ſea-coaſt, there's great danger to fear,
The ſea-ports neglected—Caſtles and Country houſes,
Will be burnt, ſack'd, or plunder'd, if the Yankies
    come there,

Never fear let us hope, that our ſailors ſo bold, boys,
Will ſoon make theſe fencies appear light as air,
And tho ſickneſs hath teſt us the Drake Sloop of War,
May ſome Cruizer ſoon bring in that bold privateer,

Beſides, brother James, we have got a brave army,
Our Militia's embodying as faſt as they can,
Had, trained and accountred like regular Forces,
And march thro their Counties out every Man,
Tho Children and Wives for their loſs are lamenting,
They are to be ſtation'd the ſea coaſts around,
And if the French Dogs ſhould perfume to invade us,
The devil ram me, but we'll drive them back home,

So puſh round the pitcher, let us drink and be merry,
Here's a health to our ſoldiers and ſoilors of fame,
And to their Commanders, both by land and by ſea,
May they chaſtiſe falſe France, and humble proud Spain;
And may Wiſdom guide the Heads of the nation,
And our Colonies once more with us united be,
Then our Foes ſhall find, that George is our Champion
And Britain ſtill flouriſh by Land and by ſea,

(12″ × 3⅝″)

A New Song,

Called, Weary of tumbling Alone.

ONE morning of late, as I walk'd in
    great ſtate,
I heard a maiden making ſad moan,
I aſk'd her the matter, ſhe ſaid, ſir, I won't
    flat er,
I am weary of tumbling alone.

O that is pity, that a maiden ſo pretty,
And the young man ſo idle are grown,
But a curſe light upon it, and worſe may
    come on it,
If I leave you a tumbling alone.

O then, ſays the ſailor, can you fancy me,
I have got gold, and got ſilver in ſtore,
I have brought from the ſea, ſuch a fine
    remedy,
That will eaſe you of tumbling alone.

O then, ſays the fair maid, if you can fancy
    me,
I have got plenty of money in ſtore,
No more croſs the main to fight France
    nor Spain,
Nor go where the cannons loud roar.

O then, ſays the ſailor, I can fancy you,
As long as your money doth laſt,
She grows thick in the waiſt, and thin in the
    face,
But the ſailor he ſteers off at laſt.

As down in the garden there grows a red
    roſe,
I'll pluck it, and call it my own,
In an hour it will fade, and ſo will a maid,
That's weary of tumbling alone.

(12⅝″ × 3⅜″)

A new SONG,

BRITONS *for arms yourselves prepare*
Honour and Glory co.. *for War,*
Reputed Sons of Ancient Fame,
Do not your Noble courage Stain,
Nor Submit Tamely to proud SPAIN.

You that Reign Masters of the Sea,
Shake of Inglorious sloath and ease;
Exert yourselves with force and might,
And show that Englishmen can fight,
And do their Injured Nation Right.

Display your Colours mount your Guns,
Batter their Castles and their Towns;
And let your thundering cannons Roar,
Till we our wanted Peace restore,
And coward Spain insults no more.

Resolved to conquor or to Die,
With armt pnrsu'd they'll soon comply,
How soon Hostilities will cease
And Britian gain a lasting Peace,
Then Trade will flourish and Increase.

THE
Wars are not Over.

AS I was travelling the country up and down,
  Until that I came to a little market town,
The drums beat loud for soldiers I am sure,
Which made me conclude the Wars were not o'er.

Then in comes the Tanner, and thus he does say:
I have trusted all my leather to a Shoemaker this day,
He's gone for a soldier, which grieveth me full sore,
And he will pay me for my leather when the wars are
    all o'er.

The next is the Taylor, and thus he does say:
They have knocked down my wages to sixpence a day
The people wear their old cloaths they are grown so
    poor,
And they will not get new till the wars are all o'er.

Then in come the Barber with razor and ball,
Do you want to be shav'd, kind gentlemen all?
The people wear their old wigs, they are grown so
    poor,
And they will not get new till the wars are all o'er.

The next trade is the Cooper, his trade is good for
    nought,
His hoops are too long and his staves are too short,
'Tis on the long settle there stands a long score,
And he will not rub it out till the wars are all o'er.

The next is the Blacksmith, his trade is worst of all,
He's sold his bed from under him for iron and coal,
He's taken up his lodgings upon the cold floor,
And there he must remain till the Wars be all o'er.

Then in comes the landlady so neat and so trim,
With her ruffles at her elbows, and thus she does
    begin,
I've let all my ale go, 'tis for an old score,
And I will pay my maltster when the Wars are all o'er

Then in came the Devil with the malt at his back,
With anger he stuff'd her in the mouth of his sack,
He took away the landlady, 'tis for an old score,
And he will bring her back again when the Wars
    are all o'er.

THE CHAUNT SELLER

Or, a New Batch of Ballads.

COME all you chanting vocalists,
   That warbles high and low, sirs,
A yard-and-a-half of music buy,
   That is of chaunting Joe, sirs;
Here is love songs, and comic songs,
   And songs of every nation,
And if you'll wait an instant,
   You shall have them in rotation.
       -- CHORUS.
A chaunt-seller I am by trade,
   As through the streets I trudge it,
Songs you'll find of every kind,
   I carry in my budget.

Here's Doctor Brown, and Alice Grey,
   Going to the Nore, sir,
With Billy Barlow and Crazy Jane,
   Capering on the shore, sir;
Why did I Love, Lost Rosabel,
   She's Bolted with Another,
The Man vot wears a Mackintosh,
   Well, Spooney, hows your Mother?

Here's the Nobby Waterman,
   Doing the Agreeable,
With the Maid of Judah, Out of Place,
   Upon the Parlour Table;
At close of Day, Bid me Discourse,
   The Pleasures of a Pipe, sir,
Oh! say not Woman's Heart is Bought,
   With Half a Yard of Tripe, sir.

I've been Roaming, Thro' the Woods,
   All Night upon the spree, sir,
With the Girl I left me,
   On the Open Sea, sir;
It was in the Merry Month of May,
   Upon the Rigs of Barley,
Gayly ye Danced down Wapping Stairs,
   Over the Water to Charlie.

If I had a Donkey wot wouldn't Go,
   All around the Room, sir.
I saw her at the Fancy Fair,
   With a Shovel and a Broom, sir;
I've Journey'd over Many Lands,
   With the King of the Forest Glade, sir,
Does you're Mother know you're Out?
   With the Mountain Maid, sir.

Come Landlord fill a Flowing Bowl,
   Begone, I say, Dull Care O!
The Flag that Brav'd a Thousand Years,
   At a Country Fair O!
When a little Farm we keep,
   On the Banks of Allan Water,
Soloman Lob, he lost his Nob,
   With the Rat Catcher's Daughter.

Here's the Parson's Clerk, the Cove wot Sings
   Amen, besides a Medley,
You'll find the Lass of Richmond Hill,
   Along with Arthur O'Bradley;
And there you have the Gipsy Girl,
   Going to Chelsea to buy a Bun, sir,
Rory O'More, Going out a Shooting,
   With my Master's Gun, sir.

Now's the Day and now's the Hour,
   Pretty Little Sally,
My Ellen is the Fairest Flower,
   She lives in our Al ey;
Tell me when, and tell me where,
   How to Spend a Dollar,
In the Days when we went Lushy home,
   With Glorious Apollo.

Here you see the Vorkhouse Boy,
   Likewise the Overseer, sir,
Going out a Gipsying,
   With the Jolly Buccaneer, sir
Come let us dance Dance an Sing,
   Mr. and Mrs. Wrangle,
Child of Earth with the Goden Hair
   Has your Mother sold her Mangle?

Love was once a Little Boy,
   Yet never go a Tossing,
I am over Young to Marry yet,
   The Man vot Sweeps a Crossing;
Meet me at the Garden Gate,
   A Fig for Pride and Riches,
Pray Goody please to moderate,
   Hodges Leather Breeches.

Far from me my True Love Flies,
   Sound the Trumpet boldly,
Drink to me only with thine Eyes,
   I am a Fashionable Coaley;
We met Bill Jones, with Sarah Sykes
   Lasses love the Sailors,
Tom Bowling, what's a Woman like?
   The Devil among the Tailors.

Ben Block, She never told her Love,
   Going out a Shooting,
Mother give your Boy a Buss,
   A Chapter upon Kissing.
You Gentlemen of England,
   We've Lived and Loved together,
God bless Prince Albert and the Queen,
   And may they reign for ever!

BIRT, Printer, 39, Great St. Andrew
    Street. Seven Dials.
Printing of every description done Cheap

(9⅞″ × 7¼″)

144

A Famous Sea Fight

BETWEEN

CAPTAIN WARD

AND THE

RAINBOW,

STRIKE up ye lusty gallants,
With musicks sound of drum,
For there is such a rover,
Upon the sea is come;
His name is Captain Ward,
Full well it doth appear,
There has not been such a rover,
Found out these thousand years.

Nor he hath sent unto the king,
The sixth of January,
Desiring that he might come in,
With all his company,

And if the king will let me come,
Till I my tale have told,
I will bestow for my ransom,
Full thirty ton of gold.

O nay, O nay, then said the king,
O nay that must not be,
To yield to such a rover,
Myself will not agree,
He hath deceiv'd the Frenchmen,
Likewise the king of Spain,
Then how can he be true to me,
Who has been false to twain.

With that the king provided,
A ship of worthy fame,
The Rainbow she is call'd,
If you would know her name,
And now the gallant rainbow,
She rolls upon the sea,
Five hundred gallant seamen,
To keep her company.

The Dutchmen and the Spaniards,
She made them for to flee,
Also the bonny Frenchmen,
As she met on the seas,
When as the gallant Rainbow,
Did come where he did lie,
Where is the Captain of that ship,
The rainbow he did cry.

O that I am, says Captain Ward,
There's no one bids me lie,
And if thou art the king's fair ship,
Thou rt welcome unto me.
I tell thee what said the rainbow,
Our king is in great grief,
That thou shouldst lie upon the seas,
And play the errant thief,

You will not let your merchantmen,
Pass as they did before,
Such tidings to our king is come,
Which grieves his heart full sore.
With that this gallant Rainbow,
She shot out of her pride,
Full fifty good brass pieces,
Charged on every side.

And yet these gallant shooters,
Prevailed not a pin,
Though they were brass on the outside,
Brave Ward was steel within.

Shoot on, shoot on, said Captain Ward,
Your sport well pleaseth me,
And he that first gives over,
Shall yield unto the sea.

I never wronged an English ship,
But Turk and king of Spain,
Likewise the blackguard Dutchmen,
As I met on the main,
If I had known your king,
But two or three days before,
I would have far'd Lord Essex life,
Whole death doth grieve me sore.

Go tell the king of England,
Go tell him thus from me,
If he reigns king of all the land,
I will reign king at sea.
With that the gallant Rainbow,
She fired and shot amain,
Then left the rovers company,
And home return'd again.

Our royal king of England,
Your ships return'd again,
For Captain Ward he is so strong,
He never will be ta'en,
O everlasting said the king,
I have lost jewels three,
Which would have gone unto the seas
and brought proud Ward to me.

The first was Lord Clifford,
Great Earl of Cumberland,
The second was Lord Mountjoy,
As you shall understand,
The third was brave Lord Essex,
From field would never flee,
Who would have gone unto the sea,
And brought proud Ward to me.

Printed and Sold by J. Pitts, 14, Great St. Andrew street, Seven Dials.
Price One Penny.

The Bold Prisoner,

Pitts, Printer, Wholesale Toy and Marble warehouse, 6, Great st. Andrew street 7 dials

AS I was a walking for my recreation,
    Across the green meadows one morning in
There I heard two brothers a talking, (May
And I listened awhile to what they did say,

Says one to the other I have got a brother
In prison so strong confined is he
But if I had forty brave fellows like myself
We soon would set the bold prisoner free

Ten of them should hold our horses head,
Ten at the prison door should be,
And ten should guard the prison all round.
While the rest should set the bold prisoner free

Dicky broke locks and Dicky broke bolts,
And Dicky made all before him to flee,
And Dicky took Arthur all up in his arms
And carried him off most manfully

Dicky looked over his left shoulder
You little do think what I do see,
Here comes the bold sheriff of bonny down dale
And a hundred bold traps in company.

O stop O stop the sheriff he cries,
O stop O stop whosoever you be
Only give us the irons from off his legs
And you may have the bold prisoner free

O no, O no you are vastly mistaken,
O no O no that never can be,
The irons will serve to shoe our horses
For we have a farrier in our company

O I will leave houses and I will leave lands,
I will leave wives and children three,
But before I'd leave my own dearest brother
I sooner would die under yonder green tree;

To dancing to dancing they went
To dancing they went most merrily
'Twas the very best dance that ever they had,
Because they had set the bold prisoner free.

The Land we *Live* in.

Pitts. Printer. Wholesale Toy & marble
Warehouse, 6, Great st, Andrew street
7 Dials

SINCE our foes to invade us have long been
    preparing
'Tis clear they consider we've something worth
    sharing
And for that mean to visit our shore,
It behoves us with spirit to meet'em.
And tho' t'will be nothing uncommon to beat'em
We must try how they'll take it once more

CHORUS.

So fill fill your glasses be this the toast given
Here's England for ever the land boys we live
    in,

Here's a health to the tars on the wide ocean
    ging,
Perhaps even now some broadsides are exchang (ing.
We'll on shipboard and join in the fight.
And when with the foe we are firmly engaging
Till the fire of guns lull's the sea in its raging.
On our country we'll think with delight

On that throne where once Alfred in glory seated
Long may our King by his people be greeted,
For to guard we'll be all in one mind,
May religion, law, order, be strictly defended
And continue the bleasings they first were intend
    ed,
In union the nation to bind,

(10″ × 7½″)

146

LORD BATEMAN.

LORD Bateman he was a noble lord,
  A noble lord of high degree,
He shipped himself on board a ship,
  Some foreign country he would go sea.

He sailed East, and he sailed West,
  Until he came to proud Turkey,
Where he was taken and put in prison,
  Until his life was quite weary.

And in the prison there grew a tree,
  And it grew so stout and strong,
Where he was chained by the middle,
  Until his life was almost gone.

This turk he had one only daughter,
  The fairest creature my eyes did see,
She stole the keys of her father's prison,
  And swore Lord Bateman she would set free.

Have you got houses, have you got lands,
  And does Northumberland belong to thee?
And what would you give to the fair young lady,
  That out of prison would set you free?

I have got houses, I have got lands,
  And half Northumberland belongs to me,
I'll give it all to the fair young lady,
  That out of prison would me free.

O then she took him to her father's hall,
  And gave to him the best of wine,
And every health that she drank unto him,
  I wish Lord Bateman that you were mine.

Now in seven years I'll make a vow,
  And seven years I'll keep it strong,
If you will wed with no other woman,
  I will wed with no other man.

O then she took him to her father's harbour,
  And gave to him a ship of fame;
Farewell, farewell, to you Lord Bateman,
  I'm afraid I shall ne'er see you again.

Now seven long years are gone and past,
  And fourteen days well known to thee:
She packed up all her gay clothing,
  And said Lord Bateman she would go see.

But when she came to Lord Bateman's castle,
  So boldly the bell rang she,
Who's there, who's there, cried the proud porter,
  Who's there come tell unto me.

O is this Lord Bateman's castle,
  Or is his lordship here within?
O yes, O yes, cried the young porter,
  He's just now taken his new bride in.

O tell him to send me a slice of bread,
  And a bottle of the best wine,
And not forgetting the fair young lady,
  Who did release him when close confined.

Away, away, went this young proud porter,
  Away, away, and away went he,
Until he came to Lord Bateman's chamber,
  Down on his bended knees fell he.

472.

I'LL DREAM OF
THEE NO MORE

London :—H. SUCH, Machine Printer, & Publisher, 177, Union-street, Boro'.—S. E.

OH ! farewell, farewell for ever,
  We shall never meet again,
Love's bright chain which now we sever,
  Ever broken must remain.
All the vows once fondly plighted,
  Back to thee I now restore,
Thou my heart's best love hath slighted,
  And I'll dream of thee no more.

Then farewell, farewell for ever,
  I never thought we thus should part,
Oh, farewell ! and may'st thou never,
  Feel the pangs that wring my heart.
Other hearts may still surround thee,
  But for me all hopes are o'er,
Thou hast broke the spell that bound me,
  And I'll dream of thee no more.

LORD BATEMAN, (Continued.)

What news, what news, my proud young porter,
  What news hast thou brought unto me?
There is the fairest of all young creatures,
  That ever my two eyes did see.

She has got rings on every finger,
  And round one of them she has got three,
And as much gay clothing about her middle
  As would buy all Northumberland.

She bids you send her a slice of bread,
  And a bottle of the best wine,
And not forgetting the fair young lady,
  Who did release you when close confined.

Lord Bateman he then in a passion flew,
  And broke his sword in splinters three,
Saying, I will give all my father's riches,
  That's if Sophia has crossed the sea.

Then up spoke the young bride's mother,
  Who never was heard to speak so free,
You'll not forget my only daughter,
  Now Sophia has crossed the sea.

I own I made a bride of your daughter,
  She's neither the better nor worse for me,
She came to me with her horse and saddle,
  She may go back in her coach and three.

Lord Bateman prepared another marriage,
  With both their hearts so full of glee,
I'll range no more in foreign countries,
  Since Sophia has crossed the sea.

(9⅞″ × 7⅜″)

THE TRUE BALLAD

OF

BARBARA ALLEN'S CRUELTY.

IN Scarlet Town, where I was bound,
　There was a fair maid dwelling,
Whom I had chosen to be my own,
　And her name it was Barbara Allen.

All in the merry month of May,
　When green leaves they were springing,
This young man on his death-bed lay,
　For the love of Barbara Allen.

He sent his man unto her then,
　To the town where she was dwelling :
"You must come to my master here
　If your name be Barbara Allen."

"For death is printed in his face,
　And sorrows in him dwelling ;
And you must come to my master dear,
　If your name be Barbara Allen.

"If death be printed in his face,
　And sorrows in him dwelling,
Then little better shall he be
　For bonny Barbara Allen."

So slowly, slowly she got up,
　And slowly she came to him ;
And all she said when she came there,
　"Young man, I think you are dying."

He turned his face unto her then ;
　"If you be Barbara Allen,
My dear, said he, come, pity me,
　As on my death-bed I am lying."

"If on your death-bed sure you be,
　What is that to Barbara Allen ?
I cannot keep you from your death,
　So farewell," said Barbara Allen.

He turned his face unto the wall,
　And Death came creeping to him ;
Then "Adieu, adieu, and adieu to all,
　And adieu to Barbara Allen."

As she was walking on a day
　She heard the bell a-ringing,
And it did seem to ring to her,
　"Unworthy Barbara Allen."

She turned herself around about,
　And she spied the corpse a-coming ;
"Lay down, lay down the corpse of clay,
　That I may look upon him."

And all the while she lookéd on
　So loudly she lay laughing ;
While all her friends cried out amain,
　"Unworthy Barbara Allen."

When he was dead and laid in grave
　Then Death came creeping to she ;
"O Mother, Mother, make my bed,
　For his death hath quite undone me.

"A cruel creature that I was
　To slight him that loved me dearly,
I wish I had been a kinder maid
　The time that he was near me."

So this maid she then did die,
　And desired to be buried by him,
And repented herself before she died
　That ever she did deny him.

PRINTED FOR THE NEW AND OLD SONG AND BALLAD COMPANY.

No. 1.

PRICE ONE HALFPENNY.

(9⅝″ × 7¼″)

148

DEATH OF Lord Nelson.

Come all you gallant seamen & give me a meeting,
   Attend to those lines that I'm going to relate,
And when that you hear it 'twill move you with pity,
   To hear how Lord Nelson he met with his fate,
For he was a bold and undaunted commander,
   As ever did sail on the ocean wide
And he made the French and the Spanish to surrender,
   By always pouring into them a broadside.
      Mourn, England, mourn, mourn and complain.
      For the loss of Lord Nelson who died on the main.

From aloft, to aloft, where he was commanding,
   All from a French gun he received a ball,
And by the contents he got mortally wounded,
   And that was the occasion of Lord Nelson's fall;
Like an undaunted hero, expos'd to the fire,
   As he give the command, on the quarter deck stood,
And to hear of his actions you would much admire,
   To see the decks covered all with human blood.

One hundred engagements he had been into,
   And ne'er in his time was he know to be beat,
For he had lost an arm, likewise a right eye too,
   No powers upon earth ever could him defeat;
His age at his death it was forty and seven,
   And as long as I live his great praises I'll sing,
For the whole navigation was unto him,
   Because he was loyal and true to his king.

Then up steps the doctor in a very great hurry,
   And unto Lord Nelson those words he did say,
Indeed then my lord, I am very sorry,
   To see you here lying and bleeding this way,
No matter, no matter, whatever about me,
   My time it is come, I am almost at the worst,
There my gallant seamen are fighting boldly,
   Go and attend to those brave fellows first.

Then with all his strength he called out to the captain,
   Pray let me know how this battle does go,
I hear that our guns they continue to rattle,
   Though death is approaching I very well know,
The antagonist ship is gone down to the bottom,
   Eighteen we have captured and brought them aboard
And two of them blown quite out of the ocean,
   So that is the news I've brought you my lord,

Come all gallant seamen that unite in a meeting,
   Always let Lord Nelson's memory go round,
For it is your duty when you unite a meeting,
   Because he was loyal and true to the crown;
So now to conclude and finish these verses,
   My time it is come, I am now to the worst,
May heaven go with you and ten thousand blessings,
   Still resting the fleet with your Lord Collingwood.

343 Printed & Sold by J. Wrigley, Junr., 3, Rochdale Road Manchester.

The Cruel SHIP CARPENTER

J. O. Bebbington, Printer, 26, Golden Street,
Oldham Road, Manchester, and sold by John
Beaumont, 176, York Street, Leeds.

In fair Worcester city and in Worcestershire,
A handsome young damsel she lived there;
A handsome young man he courted her to be his
   dear
And he was by trade a ship carpenter.

Now the king wanted seamen to go on the sea,
That caused this young damsel to sigh and to say,
O William, O William, don't you go to sea,
Remember the vow that you made to me.

It was early next morning before it was day,
He went to his Polly, these words he did say —
O Polly, O Polly, you must go with me,
Before we are married my friends for to see.

He led her through groves and valleys so deep,
And caused this young damsel to sigh and to weep
O William, O William, you have led me astray,
On purpose my innocent life to betray.

It is true, it is true, these words he did say,
For all the night long I've been digging your grave
The grave being open, the spade standing by,
Which caused this young damsel to sigh & to cry

O William, O William, O pardon my life,
I never will covet to be your wife,
I will travel the country to set you quite free,
O pardon, O pardon, my baby and me.

No pardon I'll give, there's no time to stand,
So with the knife that he had in his hand,
He stabbed her heart till the blood it did flow,
Then into the grave her fair body did throw.

He covered her up so safe and secure,
Thinking no one could find her he was sure;
Then he went on board to sail the world round,
Before that the murder could ever be found.

It was early one morning, before it was day,
The captain came up, these words he did say,
There's a murderer on board & he must be known
Our ship is in mourning, she cannot sail on.

Then up stepped one, indeed it's not me,
Then up stepped another, the same he did say,
Then up starts young William to stamp & to swear
Indeed it's not me I vow and declare

As he was turning from the captain with speed,
He met his Polly which made his heart to bleed;
She stript him & tore him, she tore him in three,
Because he had murdered her baby and she

$(9\frac{7}{8}'' \times 7\frac{1}{2}'')$

THREE MAIDS A-MILKING WOULD GO.

Three maids a milking would go,
Three maids a milking would go,
The wind it blew high the wind it blew low,
Which toss'd their milkpails to and fro.

They met with a man by the way,
And one of them did to him say,
Kind sir have you got any skill,
For to catch us a bird or two.

O yes I have a very great skill,
O yes I have a very great skill,
If you will go with me to yonder shady tree,
I will catch you a bird to your will.

To yonder shady green grove they went,
To yonder shady green grove they went,
And he catch'd her a bird upon her own ground,
As soon as he knew her intent.

Then he set her up against a green tree,
Then he set her up against a green tree,
And he beat the bush and the bird flew in,
A little above my love's knee.

Then her sparkling eyes turned round,
And if she had been in a swound,
Saying I caught a bird upon my word,
Picking upon its own ground.

This pretty fair maiden she fell sick,
This pretty fair maiden she fell sick,
The bird it stopt up and her apron tuck'd up,
Until it was forty weeks old.

Pretty maidens be ruled by me,
Pretty maidens be ruled by me,
Never catch a small bird upon the green ground,
But catch them upon the green tree.

So here's a health to the bird in the bush,
Likewise to the linnet and thrush,
For birds of a feather will all flock together,
Let their parents say little or much.

WILLIAMSON, PRINTER, NEWCASTLE.
[29]

THE BUTCHER
AND THE
TAILOR'S WIFE

There was a wealthy tailor,
In London town did dwell
He had a handsome wife,
And her name was Mary Bell;
She's gone to the market,
A joint of meat to buy:
What is your will, dear Madam
The butcher did reply.

This joint of meat was straightway cut down,
Refuse it she did not,
Straightway she fetch'd it home,
And put it in the pot;
But when the tailor he came home,
She told him what she had,
Then the poor tailor leap'd for joy,
And his heart was very glad.

Dear husband, O dear husband,
I'll tell you how it must be,
To morrow night the butcher
He has to lie with me:
Take your broad sword in your hand,
And under the bed go,
The first man that enters then,
Be sure to run him through.

I never handled sword or gun,
My dear and loving wife,
The butchers they are bloody dogs:
I'm afraid he'll have my life.
Do not you be faint hearted,
But with courage stout and bold,
And if the butcher you o'ercome,
You'll wear a chain of gold.

The butcher thinking it was time
To see the tailor's wife,
And fearing they should form a plot
Or trick to take his life.
He got a brace of pistols loaded
With powder and with ball,
The first man that molests me now,
By jove! I'll make him fall!

When the butcher he came in,
She took him by the hand,
And led him to her bed chamber;
Sir, I'm at your command,
He pull'd out a brace of pistols,
And laid them on the bed,
The poor tailor struck with fear,
He lay as if quit dead.

As he was taking of his clothes,
And going into bed,
How was he struck when he did spy
One of the tailor's legs.
Is this your husband's dog? he says,
I'll shoot him for the fright!
O spare my life the tailor cries,
And you shall have my wife.

(9⅞″ × 7½″)

THE PRETTY
Plough Boy.

Printed and Sold Wholesale and Retail by
J CATNACH, 2, Monmouth-Court,

IT'S of a pretty plough boy was gazing o'er his plough
His horses stood resting underneath the shade,
Twas down in yonder grove he went whistling to his
plough,
And he chanced there to meet a pretty maid.
And this was his song as he walked along,
Pretty maid you are of high degree,
If I should fall in love and your parents should know
The next thing, they will send me to sea.

So when her aged parents came for to know,
The plough boy was ploughing on the plain,
A press gang they sent and pressed him away,
And sent him in the wars to be slain.
Then she dress'd herself all in her best,
And her pockets were well lined with gold,
And she trudged the streets with tears in her eyes,
An search of her jolly sailor bold.

The first that she met was a jolly sailor,
Have you seen my pretty plough boy, she cry'd,
He's just cross'd the deep and sailing for the fleet,
Then he said pretty maid, will you ride.
She rode till she came to the ship her love was in,
Then unto the captain did complain,
Said she I'm come to seek for my pretty plough boy,
That is sent to the wars to be slain.

A hundred bright guineas she freely pull'd out,
And gently she told them all o'er,
And when she'd got her pretty plough boy in her arms
She hugg'd him till she got him safe on shore
And when she'd got her pretty plough boy in her arms
whereaftentimes he had been before.
She set the bells to ring, and sweetly she did sing.
Because she met with the lad she did adore.

THE
SPOTTED COW.
nach, Printer, 2, Monmouth-Court
, Dials.

ONE morning in the month of May
As from my cot I stray'd,
Just at the dawning of the day,
I met a charming maid.

Good morning, fair maid, whither said
So early tell me now,
The maid reply'd kind sir she cry'd.
I've lost my spotted cow.

No more complain no longer mourn,
Your cow's not lost my dear,
I saw her down in yonder lawn,
Come love and I'll shew you where.

I must confess that you are very kind,
I thank you, sir said she,
You will be sure her there to find,
Come sweetheart go with me.

Then to the groves we did repair,
And crossed the flowery dale,
we hugged and kissed each other,
And love was all our tale.

And in the grove we spent the day
And thought it pass'd too soon,
At night we homeward bent our way
when brightly shone the moon.

If I should cross yon flowery dale
Or go to view the plough,
She comes and calls ye gentle swains,
I've lost my spotted cow.

Canadian Boat Song.

FAINTLY as tolls the evening chime,
Our voices keep tune and our oars keep time
Soon as the woods on shore look dim,
we'll sing at St, Anne's our parting hymn,
Row, brothers, row, the stream runs fast,
The Rapids are near and the day-light's past.

why should we yet our sail unfurl,
There is not a breath the blue waves to curl
But when the wind blows off the shore.
Oh, sweetly we' rest our weary oar,
Blow, breezes, blow, the stream. &c.

Ut-away tide this trembling moon
Shall see us float over thy surges soon
Saint of this green Isle. hear our prayer,
Grant us cool heavens and safely there.
Blow, breezes, blow, the stream &c.

(10″ × 7⅝″)

THE
RATCATCHER'S DAUGHTER.

Not long ago, in Vestministier,
  There liv'ed a Ratcatcher's daughter,
She did'nt quite live in Vestministier,
  But t' other side of the vater.
Her father caught rats, and she sold sprats,
  All round and about that qua-rter,
And the gentlefolks all did lift there hats
  To the ratcatcher's pretty little daughter.
    Doodle dee, doodle dum, ri, da, doo, da, di do.

She wore no hat upon her head,
  No cap nor dandy bonnet:
And her hair hung gracefully down her back,
  Like a bunch of carrots upon it.
Now vhen she cried 'Sprats' in Vestministier,
  She 'ad such a loud sweet woice, sir,
You could hear her all down Parliament Street,
  As far as Charming-Cross, sir.
    Doodle dee, &c.

Now rich and poor from far and near,
  In matrimony sought her;
But to friends and foes she turn'd up her nose,
  Did the ratcatcher's pretty little daughter.
For there was a man sold lilly-vhite sand,
  In Cupid's net had caught her;
And right over head and ears in love
  Fell the ratcatcher's beau-tiful daughter.
    Doodle dee, &c.

Now lilly vhite sand so ran in her head,
  As she vent down to Strand, oh !
Instead of crying "do you vant any sprats?"
  She cried "D' ye vant any lilly-vhite sand, oh ?"
The people vere all amaz'd and thought she was craz'd
  As she vent down the Strand oh !
To hear the gal vith sprats on her head,
  Crying "D' ye vant any lilly-vhite sand, oh ?"
    Doodle dee, &c.

Now ratcatcher's daughter so ran in *his* head,
  He could'nt tell vhat he was arter,
For instead of crying "D' ye vant any sand?"
  He cried "D' ye vant any ratcatcher's daughter?"
His donkey cock'd his ears and laughed,
  And could'nt think what his master was arter,
When he heard a man that sold lilly-vhite sand,
  Cry "D' ye vant any ratcatcher's daughter ?"
    Doodle dee, &c.

Now they had agreed to marri-ed be
  Upon last Easter Monday ;
But the ratcatcher's daughter had a dream
  That she vould'nt be alive on the Sunday.
She vent vunce more for to buy some sprats,
  And she tumbled into the vater ;
Then over the head all kivered up with mud,
  Was the ratcatcher's pretty little daughter.

[SPOKEN.]—And, considering the state of the Thames
at this here present moment, vhat must she have swallowed!
ugh! ugh!   Doodle dee, &c.

Vhen lilly-vhite sand did hear the news,
  His eyes ran down vith vater ;
Says he" In love I've constant prov'd,
  Blow me if I'll live long arter."
So he cut his throat vith a pane of glass,
  And stabb'd his donkey arter :
So here vas an end of lilly-vhite sand,
  Donkey, and the ratcatcher's daughter.
    Doodle dee, &c.

The neighbours all, both great and small,
  Did flock unto the berre-in,
And vept that a gal who'd cried out 'sprats'
  Should be dead as any herre-in.
The Corioner's Inquest on her sat,
  At the sign of 'Jack in the Vater,'
To find what made life's sand run out
  Of the pretty little ratcatcher's daughter.
    Doodle dee, &c.

The werdick was that too much vet
  This poor young woman died on ;
For she made a hole in the Riviere Thames,
  Vot the penny steamers ride on ?
'Twas a haccident, they all agreed,
  And nuffin like self-slaughter ;
So not guiltee, *of fell-in-the-sea,*
  They brought in the ratcatcher's daughter.

[SPOKEN.]—Vell, ladies an' gen'lemen—arter the two
bodies was resusticated, they burri-ed them both in one
seminary—and the epigram vich they writ on the tomb-
stone was :—

          Doodle dee, &c

          Song 252.

(10" × 7⅝")

A NEW SONG.

THE WANTS OF PRINCESS ALICE.

'Tis said our Princess Alice
  Has a man at her command:
He is but a little German Laird,
  As we do understand.
Thirty Thousand we must give her,
  Upon her wedding day!
John Bull must forthwith draw his purse,
  Expenses large to pay.

Thirty Thousand the day she's wed,
  And six thousand every year,
We'll be taxed to give this German Laird,
  And his pretty Alice dear.

Thirty thousand, little enough,
  Lord Palmerston does think,
To uphold the merry wedding spree,
  With lots of meat and drink.
And six thousand pounds of British gold
  Every year we'll have to give
To this little German and his bride,
  So long as they do live.

She wants some of our good roast beef,
  To fill his German bags;
And she wants some thread and needles
  To patch and mend his rags:
She wants a bed-tick and two pillows,
  With blankets, sheets and rugs:
And she wants an iron bedstead,
  For it will not harbour bugs.

She wants a set of curtains,
  And they must be Turkey red;
And she wants that little useful thing
  That stands beneath the bed.
She wants to have a sofa,
  Likewise some stools and chairs;

And she wants a nice piano,
  To play some German airs.

She wants a tea and coffee pot,
  Plates, dishes, knives and forks;
And she wants some wine and brandy,
  With a screw to draw the corks.
She wants some cups and saucers,
  And she wants a frying-pan,
To fry some German sausages
  For her little German man.

She wants a cage and parrot,
  That can to her nicely talk;
And she wants a coach and horses,
  For she does not want to walk.
She wants a great big looking-glass,
  Her pretty face to see;
And she wants a German lap-dog,
  To nurse upon her knee.

She wants a German cuckoo-clock,
  To tell the time of day;
And she wants a lot of servants,
  To dress her out so gay.
And she wants to lead the fashion,
  In costly robes so fine;
She wants a Garibaldi hat,
  And a great big crinoline.

She wants to live in idleness,
  In luxury and ease;
She wants a dozen of children,
  To play around her knees.
She wants to go to sprees and balls,
  To the masquerade and play:
And she wants the British public
  The cost of all to pay.

Song 239

(10″ × 7½″)

DOWNFALL
OF POOR
OLD ROGER

Fourteen years penal servitude.

The Tichborne trial is now done,
　　Doodah, doodah,
We hear that Hawkins' side has won,
　　Doodah, doodah day.
Kenealey now deserves a rest,
　　Doodah, doodah,
For the big fat man he's done his best,
　　Doodah, doodah day.

CHORUS.

But never mind old boy,
In fourteen years you'll be free,
And if you do return again,
We'll welcome you with glee.

Now Hawkins he does feel so jolly,
He's banished care and melancholy,
He went home on Saturday night,
Jumped into bed and cuddled his wife.

And Mother Jury's got her tin,
She can go and spend it now in gin,
She saw Young Orton stripped I'm sure
And danced with him the Perfect Cure.

The claimant has to prison gone,
I think he'll find it rather warm,
For the oakum now he must pick.
And his skilly won't be very thick.

When he did to prison go,
They made of him a perfect show,
They cropped his hair so very thin,
And then his troubles did begin.

To see him strip and have a bath,
I am sure would make the people laugh
To dress him they did begin,
A knickerbocker suit they put him in.

They'll mult him down a stone or two,
For the treadmill he must have to do,
His bedstead will be such a topper,
To keep him up, he's such a whopper.

The claimant now can't blow his bacca,
He'll wish he'd stopp'd in Wagga Wagga
Oh that he will. I know quite well,
When he is in his prison cell.

The Tichborne trial is now o'er,
Of trials like that we want no more,
They cost the country lots of money,
And make some persons feel so funny.

Disley, Printer, 57, High Street, St. Giles

Nightingale in the East

On a dark lonely night on the Crimea's dread shore
There had been bloodshed and strife on the morn-
　　ing before,
The dead and the dying lay bleeding around,
Some crying for help—there's none to be found ;
And God in his mercy he pity'd their cries,
And the soldier so cheerful in the morning do rise,
So forward my lads, may your hearts never fail,
You're cheer'd by the presence of Miss Nightingale

Now God sent this woman to succour the brave,
Some thousands she saved from an untimely grave,
Her eyes beam with pleasure, she's bounteous and
　　good,
The wants of the wounded are by her understood.
With fever some brought in with life almost gone,
Some with mangled limbs,some to fragments is torn
But they keep up their spirits,their hearts never fail
Now they're cheer'd by the presence of sweet Miss
　　♪ Nightingale.

Her heart it means good—for no bounty she'll take
She'd lay down her life for the poor soldier's sake,
She pray'd for the dying, gave peace to the brave,
She felt that a soldier had a soul to be saved;
The wounded they lov'd her, as it has been seen,
She's the soldier's preserver theycall her their queen,
May God give her strength, & her heart never fail,
One of Heaven's best gifts is Miss Nightingale.

The wives of the wounded how thankful were they
Their husbands were car'd for—now happy & gay,
Bless'er her country, this gift God has given,
The soldiers all said she was angel from Heaven.
Sing praise to this woman, deny it who can !
All females was sent for the comfort of man,
Let's hope no more against them you'll rail,
Use them well & they'll prove like MissNightingale

(10¼″ × 4″)

SIR J. FRANKLIN
And his Crews.

You tender Christians I pray attend,
To these few lines that I have now penn'd,
Of Sir John Franklin and his brave band,
Who've perished far from their native land.

　So listen now while I tell to you
　The fate of Franklin and his brave crew.

It's now nine years since they first set sail,
With joyous hearts and a pleasant gale,
In frozen regions to cruise about
The North-west passage to find out.

There was many a sad and an aching heart
As from their friends these brave men did part
To plough their way o'er the raging main
For fear they should ne'er return again.

When six dreary years they had been away
Some other vessels without delay
Were sent to search for the missing crews,
But alas of them they could hear no news.

A gloomy mystery for nine long years,
Their wives and children has kept in tears ;
In deepest anguish they did await
The ships sent out to learn their fate.

Poor Lady Franklin in great despair
In anguish wild she tore her hair ;
Saying ten thousand pounds I'give for news
Of my loving Franklin and his brave crews.

The government in this present year
Did pensions give to their families dear ;
But Lady Franklin refused the grant
Crying give me my husband I no money want.

At length sad tidings of this brave band
Has reached the shores of their native land,
By which we hear that they are all dead,
Though suffering much ere their souls had fled.

As through the frozen seas they pushed
Their ships by blocks of ice were crushed,
And offering prayers for their babes and wives
Many brave souls did lose their lives.

Forty poor creatures from a watery grave
With one of the boats their lives did save,
And over the ice they now took their way
To reach in safty the Hudson's Bay.

What horrid sufferings of pain and want—
These frozen regions no food did grant ;
At length oh horrid for want of meat
Their dying comrades they had to eat.

How horrid was the sight when found
Their limbs and bodies lay scattered round.
The flesh knawed off from every bone,
Oh may their souls to heaven have gone.

Now for to finish and make an end,
May God their families from want defend,
And while their loss we sadly dep'ore,
We hope such horrors to hear no more.

151

(Trimmed to 8¾″ × 3″)

LONG LIFE TO

CAPTAIN WEBB!

THE CHAMPION OF THE SEAS

A New Song written on the wonderful task completed by Captain Webb, who Swam from Dover to Calais on the 24th of AUG. being above twenty hours in the water.

Air—Oyster Shell Bonnets.

About Captain Boynton a lot has been said,
But we're jolly well proud of our bold Captain Webb,
He wants no Cork Dresses to soothe his alarms,
He can swim like a duck, with his good legs & arms.

CHORUS.

Captain Boynton's defeated you'll see at a glance,
By Captain Webb swimming from England to France

Captain Boynton came over to take us all in,
His dresses to sell and the dollars to win,
But the Yankee's are done cork jackets and all,
Captain Webb done the journey with no dress at all.

Captain Boynton we know could'nt sink in the sea,
Paddling along he's as safe as could be,
But poor Webb had nothing but good English pluck,
He must be wet footed for he swims like a duck.

'Ere the dawn of the day he left Dover pier,
He jump'd in the water without any fear,
The fishes were startled to see his legs go,
They bob'd up their tails and they bob'd down below.

As bold Captain Webb thro' the channel did fly,
He stuck his big toe in a mackarel eye,
And in their own language the poor fishes said,
Here's a fish with two legs, knocking about over head

But he went on his way thro' the glistening tide,
Till a jelly fish gave him a nip in the side,
It was like a big flea and behaved very rough,
Perhaps he thought the bold Captain was tarnation
tough.

About twenty hours he stuck to his task,
And then by success was rewarded at last,
The astonished Frenchmen were anxious to learn,
If the Captain had got any steam in his starn.

The Captain was cheer'd as he landed on shore,
Altho' he was tired he was not done o'er,
He shook hands with friends and the truth must be
said,
Had something to drink and toddled to bed.

Now altho' Captain Boyton is a wonderful man
Let him take off his dress and do this if he can,
We've a little girl in London Miss Beckwith I mean,
Could wack all the Yankee's that ever was seen.

So let us give honor were honor is due,
Success to the Captain so fearless and true,
We hope that his bold eyes, will never grow dim,
Till every man in this Country can swim.

London :—H. P. SUCH, Machine Printer & Publisher,
177, Union-street, Borough, S.E.

Oct 1875

($9\frac{7}{8}'' \times 7\frac{1}{2}''$)

THE
Present Times,
OR
EIGHT SHILLINGS
A WEEK.

———o———

Come all you bold Britons wherever you be,
I pray give attention, and listen to me,
There once were good times, but they're gone by
    complete,
For a poor man lives now on eight shillings a week.

Such times in Old England there never was seen,
As the preasent ones now—but much better have
    been,
A poor man's condemn'd and look on like a thief,
And compelled to work hard for eight shilling a
    week.

Our venerable father remembers the year,
When a man could earn three shillings a day and
    his beer,
He then could live well, keep his family neat,
But now he must work for eight shillings a week.

The nobs of Old England of shameful renown,
Are striving to crush a poor man to the ground,
They'll beat down their wages, and starve them
    complete,
And compel them to work for eight shillings a week.

A poor man to labour, believe me 'tis so,
To maintain his family is willing to go
Either edging or ditching, to plough, or to reap,
But how does he live on eight shillings a week?

In the reign of Old George, as you all understand,
There then was contentment throughout the whole
    land,
Each poor man could live, and get plenty to eat,
But now he must pine on eight shillings a week.

So now to conclude, and finish my song,
May the times be much better before it is long,
May every poor labourer be able to keep
His children and wife on Twelve Shillings a week.

Will you
LOVE ME
THEN AS NOW.

———oo———

You have told me that you love me,
    And your heart's thoughts seem to speak
As you look on me so fondly,
    And the life-blood tints your cheek ;
May I trust that these warm feelings
    Never will grow cold and strange,
And that you'll remain unalter'd
    In this weary world of change !
When the shades of care and sorrow
    Dim my eyes, and cloud my brow,
And my spirits sink within me,
    Will you love me then as now ?

Though our youth may pass unclouded,
    In a peaceful happy home,
Yet as year on year advances,
    Changes must upon us come ;
For the step will lose its lightness,
    And the hair be changed to gray,
Eyes once bright will lose their brightness,
    And the hopes of youth decay ;
When all these have passed upon me,
    And stern age has touched my brow,
Will the change find you unchanging,
    Will you love me then as now ?

(10″ × 7⅜″)

SALE

OF

A WIFE.

Come all you lads and lasses gay, and banish care and strife,—In the market-place, a mason did by auction sell his wife;—Thirteen shillings and a penny for the lady, was the sum,—And to see the curious spree some thousands soon did run;—In the market-place, I do declare, its true upon my life,—A mason did, the other day, by auction sell his wife.—This man and wife, good lack-a-day! did often disagree;—For she often pawned her husband's clothes to go upon the spree. So he led her to the market, with a halter, I am told, And there she was, so help my bob, by public auction sold. When the auctioneer began the sale, a jolly farmer cried, Here's five and fourpence half-penny for the mason's lushy bride; A tanner cried out seven and six, and then a butcher said, I'll give you ten and seven pence, beside a bullock's head. She's going, cried the auctioneer, she's going upon my life; Tinkers, cobblers, sailors, will you buy a charming wife? Such fighting, scratching, tearing too, before no one did see; Such roaring, bawling, swearing, O! blow me, it was a spree. At length a rum old cobbler did give a dreadful bawl, Here's thirteen and a penny with my lapstone and my awl. Thirteen and a penny, when down the hammer dropt, With whiskers, apron, bustle, shawl, stays, petticoat, and——A lushy mason's lady was this blooming damsel gay, She did unto the hammer come upon a market-day; Bakers, butchers, masons, did bid for her, we hear; While a lot of rum old women pitched into the auctioneer. Young men and maids did hallo, while married folks did sneer; They frightened the old cobbler and knocked down the auctioneer. The cobbler took the lady up just like a Scotchman's pack, And the funny mason's lady rode upon the cobbler's back. Some laughed till they bursted, while others were perplexed, But the cobbler bristled up his wife with two big balls of wax. The cobbler sat her on his knee, and joyfully did bawl, While the lady knocked about the seat the lapstone and awl. Then the mason he did sell his wife, as you shall understand, And thirteen and a penny was popt into his hand; He whistled and capered, for to banish care and strife; He went into a gin-shop, singing, I have sold my wife! So the divorced mason he may go, to banish care and strife, Unto the market-place again and buy another wife. Now the cobbler and the lady are both in a stall, While the cobbler works the bristle, why the lady works the awl. And they upon the lapstone do so merry play together, Singing, heel and toe, gee up gee woe, big balls of wax and leather. And day and night, in sweet delight, they banish care and strife; The merry little cobbler and his thirteen-shilling wife.

Song 221.

$(10\frac{1}{4}'' \times 7\frac{1}{2}'')$

A NEW SONG ON THE

AMERICAN War.

Printed and Sold by J. Wrigley, Junr.
3 Rochdale Road. Manchester.
N.B.—Having Bought all Bebbington's Stock of
Stereotype Plates, Hawkers, and Shopkeepers, can
be Supplied with his Hymns, and Ballads. Cheaper
than any House in the Trade.

The Wild Irishman
IN LONDON.

I am a wild Irishman just come to town,
  To view the fine city of fame and renown ;
And when I came there I began for to walk,
  Unto that fine field, they call it Hyde Park.

CHORUS:— Tidy hi hia ! shillelah an ha !
    Long life and success to Erin go Bragh.

I hurried myself until I came there
  Thinking it might be sweet Donnybrook Fair ;
And what should I see in the middle of a crowd,
  Two naked fellows a boxing about.

They jumped and they capered and gave me aroke,
  Says I to myself its all but a joke :
Says I my tight fellows no more of your trick
  Its my country fashion to fight with two sticks.

A big headed butcher being standing hard by,
  He says Irish Pat I will knock out your eye ;
For fear of my eye, not a word did I speak,
  And then my poor heat began for to shake.

I looked all around to try if I'd see,
  Any lad that I knew in my own country,
Till a hearty young fellow come close to my back,
  Bulu a rue boughel lagus bulu me lath.

Then I being put up to the word of command,
  I took my shillelagh all in my right hand,
I gave one of those fellows a blow on the head,
  I streched him as if he was seven years dead.

In less than five minutes the field it was clear,
  There never was an Englishman dare to appear,
Says one to another come let us be quick,
  Don't you see the wild Irishman with the big stick

Then up St. Giles I straight took my way,
  It happened to be on a Patrick's day,
And there I was created to bumpers of beer,
  And then my poor heart it began for to cheer.

Come all you tender Christians with patience lend an ear,
And listen to those feeling lines that I have written here,
I'm sure each eye will shed a tear. if you attention pay,
While thinking on your loving friends that's in America.

For many years our Irish boys have laboured hard in store,
To help their friends and parents all round the Shamrock shore,
But now the cry of war is raised, they're watching night and day,
To save their lives and property, all in America.

The 26th of June, in New York town, its awful to behold,
Some thousands of the Americans they could not be controlled,
They robbed and plundered right and left, upon that awful day,
And swore they'd banish Irishmen out of America.

The blacks and slaves of New Orleans and Philadelphia joined,
With Boston, Quebec, and New York, with one accord combined,
To free the British settlements and claim them as their own,
Which leaves our Irishmen to weep far from their native home.

To see our Irish females, your heart would tear with grief,
For mercy they did loudly cry, but could not find relief;
Far from their friends and native land, there's many fell a prey,
A victim to those savage blacks, all in America.

Through streams of blood they waded, where cannans loud did roar,
And many a gallant Irishman lay weltering in his gore.
The children cried ! Oh ! Mamma we may rue the day,
That we have lost our fathers, all in America.

There's many in this country may shed a briny tear,
While thinking on their children and them they loved so dear,
But if they were back in Erin's Isle, among their friends the y'd
    stay,
And thank the LORD to see themselves, far from America.

Our Irish priests and bishops, they undergo great pain,
To save their loving parishioners from this tormenting train,
Like St. Francis in the wilderness they earnestly did pray,
For peace and unity once more, all in America.

Now since these lines, I must conclude, let each Irish heart unite,
To offer up a fervent prayer, both morning, noon, and night,
Unto the LORD of MERCY, do not neglect to pray,
That He may save our loving friends that's in America.

(10″ × 7½″)

159

The Vocal Grove; a variety of Songs.

LONDON:
PRINTED AND PUBLISHED BY
J. Catnach, 2. Monmouth Court, 7 Dials.
Cards, Bills, &c. Printed Very Cheap.

The Chevalier's Daughter. A favourite Song.

AH! tell me, ye twains, have you seen my Pastora,
A Cry, have you met the sweet nymph on your way
Transcendant as Venus, and blythe as Aurora,
From Neptune's bed rising, to hail the new day:
The fairest, the meekst, for ever my theme;
Foreon do I wander, & long time have sought her
A goddess in form, tho' a cottager's daughter.
That dwells on the borders of Aln's winding stream.

Tho' loathing to grief, & young squires have fought her
To think her behind in the cottage chain; (her
Devoid of ambition, the cottager's daughter
Convnc'd them there offens & flatt'ry were vain:
When first I beheld her, I fondly besought her,
My heart did her homage, & love was her theme,
She vow'd to be mine, the sweet cottager's daughter
That dwells on the borders of Aln's, &c.

Then why thus alone does the lover me to languish!
Pastora (ô ponder could ne'er yield her heart:
Ah! no, the returns to remove my fad anguish,
O'er her heart love & truth retain the command:
The wealth of Golconda could never have bought her
For love, truth, & constancy, still is her theme:
Then grant me, kind Hymen, the cottager's daughter
That dwells on the borders of Aln's, &c.

The GREEN-WOOD Shade.

ON an arbor of woodbine ye bolt shall be led;
So leaves for your pillow the grass for your bed
While wanton young sparrows chirp over your head
All under the green-wood shade.

When the moon with pale lustre, just peeps through
the grove,
And oft perches near, the chaste turtle-dove,
The mask without blushing, shall chip her true-love
All under the green-wood shade.

Our pleasure, quite harmless, begin with the day,
We ever are buxom, we ever are gay,
No virgins diffemble, no shepherds betray;
All under the green-wood shade.

The Forsaken SHEPHERDESS.

"BENEATH some hoary mountain,
I'll lay me down and weep,
Or near some warbling fountain
Bewail myself asleep."
By my false swain deserted,
Ungrateful and unkind,
Forlorn and broken-hearted,
No comfort can I find.

Each valley, field, and bower,
And every dewy flower,
Remind me of my love.
My ewes and lambs neglected,
Run bleating o'er the plain,
Whilst lonely and dejected,
I sing my love-lorn strain.

The Broom of COWDEN-KNOWS.

WHEN summer comes, the chains on Tweed
Sing their faceful, loves,
Around the ewes and lambkins feed,
And music fills the groves.

But my lov'd long is then the broom
So fair on Cowden-knows;
For sure to sweet, so soft a bloom
Elsewhere there never grows.

O the broom, the bonny, bonny broom,
The broom of Cowden-knows!
For sure so feeth, so bright a bloom,
Elsewhere there never grows.

There Comyx tun'd his oaten reed,
And won my yielding heart;
No shepherd e'er that dwelt on Tweed,
Could play with half such art.
He fung of Tay, of Forth, and Clyde,
The hills and dales all round,
Of Leader-haughs and Leader-side,
Oh! how I lov'd the found.

Not Tiviot braes so green and gay,
May with this broom compare,
Nor Yarrow banks in flow'ry May,
Nor the Bufh about Traquair.
More pleasing far are Cowden-knowes,
My peaceful happy home,
Where I was wont to milk my ewes,
At even among the broom.

A FAVOURITE SONG

SOFTLY found the martial trumpet,
Now the din of war is o'er:
Peace, fair maid, prepares a banquet,
Laurel'd heroes, part no more.

A calm retreat where myrtles tutor,
With mufly rofe, and fweet woodbine,
You've sheath'd the fword, now guard life fair.

LIBERTY.

SINCE ev'ry charm on earth combines

The Mermaid's Song.

NOW the dancing fun-beams play,
On the green and glassy sea;
Come, and I will lead the way,
Where the pearly treasures be.
Come with me, and we will go,
Where the rocks of coral grow,
Follow, follow, follow, me,
Follow, &c.

Come, behold what treasures lie,
Far below the rolling waves;
Riches hid from human eye,
Dimly shine in Ocean's caves:
Taking tides hear no delay,
Stormy winds are far away,
Come with me, &c.

LOVE among the ROSES.

YOUNG Love flew to the Paphian (bower
And gather'd sweets from many a
From roses and sweet jessamine,
The lily and the eglantine,
The Graces there were culling posies,
And Cupid's young Love among the roses.
Oh! happy day, O! joyous hour,
Compose a wreath from ev'ry flower,
Let's bind him to us, ne'er to sever,
Young Love shall dwell with us for-ever,
Eternal springs the wreath encompass,
Content to live among the roses.

The COTTAGE R's Daughter.

DOWN in yon valley my father does dwell,
See yonder on Mary he's leaning;
All that his cottage produces he fells,
But I must away by the break of the day,
My basket to fill by the water,
To earn what I can, for my father poor own,
For I am his only daughter.

The ladies they offer'd me places three,
And told me to choose which I'd rather:
But this is the answer they all get from me,
Oh! Ladies this I think of my father!
If I was to leave the cottage would grieve,
Forgetting the duties he taught her,
If I was to leave the cottage would grieve,
For I am his only daughter.

Young Jockey he fetch'd from the fields below,
Three pretty cows from old Mary:
And soon he shall want, he told me so,
A maid to look after his dairy;
Should he ask me to go, I could not fay No,
For its only just over the water,
Should he ask me to go, I could not fay N♫,
But still I'm the cottager's daughter.

Where is my LUBIN.

Sung by Mrs. BLAND.

AH! where is my Lubin? ye fongfters ah
Say what can occasion his stay; (where!
He profit me to go with him once to the fair,
And I told him it would be his way.

Chorus of Huntsmen in Der Freischütz.

WHAT equals on earth the delight of the
huntsman,   (how,
For whom does life's cup more enchantingly
To follow the flag thro' the forefts & meadows,
When brightly the beams of the morning
first glow.

Oh, this is a pleasure that's worthy of Princes,
and health is the fure invigorate let found,
When echoing caverns and forefts furround us,
More blightly the pledge of the goblet will
found.   Hark, follow, &c.

The light of Diana illumines our forest,
The fhades where in fummer we often retreat,
Not is then the fell wolf in his covert fecurer,
The boar from his lair is laid at our feet.

Sung in Love in a Village.

O that I been by fate decreed,
In fair Rosetta's fight to feed,
    My flocks upon the plain.
What blifs what I been born to tafte
    Which now I ne'er muft know;
Ye envious powers why have ye plac'd
    My fair one's lot fo low.

The words from CLARE'S POEMS.

Sung by Miss STEVENS.

HERE we meet too foon to fart,
Here to leave will raife a fmart,
Here I'll prefs thee to my heart,
    Where none have place above thee;
Here I vow to love thee well,
Could but words unfeal the fpell,
Had I but language, strength to tell,
    I'd fay how much I love thee.

Here the rofe that decks thy door,
Here the thorn that fpreads thy bow'r,
Here the willow on the moor,
    The birds at reft above thee;
Had thy light of life to fee,
Senfe of foul like thee and me,
Soon might each a witnefs be,

There's the church upon the hill,
Here the pure and murm'ring rill,
Where off I've vow'd to love the ftill,
    Till death our love fhall fever;
Then to the altar let's away,
Make this my love our bridal day.
No longer happinefs delay,
    But make me thine for ever.
For then my love no more we'd part,
No more by leaving raife a fmart,
I'd fondly prefs thee to my heart,
    And ftill for ever love thee.

PARODY on the Rofe-bud of Summer.

WHEN gooseberries grow on the ftem of
    a daisy,   (chops,
And julap is made from the curls of a jazz,
When fteam-boats no more on the Thames
    fhall be going,
And a caft-iron bridge reach Vauxhall from
And the Grand Junction Water-Works ceafe
    to be flowing.
Oh! then, Molidusia, I'll love thee, &c.

At which mamma will fcold,
So to revenge Love thinks it fair
    To fhoot fometimes the old.
With Love fome folks go mad,
Try'd by thofe fome quite this,
Some find themfelves too fond,
    The fea they muft jump in.—Oh! 'tis, &c.
Great people and the fmall,
Love rules alike both high and low,
Exciting always married pairs
    Which Love can't rule at all.
Yet angels now will fee,
In thofe dear forms they wed,
What angels thofe muft be
    Who crack a hufband's head.
In all your letters fill'd with Love,
Take care you won't appear,
For if they ever go to Court,
    You'll look a little queer.
Not Hymen's Court I mean,
With burning Loves and Graces,
But where inftead are feen
    Long wigs and longer faces.
Then why fhould lovers ever pine,
For any fair they fee,
If twenty-one your fuit decline,
    Chufe you'll agree at laft,
And tho' your maidens jeer,
And fay the choice is wrong,
One confolation's clear,
    She can't live very long.—Oh! 'tis love, &c.

Reflecting on the pains of love,
And envy ev'ry down I fee,
Enjoy the fweets of LIBERTY.
We'll live in fweet tranquillity,
Nor with for greater LIBERTY.

HOME! SWEET HOME!

Song by Miss M. TREE.

MID pleafures and palaces though we may
    roam,
Be it ever fo humble there's no place like home;
A charm from the fkies feems to hallow us there,
Which feek through the world is ne'er met with
    elfewhere.
Home! home! fweet, fweet home,   (home.
There's no place like home, there's no place like
An exile from home, fplendour dazzles in vain,
Oh! give me my lovely thatch'd cottage again,
The birds finging gaily that came at my call,
Give me them with the peace of mind dearer than
    Home! home! &c.   (all.

LOCH-EROCH SIDE.

AS I came by Loch-Eroch fide,
    The lofty hills furveying,
The water clear, the heather blooms,
    Their fragrant fweets conveying.
I met, unfought, my lovely maid,
    I found her like May morning;
With graces fweet, and charms fo rare,
    Her perfon all adorning.

How kind her looks, how blifs was I,
    While in my arms I prefs'd her!
And her her wishes fcarce conceal'd,
    As fondly I carefs'd her.
She faid, If that your heart be true,
    And constantly you'll love me,
I heed not care, nor fortune's frown,
    For nought but death fhall move me.
But faithful, loving, kind, and true,
    For ever you fhall find me,
And of our meeting here fo fweet,
    Loch-Eroch fide fhall mind me.
Enraptur'd then, My lovely laff,
    I cried, no more we'll tarry;
But leave the fweet Loch-Eroch fide,
    For lovers foon fhould marry.

A Dawn of HOPE.

A Dawn of HOPE my foul reviews,
    And banifhes defpair;
If reft my deareft Damon lives,
    Make him, ye gods, your care.
Difpel thefe gloomy fhades of night,
    My tender grief remove;
Oh! fend fome cheering ray of light,
    And guide me to my love.
Thus, in a fecret friendly fhade,
    The penfive Celia mourn'd,
White courteous Echo lent her aid,
    And figh for figh return'd.
When fudden Damon's well-known face,
    Each rifing fear difarms;
He, eager fprings to her embrace
    She finks into his arms.

Sung by Miss Tree, in the Opera of Maid Marian.

A Damfel ftool to watch the fight,
    On the Banks of Kingflie Mere,
and they brought to her feet her own true
    Sore wounded on a bier;   [Knight,
Oh, let not, he faid, while yet I live,
    The cruel foe me take,
But with thy lips one fweet kifs give,
    And caft me in the lake.
About his neck the wound her arms,
    And the kifs'd his lips fo pale,
And evermore the war's alarms
    Came loudly up the vale.
She drew him to the lake's deep fide,
    Where the red heath fringed the fhore,
She plunged with him beneath the tide,
    And they were feen no more.

The SLAVE. Sung by Miss Stephens.

SONS of Freedom! hear my ftory,
    Mercy well becomes the brave;
Humanity is Britain's glory,
    Pity and protect the SLAVE.
Free-born daughters who poffefs'd,
    Eyes that conquer, hearts that fave;
Greet me with a after's blefsing,
    Oh! Pity and protect the SLAVE.

Published by Chas Magnus, 12 Frankfort St NY.

The Dying Soldier to his Mother.

Words by Thos. MacKellar. Music by Wm. U. Butcher.

„Kiss my little Brother and my Sisters, and tell them I died for my Country".

The Music to these Words Published by Lee & Walker, 722 Chestnut St.

On the field of battle, mother,
 All the night alone I lay,
Angels watching o'er me, mother,
 'Till the breaking of the day.
I lay thinking of you, mother,
 And the loving ones at home,
'Till to our dear cottage, mother,
 Boy again I seemed to come.

He to whom you taught me, mother,
 On my infant knee to pray,
Kept my heart from fainting, mother,
 When the vision passed away.
In the gray of morning, mother,
 Comrades bore me to the town;
From my bosom, tender fingers,
 Washed the drops that trickled down.

I must soon be going, mother,
 Going to the home of rest;
Kiss me as of old, my mother,
 Press me nearer to your breast.
Would I could repay you, mother,
 For your faithful love and care;
God uphold and bless you, mother,
 In this bitter woe you bear.

Kiss for me my little brother,
 Kiss my sisters, loved so well,
When you sit together, mother,
 Tell them how their brother fell.
Tell to them the story, mother,
 When I sleep beneath the sod,
That I died to save my country,
 All from love to her and God.

Leaning on the merit, mother,
 Of the One who died for all,
Peace is in my bosom, mother,
 Hark! I hear the angels call.
Don't you hear them singing, mother?
 Listen to the music's swell
Now I leave you, loving mother—
 God be with you—fare you well!

500 Illustrated Ballads, lithographed and printed by CHARLES MAGNUS, No. 12 Frankfort Street, New York. Branch Office: No. 520 7th St., Washington, D. C.

(8″ × 5″)

162

THE DOWNFALL
OF THE
Tyrant
BONAPARTE,
Revolution in France---Bonaparte's Arrest---Riseings in Paris & throughout France.

The battle of Waterloo has decided the fate of Bonaparte and of France. The Emperor is no longer the Emperor! He has been forced, *unconditionally, to abdicate the Throne*, in order to afford his partizans something to offer in propitiation to Europe, which they have roused and insulted.

BUONAPARTE HAS BEEN, AND STILL IS A PRISONER IN THE PALACE ELYSEE! (no Elysium to him!) having been placed under arrest by the Legislative Bodies.

All the Ports of France on the Coast opposite to England, have already shown themselves well disposed for the King.

At nine o'clock on Wednesday morning, the arrival of Bonaparte was universally known in Parris, and the public consternation became general. In the course of the day, he summoned the Ministers, and stated to them explicitly, that *his Army was no more!* A second edition of the Moniteur was published, a measure deemed absolutely necessary, in order to satisfy the impatient curiosity of the people, as to the fate of the army. *It was acknowledged to have been annihilated.*

On Thursday, Regnault de St Angely, told Bonaparte in plain terms, that he must immediately abdicate the Throne. Bonaparte sent word to the Chambers, that they might expect a Message from him in *a few hours.* They returned for answer, that they expected it in *one*—and in *one* it came—proposing *to abdicate in favour of his Son.* This proposal was rejected, and an *unconditional surrender* of the Government *alone* satisfied the Chambers.

The debates of the Chambers were of the most tumultuous description. The Minister of the Interior, it is said, attempted to shew that Soult had rallied 60,000 men on the north frontiers; but Ney, with great violence, denied this assertion, affirming that 25,000 were the whole that could be collected, He added, that no succesful resistance could be opposed to the Allies, in any direction, to the heart of the kingdom. It was then observed, that there were the remains of the Imperial Guards, to which Ney replied, that he had commanded them, and knew best what had become of them.

Letters from the Duke of Wellington, dated the 20th inst at Calane Cambracis, beyond Cambray. Prince Blucher and his Army had advanced to Auvergue!

Bonaparte's Abdication has been sanctioned by the Legislative Body.

Lord Castlereagh is going to Brussiels.

The fall of Bonaparte is most complete: he has lost all, and even in France it is stated plainly and roundly at 60,000 men, the flower of his army, and the whole Materiel,

Printed by J. Aston, Coventry, and may be had gratis.

$(12\frac{1}{2}'' \times 8\frac{1}{8}'')$

AN ACCOUNT

OF THE

TERRIBLE

STORM,

On Land and at Sea,

On Tuesday and Wednesday, the 13th and 14th inst. upwards of 26 Vessels were lost at, and near Sunderland, and 12 Persons perished in the Storm. Also, the Damage done on Land, by the Flooding of the Rivers.

In the night of Tuesday last, there was a very strong gale from the eastward, accompanied with heavy and long continued rain. Much damage has been caused at sea, and great floods on land. The Tyne was alarmingly swelled on Wednesday morning, overflowing all the low lands in its vicinity, and reaching the cellars on the Quayside and in the Close, and occasioning considerable loss of goods and liquors.

On Wednesday last, a small vessel laden with corn, &c. struck on the rocks near Marsden, between Shields and Sunderland. She went to pieces, and all on board, consisting of eight persons, perished. They were seen to suffer by some pilots, who were not able to render them any assistance.

On Tuesday last, about 150 colliers arrived safely in Sunderland harbour, and several sailed laden, with a fine north-west wind a smooth sea; but during the night, the wind having shifted to the north-east, with a most tremendous sea, Wednesday presented one of the most awful spectacles witnessed for these many years. There were four vessels lying on their broad-side on the South Rocks, and by 3 o'Clock there were 15 vessels on shore and wrecked between the South Pier and Hendon. The following vessels are among those that are wrecked:—The Adriatic, Wardell, of Shields; the Thomas. Gales, and the Margaret, of Sunderland; the Blagdon, and the Phœnix, of Shields, the Hunter, the Vine, the Louisa, the Caledonia, the Sythe, the Friends, the Barbara, the Nœvius, and the Thorney Close, all of Sunderland, and the sloop Catharine, of Perth, were all driven on shore at Sunderland; crews saved. The brig Thomas Fenwick, of Shields, is supposed to have sunk in deep water off Sunderland, after having been abandoned by her crew on the night of Tuesday. On the afternoon of Wednesday last, as the sloop Eleanor, of Sunderland, was attempting to take that harbour, she sunk, and was afterwards washed on shore. The crew, four in number, perished in the presence of some thousands of spectators, who were unable to lend the slightest assistance. The life-boat was repelled by force of the sea, the crew of the sloop then giving signs of distress. There are five or six vessels a-shore on the sand at Stranton, near Hartlepool; we have not been able to learn their names, except the William and the Clio, of Sunderland.

The same night the river Tees swelled to a height not exceeded within the memory of the oldest inhabitant of Barnardcastle. In the Street of Bridge-gate it entered several of the houses, and swept away from some of the inhabitants, a great part of their furniture, clothes, &c. while asleep in bed, and left them in a situation truly deplorable.

The rivers in the North Riding of Yorkshire overflowed their banks to an extent never remembered by the oldest people now living, and have done an immense damage to the adjoining country.

On Wednesday morning, the rivers that run through Carlisle rose to an alarming height. The temporary bridge lately erected across the Petteril at Harraby, about a mile and a half from Carlisle, was nearly washed away, and the carriages from the south were obliged to go round by Botcherby. The Caldew was so much swollen that all the houses in Caldewgate were completely inundated, and the watchmen were called off duty to render assistance in saving the lives and property of the inmates.   [From the "Newcastle Courant."]

Returns have been made by several of the gentlemen in Inverness and Moray Shires, who sustained losses by the late unprecedented floods, which sufficiently evince the extent of that great national calamity. We extract the following:—Earl of Seafield, 20,600l. Duke of Gordon. 16,494l. 6s. 4d. Mr. Grant of Ballindalloch, 8,500l. Mr. Frazer, of Relig, 500l. Several heavy losses have not as yet been stated, and there are various returns of one and two hundred pounds each. Much as the landlords may have lost, the tenants we fear, have suffered still more severely.

Fordyce, Printer. Newcastle.

RATE BY
Edward Mann
Always making fashion news

WORLD'S
LARGEST
EVENING
SALE

The Evening News

LATE
EDITION

© Associated Newspapers Ltd. 1959   NO. 24,239   LONDON. MONDAY, DECEMBER 7, 1959   PRICE 2½d.

TIO PEPE
Spain's dry sherry
GONZALEZ BYASS

TWO people were injured when a 151 bus and two cars were in collision at Morden (P5)

JUDGES should have training in both law and criminology, said the Howard League (P9)

500 PEOPLE appealed to the Duke of Edinburgh for help to save open spaces in Lee (P3)

CYCLING to school is no longer safe in East Suffolk because of high - speed traffic (P5)

Distress Calls Go Out . . Atlantic Liners Battered

SEA STORM TERROR

15 Feared Lost In Ship Wrecks

"EVENING NEWS" REPORTER

THE GREAT STORM BROUGHT DEATH AND DISASTER TO SHIPPING OFF BRITAIN TO-DAY.

A trawler with her crew of 12 were lost off the Caithness coast and the crew of another trawler clung to liferafts when their vessel began to sink off the Yorkshire coast.

Crack Atlantic liners were delayed, smaller vessels sent distress calls and Channel ships raced for shelter.

THE GALE BABY

TWO CALLS
Sinking Fast

ROADS
Flooded

ROCKETS
And An S O S

A NEW PERIL IN STRICKEN FREJUS

YOUR WEATHER
UNTIL NOON TO-MORROW

Dicey Vegetables

Fighting Stock

Sliding Scale

Moscow Drivers

TV and Radio—P5
CHANNEL 10 ON BACK PAGE

HELLO, MUMMY

Little ten-month-old Francesca was at the airport to greet her mother, Baroness von Thyssen, when she arrived in London from a holiday in the West Indies. Francesca had been staying with the Baroness's parents Admiral Keith Campbell Walter and his wife. The Baroness will fly out again to-morrow on a two-day business trip.

A LONDON MUSEUM? WE'LL HELP YOU, SAYS CAIRO

LUCKY NUMBERS THAT WIN £50

Winners of £50 in this month's Premium Bonds draw were announced to-day. The lucky numbers are in Page NINE.

PINK ZONE PEPS UP AGAIN

OXYGEN RAID

ROAD CLOSED

FILLING THE GAP

Have you a staff vacancy to fill urgently? Whether it is a secretary, clerk, salesman or representative you are seeking, the cheapest and quickest way of filling the gap is by a small ad in "The Evening News."

PHONE
FLE 6000
BEFORE 9 O'CLOCK
TO-NIGHT

Going Strong

Shock Wave

Loaded

THE DUKE'S HOLIDAY

Small Bore

The Seadragon

A-Bomb Protest

Ike Flies On After Ankara Triumph

Ankara, Monday.—President Eisenhower left here to-day for Karachi, after a triumphant visit and talks with Turkish leaders.

Pakistan is the third stop on his 11-nation, 22,000-mile tour of the Middle East and Far East.—B.U.P.

GRUNWALD IN COURT

FRIEDRICH GRUNWALD was appearing at the Mansion House to-day on a charge of fraudulent conversion, involving £2,235,000 entrusted to him by the State Building Society in this case.

He was appearing on remand of £500,000.

MR. K AND KADAR LEAVE BUDAPEST

LONDON ALERT FOR SAFE RAIDERS

S. AFRICA DROPS BRITISH RANKS

SWART FOR LONDON

BUFFERS CRASH

"FIGHTING ON ALGERIAN BORDER"

Cafes, Clubs Searched : Police Are Warned 'This Man Is Dangerous'

SOHO SWOOP IN HUNT FOR GUNMAN

Parsons Still On Run

"Evening News" Reporter

RONALD PARSONS, one of Britain's most dangerous criminals, was still at large to-day, 12 hours after he escaped from Wormwood Scrubs.

Police searching the 34-year-old Parsons occupied London and the Home Counties have sent warnings to all police stations that this man is dangerous.

OVER FENCE
And Away

Ronald Parsons

Golf Club Safe Gang Tie And Gag Two Men

"Evening News" Reporter

FOUR raiders bound and gagged two night watchmen and burst open and stole a safe containing over £500 from World Golf Club early to-day.

POLICE HUNT MAN AFTER CAR CHASE

BOGUS P.C. ATTACK

DOGS HUNT ARMED RAIDERS

HAMMER 'CONTRACT'

The Princess Back

The Post Boy.

From **Tuesday** March 24th. to **Thursday** March 26th. 1696.

London, March 28th. 1696.

ON *Tuesday* came on the Tryal of Sir *William Perkins* at the *Old Baily*, before the Lord Chief Justice *Holt*, the Lord Chief Justice *Treby*, Mr. Justice *Rookeby*, &c. the Prisoner being brought to the Bar, the Indictment was Read, setting forth that he had Conspired with *R. Charnock* and divers other false and Traiterous Persons to Assassinate His Sacred Majesty, and to levy War by inviting over Foreign Force, promising to assist them; and for that purpose, provided Horses, Men and great Quantities of Arms, contrary to his Allegiance, to which he pleaded Not Guilty: The Court bid him take care of his Challenge; the Jury was called over, he challenged 37, saying, two of them were the King's Servants; to which the Court answered, that it was no cause of Challenging, but the King's Council consented, there being Jurors enough. These Sworn were *Will. Northy, Edw. Gould, Dan. Thomas, Hen. Whitchot, Robert Babington, Tho. Sutton; Tho. Edlin, Rob. Saunderson, Ralph March, Joseph Wilson, Tho. Reames* and *Jeb. Rufford*. The Indictment was read the second time, Mr. *Montague* opened the same against the Prisoner briefly, Mr. Atturney General opened the nature of the Indictment, and the order they intended to proceed in the King's Evidence. Mr. Sollicitor General ordered the Witnesses to be called. Captain *Porter* the first Witness being Sworn, Deposed that in *May* he met the Prisoner at the *Old King's Head Tavern* in *Leaden-hall-street*, there being present the Earl of *Ailsbury*, Lord *Montgomery*, *Charnock*, Sir *J. Friend*, Sir *J. Fenwick*; Mr. *Cooks*, and Mr. *Goodman* came in after Dinner; that they consulted there how to bring King *James* in, and it was agreed to send *Charnock* to King *James* in *France*, to propose to him the bringing over 8000 Foot 1000 Horse, and as many Dragoons, with this assurance, that the Gentlemen present would join him with 2000 Horse; *Charnock* said, then he would not go a Fools Errand, intimating that the design was not so certainly resolved upon as it ought to be, so that they were forced to agree that the several Persons then in Company should be at the Head of those 2000 Horse. At a second meeting in *June* afterwards, which *Charnock* had ordered to propose something for the more certain carrying on of their Design, there were present Sir *J. Friend*, Sir *G. Barclay*, the Prisoner and others, it being at the *Nagg Head Tavern* in St. *James's street*, there *Charnock* promised after assurance, that all persons continued their former Resolutions, to go in 2 or 3 days for *France*. A little before the Riot in *Drury Lane*, Captain *Porter* met *Charnock*, who informed him he had been in *France*, and had seen King *James* Some time after Captain *Porter* being sick of the Gout at his Lodgings in *Norfolk street*, where *Charnock* then Lodged, and the Prisoner used to Lodge there when he came to Town; discoursing with *Charnock* about the intended Invasion and Assassinating the King's Person, the said *Charnock* told Captain *Porter* that there was a Commission brought over by Sir *George Berclay* from King *James* to levy War, and that King *James* had ordered one Mr. *Caroll* to pay a summ of Money to carry on the design; afterwards discoursing with the Prisoner, Captain *Porter* asked him if he had seen the Commission from King *James*, he said, Yes, and that King *James* had wrote it all with his own Hand; they had several meetings afterwards at the *Globe Tavern*, at the *Nagg Head Tavern*, and at the *Sun Tavern* in the *Strand*, at one of which it was proposed, that *King*, lately Executed, one *Knightley* and Captain *Porter*, should go and view what place was most convenient to attack the King's Person; there were present Sir *George Berclay*, the Prisoner and others; accordingly they went, and being returned, it was agreed to Assassinate the King by shooting him in his Coach, and the persons with him, as he came from *Richmond*, at the end of a narrow Lane leading into *Turnam Green*. At another meeting where the Prisoner, Captain *Porter*, and others

were present, it was agreed to put their design in Execution the 15th. of *February* last, and for that end there were 2 Men called Orderly Men, lodged at *Kensington*, by Name, *Chambers* and *Durance*. Captain *Porter*, the Prisoner, *Charnock*, Sir *George Berclay* and others were to command several Parties, and for that purpose, the Prisoner was to provide 5 Horses, and Captain *Porter* soon after complained two of his Horses were Lame, the Prisoner offered two of his Horses to him, and said, he could have three Horses more of one Mr. *Lewis*, formerly Gentleman of the Horse to the Earl of *Feversham*. Captain *Porter* further Deposed, that the Design of the 15th. being miscarried by the Kings not going to *Richmond*, Sir *George Berclay*, the Prisoner, Captain *Porter* and others suspected some Discovery, but Captain *Porter* told them, if any such Discovery had been made, they had not then been there; so the Design was put off till the 21st of *February*, and then all Persons being met, and the King not going abroad, it was agreed by the Prisoner, Sir *George Berclay*, Captain *Porter* and others, that all was Discovered, and they resolved to keep out of the way. The Court asked Captain *Porter* if the Prisoner was to Assassinate the King in Person, Captain *Porter* said, No; then one of the Jury prayed the Question might be put to Captain *Porter*, whether the prisoner was present at any time when the Discourse was of killing the King; Captain *Porter* said, he was there at every time, and did agree it was necessary to be done.

Then Mr. *Sweet* another Evidence was sworn, and gave Account that he discoursed with the prisoner in *February* last, at his House in *Hartfordshire*, where he told him he expected the King's landing, and that his own Troop was composed of old Troopers; and that he had bought 30 Sadles: The Prisoner told Mr. *Sweet* he was to go to *Leicester*, to meet some Gentlemen; upon his return Mr. *Sweet* asked the prisoner what Gentlemen he had seen, he said, Several; and, *That she West was as well disposed as the North*. On the 11th. of *February* Mr. *Sweet* met the prisoner in *Norfolk street* upon his Letter, where he acquainted him with the Business intended to be done by him was to be done by another, Mr. *Sweet* having a Family, he sent him back into *Hartfordshire*, but upon another Letter soon after of the Prisoner's to Mr. *Sweet* he came to Town, the prisoner asked him if he had provided for his Family, he said No, then the prisoner said, *Why did you come to Town?* On the 14th of *February* Mr. *Sweet* met *Chambers*, one of the Orderly-men, and discoursing with him over a Glass at *Kensington, Chambers* said, he had received a Wound at the *Boyne, &c*. Then the Court asked Mr. *Sweet* how many Horses he had sent to Town by the prisoner's man from *Hartfordshire*, he said, Three. The prisoner insisted, the Words about King *James* were spoken in *Hartfordshire*, and not in the County where he is now Indicted; the Court answered, That were there several Overt-Acts of the same Species of Treason in several Counties, the Overt Act in one County may be given in Evidence in another. Then the third Witness *James Ubank* was sworn, being the prisoner's man, he gave account that in *January* last he went with his master to *Leicester*, and that one Mr *Skismore* went with them; that at *Leicester* they met several Gentlemen, particularly one Mr. *Turbrough*, and another person said to be a Parson, with several others, which this Witness could not take notice of. After their return from *Leicester*, this Witness brought Horses to *London* by the Prisoner's Orders, 3 at one time, and 4 at another, each of the last having pistols; they were left at the *George Inn* in *Holborn*. The same Evidence deposed, that he had seen Mr. *Lewis*, Gentleman of the Horse to the Earl of *Feversham*, with the prisoner, where they discoursed about several Horses and Sadles, but the Witness was not privy to their Design. Some time after the Witness was sent to *Warwickshire* to the prisoner's house, and was ordered to go to one *Haywoods*, and one *Evans*, with a Team to fetch some Boxes, which was done about 11 a clock at night, and the Witness said he saw those Boxes buried in the Prisoner's Garden. Then

(11½″ × 6⅝″)

PRINCE OF WALES'
MARRIAGE.

Everybody stop and listen to my ditty,
And let the news spread from town to city,
The Prince of Wales has long enough tarried,
And now we know he's going to be married,

   For he's going to sleep all night
     And part of the next day,
   The Prince of Wales must tell some tales,
    With his doo da, doo da, day.

His pastime for a week there's no disputing,
For the first three days he'll go a shooting,
He's like his father, I don't deceive yer,
And she like Vick is a good feeder.

The next two days, so it is said, sir,
He'll begin to dig out the parsley bed, sir,
Like his dad, he does understand,
And knows how to cultivate a bit of land.

The first day over he'll lay in clover,
And just alike he'll feel all over.
At fox hunting he's clever, and all races,
Yet she might kick him out of the traces.

She must not go larking along with the gals,
Keep out of the Haymarket, and Pall Mall,
And to no married women must he speak,
He'll stand no nonsense or half-crowns a-week.

In November next she must not fail,
But have a little Prince of Wales,
Young Albert he must not be beat,
But contrive to make both ends meet.

When his wife is in a funny way,
Then he must not go astray,
Of all those things he must take warning,
Nor go out with the girls, and stop till morning.

The last Prince of Wales was a good'un to go,
He would ride with the girls in Rotten Row,
He used to flare up, he was no joker,
He was as fat as a Yarmouth bloater.

He must look to his stock and cultivation,
He must be a father to the nation,
He must begin to reap and sow,
Be a rum'un to look at, but a good'un to go.

He wants six maids as light as fairies,
To milk the cows, and look to the dairy,
To his wife the household affairs confiding,
With the Prince of Wales goes out a riding.

Long life to the Prince and his fair lady,
May she have health and bouncing babies,
May the Prince be King, we want no other,
And take the steps of his father and mother.

J. CATNACH, Printer, London.

$(9\frac{7}{8}'' \times 7\frac{1}{2}'')$

THE
Outrage & Murder
On a Little Child at PURFLEET.

A Little girl named Alice Boughen, was supposed to have been dreadfully outraged and murdered by a School-master, on Wednesday: she left her home at 2 o'clock, to go to school. At half-past 3 she left the room to go into the back, and was not seen alive afterward.

TUNE:— Just before the Battle Mother.

The Dreadful Murder
OF A WIFE
And Six Children.

Early on Monday morning a whole family, consisting of the father, mother, and six children named Duggin were found poisoned at a house in Hosier-lane, City. The father

MURDER AT CAMBRIDGE.

Robert Brown, stands charged with the murder of Emma Rolfe, by cutting her throat with a razor, on a Common near Cambridge, on Thursday night, Aug. 28th, 1876. The Prisoner has confessed the crime to Police Constable Wheel.

The victim was an " UNFORTUNATE GIRL,"

Tune:—Driven from Home·

In the quiet town of Cambridge a deed has been done,
That I'm sure has surprised and startled each one ;
An unfortunate woman but just in her prime,
Alas ! is the victim of this cruel crime.
Well known in Cambridge, from virtue betrayed,
In the path of dishonour too early she strayed ;
But whatever she's been we can all understand,
Her life was as sweet as the best in the land.

CHORUS.

Poor Emma Rolfe had no time to repent,
On Midsummer common to eternity sent ;
Robert Brown was her murderer, in prison he's cast.
From virtue she strayed to be murdered at last.

A policeman was brought and the murderer confess'd,
For the crime he committed he now has no rest,
He would give all the world to recall that sad hour,
But what has been done is beyond earthly power.
She was murdered that night, with her sins on her head,
We hope they're forgiven now she's laying dead ;
Tho' lost to the world, despised and forlorn,
Someone will miss the poor girl now she's gone.

Robert Brown will be tried for this unmanly crime,
And if he's found guilty must suffer in time ;
We pity his brother and relations as well,
Who are grieving for him as he lies in his cell :
His poor victim lies in her cold narrow be,
Never no more to her ruin be led ;
Young girls beware you are not led astray,
For plenty will quickly decoy you away.

(*Top:* 9⅞″ × 7½″)   (*Centre:* 9⅞″ × 7½″)   (*Bottom:* 10″ × 7½″)

168

George Cohen's
Plant & Machinery
Tel: Shepherds Bush 2070

Evening Standard

42,614   MONDAY, JUNE 19, 1961   ●● 3d.

WEST END FINAL
CLOSING PRICES

Frank Bustard
& SONS LIMITED
TRAVEL AGENTS
26 WHITEHALL·LONDON SW1 Tel Whitehall 5564

BRENDA NASH

Jones: Jury out only seven minutes —judge talks of his 'evil crimes'

HE RAPED BARBARA, MURDERED BRENDA

Life sentence added to 14 years

Evening Standard Reporter

Arthur Albert Jones, 44, of Ely Road, Hounslow, was sentenced to LIFE IMPRISONMENT at the Old Bailey today for the murder of 12-year-old Girl Guide Brenda Nash, of Bleriot Road, Heston, last October.

The judge, Mr. Justice Sachs, ordered that Jones should start the sentence at the end of a 14-YEAR term he is at present serving for raping an 11-year-old Girl Guide referred to merely as Barbara at the trial last March.

Today's jury was out for SEVEN MINUTES.

Mr. Justice Sachs told Jones: " You have been found guilty now of two crimes evil to a degree beyond all adjectives.

" It is proper that you should serve your sentence for the first crime and neither as a matter of fact nor appearance should it cease to operate.

I pass upon you . . .

" In the circumstances I pass upon you the sentence laid down by statute . . . that you be sentenced to imprisonment for life and for the protection of the public I think, firstly, it should be a sentence to commence upon the expiration of your existing sentence and, secondly, it will be lamentable indeed if upon the second sentence you do not serve a far longer time than upon the first."

Jones, his face tense, appeared outwardly composed as the judge spoke.

Then a touch on the shoulder by a prison officer ended the courtroom drama. He turned round and walked to the cells below. His face was now flushed . . . his head bowed.

Jones's solicitor, Mr. Harold Matthissen, said an appeal was being considered.

Mrs. Jones was not in court when her husband was sentenced. The news was taken to her by a court matron. She broke down and sobbed.

Mrs. Jones was refused permission to see her husband after sentence.

Jones's married daughter, Christine, giving no sign of emotion, hurried from court to comfort her mother.

The first

Jones is the first person ever to get ' life plus ' and this afternoon a Home Office spokesman said " A person sentenced to life imprisonment can be detained for the rest of his life."

ON PAGE SIXTEEN: Seven-minute jury surprises the Old Bailey. Empty windows where Brenda lived.

THIS MAN JONES

By JOHN MILLER

Cider-loving Arthur Albert Jones has been exposed after months of suspicion as the murderer of Brenda Nash. He was trapped by whispers in Wandsworth prison—and by his fantastic blunder in twice putting up a wrong alibi.

But it was a girl in a Mayfair hairdressers who first put police on the trail of this scar-faced man's lies to hide his crime.

Now medical men will try to assess the true character of this strange family man who lured Brenda to a violent death on a lonely Hampshire common.

After being charged with murder, Jones was transferred from Wandsworth Prison to Brixton Prison to await the murder-court hearings in case any clash with prisoners might have affected his trial.

For sex-offenders are notoriously disliked by other men jailed for different kinds of offence, such as theft or fraud.

Devoted wife

Impeccable Mr Mervyn Griffith-Jones, old Etonian, who was at the Nuremberg war crimes tribunal and who prosecuted Jones, had no hesitation in calling him " a devil at work."

Suburban neighbours still found it hard to imagine that this rosy-cheeked man with a devoted wife and two children could turn into such a guise.

He was a " lone wolf " every Friday but the rest of the week was an £18-a-week workman who had a nice council house in Hounslow and tinkered with his car in his spare time.

But the truth came out after Jones had given himself away by his own mistakes.

When Brenda vanished at 10 p.m. on Friday, October 28, the district where she lived was already in anxiety because another little girl—also a Girl Guide—had been attacked seven weeks before.

Dilemma

He was in a dilemma. He put up probably the only explanation he could think of. He claimed he had been in the West End that night.

But his luck was turning against him. He had put up a similar explanation a few weeks before.

And though in the weeks that followed he boldly bluffed the police into the belief that he knew anything about Brenda's disappearance.

● Page Sixteen, Col. 4

ARTHUR JONES
Already serving 14 years.

WEATHER—sunny periods—see Page 17.

(10⅞″ × 8½″)   (*Inset:* 6″ × 3¾″)

(7" × 5½")

ROBIN HOOD'S GARLAND,

BEING A COMPLEAT

HISTORY

OF ALL THE

NOTABLE and MERRY EXPLOITS

Performed by him and his Men on divers Occasions:

GIVING

A more full and particular Account of his Birth, &c. than hitherto published.

I fend this Arrow from my Bow,
And in a Wager will be bound,
To hit the Mark aright, altho'
It were for Fifteen Hundred Pounds.
Doubt not I'll make the Wager good,
Or ne'er believe bold Robin Hood.

LONDON:

Printed and Sold by T. SABINE, at the LONDON and MIDDLESEX PRINTING OFFICE, No. 81, Shoe-lane, Fleet-ftreet; where Printing is expeditioufly performed in all its various Branches of Letter-prefs and Copper-plate, on the moft reafonable Terms.

(7¾" × 5")

CATALANI JOE, THE BALLAD MONGER !

A popular Comic Song. written by Mr. J. La'Bern, and sung by Mr. Tanner, and Mr. Manclark at the London Concerts.

Music sold by John Duncombe and Co. 10, Middle Row, Holborn.

Come all you chaunting wocalists, that vorbles high and low, sirs,
A yard and half of music buy of Catalani Joe, sirs—
Here's love songs, and comic songs, and songs of ev'ry nation,
But if you'll vait a hinstant you shall have 'em in rotation.
                    Tol de rol, &c.

' My wife she is a vouder quite'—' I cannot love another'—
' That's the ticket'—' Take a sight'—' Roger how's your mother ?'
' I couldn't think of sich a thing'—' While the stormy winds do blow,' sir—

No. 10

' What's a house without a woman ?'—' With a helmet on his brow, sir.'
                    Tol de rol, &c.

' When a little farm we keep'—' On the banks of Allan Water'—
' We met'—' The moralizing Sweep'—and ' The Ratcatcher's Daughter'—
' Thump thump, scold scold'—' The Washerwoman's wrangle'—
' Lor bless me who'd ha' thought it'—' Has your mother sold her mangle ?'
                    Tol de rol, &c.

' Moggy Lauder'—' Who are you ?'—' The sun is o'er the mountain'—
' John White'—' To-day I'm sixty-two'— ' Let's wander by the fountain'—
' Sweet Eyes'—' Deep in a forest dell— ' Doctors they can ease ills.'
' Feyther, thankee's, pretty well, and mother' got the measles.
                    Tol de rol, &c.

(9″ × 5½″)

Sing

To all our readers
**A VERY MERRY
CHRISTMAS**
and a happy new year

VOL.6 NO.4   DECEMBER 1961   NINEPENCE

Every Star Shall Sing a Carol

A carol for the space age.
Words and music by Sydney Carter.

Every star shall sing a carol Every creature high and low,

Come and praise the king of heaven By whatever name you know.

God above, man below, Holy is the name I know.

When the king of all creation
Had a cradle on the Earth,
Holy was the human body
And the day that gave him birth.

Who can tell how many crosses,
Still to come or long ago,
Crucify the king of heaven?
Holy is the name I know.

Who can tell what other cradle
High above the Milky Way
Still may rock the king of heaven
On another Christmas Day?

Every creature he will gather,
All shall know him for their own.
I will praise the son of Mary,
Brother of my blood and bone.

Every star and every planet,
Every creature high or low,
Sing the everlasting carol:
Holy is the name I know.

Sydney Carter argues that the conquest of space is causing us
to revise our ideas of the revelation of God through Christ
that is at the core of the Christian religion. This carol is a
thoughtful attempt to pose the question on a spacial scale.

(8½″ × 5½″)

THE FROG AND MOUSE

2
This Frog he wou'd a Wooing ride,
  With a rigdum bonna duo Coinno,
With a Sword and Buckler by his fide,
  With a rigdum bonna duo Coinno;
Cho: Koy min ero &c.
3
And when he came to Moufes Hall,
  With a rigdum bonna duo Coinno,
There he did moft loudly bawl,
  With a rigdum bonna duo Coinno.
Cho: Koy min ero &c.
4
Miftrefs Moufe are you within?
  With a rigdum bonna duo Coinno,
Yes, Mr Frog pray do walk in,
  With a rigdum bonna duo Coinno.
Cho: Koy min ero &c.
5

7
Sir I am come to Woo your Neice,
  With a rigdum bonna duo Coinno,
Yes, and welcome to this Place,
  With a rigdum bonna duo Coinno.
Cho: Koy min ero &c.
8
Juft as fhey had fill'd their Beek,
  With a rigdum bonna duo Coinno,
In comes Miftrefs Pufs and her Chick,
  With a rigdum bonna duo Coinno.
Cho: Koy min ero &c.
9
Pufs feizd Uncle Rat by the Crown,
  With a rigdum bonna duo Coinno,
Chick pull'd Moufe up and down,
  With a rigdum bonna duo Coinno.
Cho: Koy min ero &c.
10

(*Top:* 13½″ × 8¾″)

(*Bottom:* 13¼″ × 9¼″)

THE BATTLE OF

BALTINGLASS

By Sylvester Gaffney.

PRICE 1/- NET

Published by
WALTON'S PIANO & MUSICAL INSTRUMENT GALLERIES
(Publications Dept.) LTD.
2, 3, 4 & 5 NORTH FREDERICK STREET and 90 LOWER CAMDEN STREET, DUBLIN

$(11\frac{1}{8}'' \times 8\frac{5}{8}'')$

THE
GREAT EXHIBITION
SONGSTER
1851

A tidy suit for all that	I turn to thee	Sweeter vow was never
As I view those scenes	Jolly Waggoner	spoken
A light heart	Jolly Beggars	Scenes that are bright
A Soldier and a Sailor	Jeannette and Jeannot	Together, dearest let
An Ape, a Lion, a Fox	Lilly of St. Leonard's	us fly
Beautiful Maid	Love one another	The Keepsake
Busy, curious fly	Little Fools and great	There's a good time
Cavalier	Life on the ocean wave	coming (Comic)
Come, let us be happy	Last Rose of Summer	The Beggar and Pope
together	Minstrel Boy	The Windmill
Child of good-nature	My pretty Jane	Take back those gems
Dearest, then, I'll love	Meet me, deares	The Moon is up
thee more	Madeline	Uncle Ned
Do not mingle	My Mother's customs	Where is the Rover ?
Farewell, thou coast	Nelly Machree	William was a seaman
of glory	Nay, smile again	Why, the world are all
Haste, for the Summer	One kindly word before	thinking about it
is flying	we part	Wine does wonders
I love but thee	Rosa May [member	Woman rules you still
If I live to grow old	Remember, love, re-	When thou art near

London :—Printed and Published by W. S. Johnson, 60, St. Martin's Lane, Charing Cross.

(8¾″ × 6⅞″)

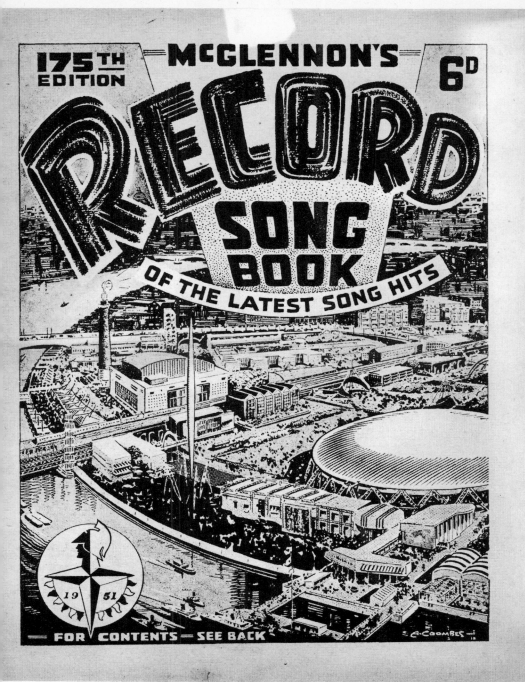

McGLENNON'S

175TH EDITION

RECORD

6D

SONG

BOOK

OF THE LATEST SONG HITS

19 51

FOR CONTENTS — SEE BACK

C. COOMBES

$(11'' \times 8\frac{5}{8}'')$

THE BROADSHEET

A weekly magazine of art and epicurianism

No. 1   OCTOBER 23   1954

Price sixpence.

EDITORIAL

"The Broadsheet" is not a pastiche of the publications of the eighteenth and nineteenth century; it is designed as a service for the Cafephile and those in search of entertainment. The first edition is published at the same time as the opening of MR. FELIKS TOPOLSKI'S exhibition of "Historical and Contemporary Broadsheets," and this issue is devoted to the reproduction of some of the exhibits.

Topolski, in his fortnightly "Chronicle," has revived the manner of retaining the simple and direct expression of the artist, by controlling the print production of his drawings himself, without being hampered by the vestigial conventions of the print technologist, with his *Valhalla* of facsimile reproduction and the layout man's typographical hoohaa.

The Chronicle is a graphic survey of the current way of life. Topolski, having been persuaded that he was good at trapping the spirit and shape of our time, assumed that such a continuous panorama, when collected and preserved over the years would become a unique document. The content is not subdued by any rules and swings from a number of issues given to one theme to single "omnibus" issues, with serial features, textual decorations and round the world experiences included. Folders are made for the 24 broadsheets which appear yearly to form a handsome line on the bookshelves; and each year is closed with a list of drawings and an index of the people, places and events recorded.

We devote part of THE BROADSHEET every week to reproducing a reduced in size version of the Chronicle—not as a collector's piece, but as a topographical statement to a wider audience than can be met by the limited and more expensive editions of the "originals."

In subsequent issues THE BROADSHEET will publish critical surveys on entertainment, epicurianism, exhibitions and fashion, and will include sectional maps in colour of London streets, showing the location of the coffee houses, restaurants and places of entertainment in fashion.

BROADSHEET EXHIBITION

On Tuesday, Topolski opened his exhibition of historical and contemporary broadsheets, his own being sold by street literature sellers dressed in early nineteenth century costume loaned by the Players Theatre.

Although millions of these sheets were sold by the flying "stationers" in Georgian and Victorian days few have survived, for during subsequent generations, which experienced so great a change in printing design and technique and frowned on this crude ephemera, such things quickly disappeared. Further, their flimsy nature and awkward size made their survival in domestic hands very difficult. They are of interest today from a social point of view and also

Photo. by courtesy of Keystone

$(8\frac{1}{2}'' \times 6\frac{1}{4}'')$

178

... THE WILD COLONIAL BOY ...

There was a wild colonial youth, Jack Doolan was his name;
Of poor but honest parents he was born in Castlemaine.
He was his father's only hope, his mother's only joy,
The pride of both his parents was the wild colonial boy.

Chorus: Come all my hearties, we'll range the mountain side;
Together we will plunder, together we will ride.
We'll scour along the valleys and gallop o'er the plains,
We scorn to live in slavery bowed down with iron chains.

In sixty-one this daring youth commenced his wild career;
With a heart that knew no danger, no foeman did he fear:
He held up the Beechworth mailcoach and he robbed Judge MacEvoy
Who trembled and gave up his gold to the wild colonial boy.

Chorus:

One day as he was riding the mountain side along,
A listening to the little birds their pleasant laughing song,
Three mounted troopers came in view, Kelly, Davis and Fitzroy.
And thought that they would capture him, the wild colonial boy.

Chorus:

Surrender now, Jack Doolan, you see there's three to one,
Surrender now, Jack Doolan, you daring highwayman!
He drew a pistol from his belt and spun it like a toy.
I'll fight but I won't surrender, said the wild colonial boy.

Chorus:

He fired at trooper Kelly and brought him to the ground.
And in return from Davis received a mortal wound,
All shattered through the jaws he lay still firing at Fitzroy,
And that's the way they captured him, the wild colonial boy.

Chorus:

(Other tunes for this ballad exist; this tune is also used for 'Bald Jack Donahue')

PUBLISHED BY BANDICOOT BALLADS J. MANIFOLD WYNUM N⁴ʰ ROAD
PRINTED BY SIMPSON HALLIGAN, BRISBANE

(11⅜″ × 8½″)

179

Go Down, You Murderers!

Words and music by EWAN MacCOLL.

Tim Evans was a prisoner,
Fast in his prison cell,
And those who read about his crimes,
They damned his soul to hell.
    Saying, go down, you murderer, go down!

For the murder of his own true wife,
And the killing of his own child,
The jury found him guilty
And the hanging judge he smiled.
    Saying, go down, you murderer, go down!

Now Evans pleaded innocent
And swore by him on high,
That he never killed his own dear wife
Nor caused his child to die.
    Saying, go down, you murderer, go down!

They moved him out at nine o'clock
To his final flowery-dell,
And day and night two screws were there
And never left his cell.
    Saying, go down, you murderer, go down!

Sometimes they played draughts with him
And solo and pontoon,
To stop him brooding on the rope
That was to be his doom.
    Saying, go down, you murderer, go down!

They brought his grub in on a tray,
There was eggs and meat and ham,
And all the snout that he could smoke
Was there at his command.
    Saying, go down, you murderer, go down!

The governor came in one day,
The chaplain by his side;
Says, "Your appeal has been turned down,
Prepare yourself to die."
    Saying, go down, you murderer, go down!

So Evans walked in the prison yard
And the screws they walked behind,
And he saw the sky above the wall
And he knew no peace of mind.
    Saying, go down, you murderer, go down!

They came for him at eight o'clock
And the chaplain read a prayer,
And then they walked him to that place
Where the hangman did prepare.
    Saying, go down, you murderer, go down!

The rope was fixed around his neck,
And the buckle behind his ear;
And the prison bell was tolling
But Tim Evans did not hear.
    Saying, go down, you murderer, go down!

A thousand lags were cursing
And a banging on the doors.
Tim Evans could not hear them,
He was deaf for evermore.
    Saying, go down, you murderer, go down!

They sent Tim Evans to the drop
For a crime he didn't do.
It was Christy was the murderer
And the judge and jury too.
    Saying, go down, you murderers, go down!

★★★★★

New verses, new ballads, suggestions,
donations, to John Foreman & Ron Baugh,
15, Mortimer Terrace, Highgate Road, N.W.5.

"The Women are worse than the Men!"

⸻●⸻

It is true that the women are worse than the men,
  Right fol right fol tid-dy fol lay,
It is true that the women are worse than the men,
  That they went down to hell and were thrown out again
With your right fol lol tid-dy fol lol,
  Fol the-dol lol the-dol, lol the-dol day.

Now there was an old man lived at Kellyburn braes
  And he had a wife was the plague of his days.
The divil he came to the man at the plough
  Saying, "One of your family I must take now."

Said he, "My good man, I've come for your wife,
  For I hear she's the plague and torment of your life."
So the divil he hoisted her up on his back,
  And landed at hell's hall-door with a crack.

There two little divils a-playing with chains,
  She upp'd with her stick, and knocked out their brains.
There were two other divils looked over the wall,
  They said, "Take her away or she'll murder us all."

So the divil he hoisted her up on his back
  And back to the old man hurried the pace.
They were seven years going and nine coming back,
  Yet she asked for the scrapings she left in the pot.

Said he, "My good man here's your wife back again
  For she wouldn't be kept, not even in hell!
Now I've been a divil the most of my life,
  But I ne'er was in hell till I met with your wife!"

"THE WILD COLONIAL BOY"

ORIGINAL VERSION—FIRST PRINTED 1880

It's of a wild Colonial Boy, Jack Doolan was his name,
Of poor but honest parents, he was born in Castlemaine,
He was his father's comfort, his mother's pride and joy,
And dearly did they always love their Wild Colonial Boy.

So now away my hearties that roam the mountain side,
Together we will plunder, together we will ride,
We'll wander over hills and we'll gallop over plains
Before we'll work in slavery bound down in iron chains.
At the tender age of sixteen years he left his native home,
And to Australia's sunny land a stranger did he roam,
He robbed the wealthy squires and their arms he did destroy,
And a terror to Australia was the Wild Colonial Boy.
At the early age of eighteen years he began his wild career,
With a heart that knew no danger and a spirit knew no fear,
He stuck up Beechwood Mail Coach and robbed Judge McAvoy,
Who trembling gave his money to the Wild Colonial Boy.
He bade the Judge " Good Morning " and told him to beware
And never lag a lantry cove that acted on the square,
And never part a mother from her son and only boy,
For fear he might turn robber like the Wild Colonial Boy.
One morning as he gaily rode along the mountain side
A-listening to the lyre birds that pleasantly did chide,
When lo—three mounted troopers—Evans, Kelly and Fitzroy.
Rode up and tried to capture the Wild Colonial Boy.
Surrender now, Jack Doolan, you see we're three to one,
Surrender in the King's name, you daring highway man,
Jack drew a pistol from his belt and shook the little toy,
I'll die, but not surrender, cried the Wild Colonial Boy.
He fired a shot at Kelly which brought him to the ground,
Returning fire from Evans he received a mortal wound,
But with his life fast ebbing he kept firing at Fitzroy,
And that's the way they captured the Wild Colonial Boy.

(13" × 4")

(*Top:* 7" × 4⅝")

(*Bottom:* 7" × 4¾")

The Silly Sentry.

IT'S A LAUGH.

The General walking down a lane
Saw a sight that gave him pain
It was a Sentry, whose name was Pritt
Who sat smoking a fag, he had just lit.

My man, said the General loudly
What are you suppose to do?
Oh, I'm a bit of a Sentry Sir
Now who the blazes are you?

I'm your General he said sternly
And you, I've a good mind to shoot

Hold it a minute, said the Sentry
And I'll give thee a bit of salute.

Sargeant, arrest this man, said the General
He's lazy or else balmy
He gave me cheek when I questioned him
He's no good for the Army.

I knew I was no good for the army, Sarge
And I hope the General gets me discharged
All this shooting, while laying in dirt
I would'nt mind betting, somebody gets hurt

Is your family as soft as you, said the General. Oh yes, said Pritt. Mother said the army would make a man of me. I said maybe a dead one. Dad said it would put new life in me. I said in my shirt you mean. Still I may get time to scratch. My Sister said you may become a General. Yes I said a General Servant to anyone. Still its all for peace the blinking liars.

Composed & issued by J. Smith, 3, Ropley St., Bethnal Green.

The Hackney Press 407 Hackney Road E.3

ARMY LIFE

The uniform they give you they say is mighty fine,
But me and my two buddies can all get into mine!

Chorus: I don't want no more of army life,
    Gee, but I want to go home.

They treat you like a monkey and stand you in a line.
They pay you thirty shillings and take back twenty-nine!

The sausages they give you they say are mighty fine;
One jumped off the table and bit a friend of mine!

Last Xmas we had chicken and it looked so mighty fine,
Then it stood up on the table and started marking time!

The coffee that they give you they pour it out like wine;
It's good for cuts and bruises and it tastes like iodine!

    I don't want no more of army life,
    Jesus I want to go - but they won't let me go.
    Gee, but I want to go home.

★★★★★

 New verses, new ballads, suggestions,
donations, to John Foreman and Ron Baugh,
15, Mortimer Terrace, Highgate Road, London, N.W.5.

(*Top:* 6¼″ × 3¾″)   (*Bottom:* 8″ × 6″)

SONGS FOR THE
MARCH FOR
LIFE *against*
nuclear death

2d

28 June LONDON

The H-Bomb's Thunder

Words by JOHN BRUNNER
Tune: MINERS' LIFEGUARD

Don't you hear the H-bombs' thunder
Echo like the crack of doom?
While they rend the skies asunder
Fall-out makes the earth a tomb.
Do you want your homes to tumble,
Rise in smoke towards the sky?
Will you let your cities crumble,
Will you see your children die?

Chorus:
  Men and women, stand together.
  Do not heed the men of war.
  Make your minds up now or never,
  Ban the bomb for evermore.

Tell the leaders of the nations
Make the whole wide world take
     heed:
Poison from the radiations
Strikes at every race and creed.
Must you put mankind in danger,
Murder folk in distant lands?
Will you bring death to a stranger,
Have his blood upon your hands?

Shall we lay the world in ruin?
Only you can make the choice.
Stop and think of what you're doing.
Join the march and raise your voice.
Time is short; we must be speedy.
We can see the hungry filled,
House the homeless, help the needy.
Shall we blast, or shall we build?

The Family of Man

Words and music
by FRED DALLAS

I belong to a family, the biggest on earth
A thousand every day are coming to birth.
Our surname isn't Dallas or Hasted or Jones
It's a name every man should be proud he owns.

  It's the family of man keeps growing,
  The family of man keeps sowing
  The seeds of a new life every day.

I've got a sister in Melbourne, a brother in Paree,
The whole wide world is dad and mother to me.
Wherever you turn you will find my kin
Whatever the creed, or the colour of the skin.

The miner in the Rhondda, the coolie in Peking,
Men across the world who reap and plough and spin.
They've all got a life and others to share it,
Let's bridge the oceans and declare it.

From the North Pole ice to the snow at the other,
There isn't a man I wouldn't call brother.
But I haven't much time, I've had my fill
Of the men of war who want to kill.

Some people say the world is a horrible place
But it's just good or bad as the human race:
Dirt and misery or health and joy,
Man can build or can destroy.

(8″ × 6⅛″)

WAYSIDE PULPIT
A Thought for the Week

WAR
never settles
who is right,
but who is
strong.

Issued by the CHURCH PUBLICITY AND SERVICE CENTRE of the NATIONAL FREE CHURCH COUNCIL, 27a, Tavistock Square, London, W.C.1

183   (30" × 20")

Mr. J. Smith, a modern bard, at his pitch in
Oxford Street, London.

(*Photograph : Teddy Schwarz*)

SELECTED BIBLIOGRAPHY

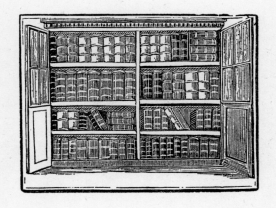

SELECTED BIBLIOGRAPHY

*BROADSIDES, EARLY NEWSPAPERS, CHAPBOOKS AND
TRACTS:*

ARBER, Edward (ed.). An English Garner, Ingatherings from our History and Literature. 8 vols. London, 1895.

ASHTON, John. Chapbooks of the Eighteenth Century. London, 1882.

BEATTIE, William (ed.). The Chepman and Myllar Prints, Nine Tracts from the First Scottish Press Edinburgh 1508 followed by the two other tracts in the same volume in the National Library of Scotland. (facsimile with bibliographical note). Edinburgh, 1950.

CATALOGUE OF THE COLLECTION OF BROADSIDES IN THE UNIVERSITY LIBRARY. (Goldsmith's Library of Economic Literature.) University of London Press, 1930.

CUNNINGHAM, Robert Hays. Amusing Prose Chapbooks Chiefly of Last Century. London and Glasgow, 1889.

DAHL, Folke. A Bibliography of English Corantos and Periodical Newsbooks 1620–42. London, 1952.

DRAPER, John W. A Century of Broadside Elegies, being ninety English and ten Scotch broadsides illustrating the biography and manners of the seventeenth century. London, 1928.

FEDERER, Charles A. Yorkshire Chapbooks. London, 1889.

FRASER, John. Scottish Chapbooks. New York and Glasgow, 1873.

GERRING, Charles. Notes on Printers and Booksellers with a Chapter on Chapbooks. London and Nottingham, 1900.

HALKETT, S., and LAING, J. Dictionary of Anonymous and Pseudonymous English Literature. 7 vols. and supplementary vol. 1926–34, 1900–1950.

HARVEY, William. Scottish Chapbook Literature. Paisley, 1903.

HODGKIN, John Eliot. Rariora (Vol. 3)—Notes on some of the printed books, MSS., etc., collected 1858–1900.

JOHN CHEAP THE CHAPMAN'S LIBRARY: The Scottish Chap Literature of Last Century, Classified. With Life of Dougal Graham. 3 vols. Glasgow, 1877–8.

MacGREGOR, George (ed.). The Collected Writings of Dougal Graham, "Skellat" Bellman of Glasgow. 2 vols. Glasgow, 1883.

MacMurtrie, Douglas Crawford. Instructions for the Description of Broadsides (American Imprints Inventory). U.S.A., 1939.

Morison, Stanley. The English Newspaper. Some account of the physical development of journals printed and published in London from 1622 to the present day. London, 1932.

Roth, H. Ling and Jolley, J. T. War Ballads and Broadsides of Previous Wars, 1779–95. (County Borough of Halifax, Bankfield Museum Notes, 2nd Series, No. 5.) Halifax, 1915.

Thomason, George. Catalogue of Pamphlets, Books, Newspapers and Manuscripts relating to the Civil War, the Commonwealth and Restoration, collected by G. Thomason, 1640–61. London, 1908.

Watt, William H. Shilling Shockers of the Gothic School (Harvard Honors Theses in English). Harvard University Press, 1932.

Welsh, C., and Tillinghurst, W. H. Catalogue of English and American Broadsides at Harvard College Library. U.S.A., 1905.

TRADITIONAL BALLADS AND SONGS:

Barry, P., Eckstorm, F. H., and Smyth, M. W. British Ballads from Maine. Yale, 1929.

Bryant, F. E. A History of English Balladry and other studies. Boston, 1913.

Child, Francis James. *The English and Scottish Popular Ballads, 1882–98.* Reprint: The Folklore Press/Pageant Book Co. New York, 1957. 5 vols. in 3. . . . Since the welcome reprint of this indispensable work, it has become unnecessary to list separately many of the standard titles by Motherwell, Buchan, Maidment, Herd, Jamieson and others, which have been admirably subsumed in Prof. Child's magnificent compilation.

Duncan, Edmondstoune. The Story of Minstrelsy. London and New York, 1907.

Gerould, Gordon Hall. The Ballad of Tradition. Oxford, 1932. . . . Also contains an excellent chapter on Broadside Ballads.

Greig, G., and Keith, A. Last Leaves of Traditional Ballads and Ballad Airs. Aberdeen, 1925. . . . This very important work is a valuable adjunct to the Child Collection, as it reinstates Peter Buchan as a collector of integrity.

Henderson, T. F. The Ballad in Literature. Cambridge, 1912.

Hodgart, M. J. C. The Ballads. London, 1950.

Hustvedt, S. B. Ballad Books and Ballad Men. Harvard University Press, 1930.

JOURNAL OF THE FOLK SONG SOCIETY, 1899–1931. London.

JOURNAL OF THE ENGLISH FOLK DANCE AND SONG SOCIETY, London, 1932, in progress.

. . . These journals contain invaluable studies on most aspects of Folk Dance, Song and Balladry, as well as important field collections.

KIDSON, Frank, and NEAL, Mary. English Folk-Song and Dance. Cambridge University Press, 1915.

. . . Contains an important chapter on "The Ballad Sheet and Song Garland", condensed from Journal of the Folk Song Society, No. 7, 1905.

KIDSON, Frank. Traditional Tunes. A Collection of Ballad Airs, chiefly obtained in Yorkshire and the South of Scotland; together with their appropriate words from Broadsides and from Oral Tradition. Oxford, 1891.

KINLOCH, George Ritchie (ed.). The Ballad Book. Reprint (Bibliotheca Curiosa, ed. E. Goldsmid). Edinburgh, privately printed, 1891.

LLOYD, A. L. The Singing Englishman. An Introduction to Folksong. London, n.d.

MAIDMENT, James (ed.). A North Countrie Garland. Reprint (Bibliotheca Curiosa, ed. E. Goldsmid). Edinburgh, privately printed, 1884.

NETTEL, Reginald. Sing a Song of England. London, 1954.

REEVES, J. The Idiom of the People. (English Traditional Verse from the Manuscripts of Cecil Sharp). London, 1958.

REEVES, J. The Everlasting Circle. London, 1960.

SCOTT, Sir Walter. Minstrelsy of the Scottish Border. 3 vols. Edinburgh, 1806.

SHARP, Cecil. English Folksongs. Collected and Arranged. 2 vols. London, 1919.

SHARP, Cecil. English Folk Songs from the Southern Appalachians ed. Maud Karpeles. 2 vols. London, 1932.

SHARP, Cecil. English Folk-Song, Some Conclusions. London, 1907.

SHARPE, Charles Kirkpatrick. A Ballad Book of Popular and Romantic Ballads and Songs current in Annandale and other parts of Scotland. Reprint (Bibliotheca Curiosa, ed. E. Goldsmid). 2 parts. Edinburgh, privately printed, 1883.

WELLS, Evelyn Kendrick. The Ballad Tree. A Study of British and American Ballads. Their Folklore, Verse and Music. New York, 1950.

... Includes valuable chapters on Minstrel and Broadside Ballads, and the eighteenth century English Ballad Revival.

WILLIAMS, Alfred. Folk-Songs of the Upper Thames. With an Essay on Folk-Song Activity in the Upper Thames neighbourhood London, 1923.

OLD BALLADS (MSS. AND BROADSIDES), sixteenth to eighteenth century:

ASHTON, John. A Century of Ballads illustrative of the Life, Manners and Habits of the English Nation during the Seventeenth Century. London, 1887.

ASHTON, John. Humour, Wit and Satire of the Seventeenth Century. London, 1883.

BAGFORD BALLADS (ed. J. W. Ebsworth). The Ballad Society. 2 vols. and supplement. Hertford, 1876–80.

(A) CATALOGUE OF AN UNIQUE COLLECTION OF ANCIENT ENGLISH BROADSIDE BALLADS. Printed Entirely in the Black-Letter. London, 1856.

CHAPPELL, William. Popular Music of the Olden Time. 2 vols. London, 1855–9.

CHRISTIE-MILLER, W. Alphabetical List of Black-Letter Ballads and Broadsides, known as the Heber Collection. In the possession of S. Christie-Miller, Esq., Britwell, Bucks. London, 1872.

CLARK, Andrew (ed.). The Shirburn Ballads, 1585–1616. (Oxford English Texts.) Oxford, 1907.

(A) COLLECTION OF SEVENTY-NINE BLACK-LETTER BALLADS AND BROADSIDES, Printed in the Reign of Queen Elizabeth, between the Years 1559 and 1597. London, 1870.

COLLIER, J. Payne. Twenty-five Old Ballads and Songs: from Manuscripts in the possession of J. Payne Collier, Octogen. A Birthday Gift. London, "Printed for Presents only", 1869.

DANIEL, George. An Elizabethan Garland ... Catalogue of Seventy Black-Letter Ballads. London, privately printed, 1856.

EVANS, R. H. Old Ballads, Historical and Narrative, with some of modern date; collected from rare copies and MSS. (New edition, enlarged) 4 vols. London, 1810.

FAWCETT, F. Burlington (ed.). Broadside Ballads of the Restoration Period from the Jersey Collection, known as the Osterley Park Ballads. With Introduction and Notes. London, 1930.

FIRTH, C. H. The Ballad History of the Reigns of Henry VII and

Henry VIII. (Reprinted from Transactions of the Royal Historical Society, 3rd Series, Vol. II.) London, 1908.

FORD, Worthington C. Broadside Ballads . . . Printed in Massachusetts, 1639–1800. Massachusetts Historical Society Collections LXXV. Boston, 1922.

FORD, Worthington C. The Isaiah Thomas Collection of Ballads. Worcester (U.S.). The American Antiquarian Society, 1924.

FURNIVALL, F. J. Captain Cox, his Ballads and Books; or, Robert Laneham's Letter; On the Entertainment at Kenilworth in 1575. Re-edited, with an account of all the books in the Captain's Library. The Ballad Society, Hertford, 1871.

JOHNSON, Richard. The Crown Garland of Golden Roses: Consisting of Ballads and Songs. (Ed. W. Chappell, from the edition of 1612) 2 parts. Percy Society, 1842, 1845.

LEMON, Robert (Comp.). Catalogue of a Collection of Printed Broadsides in the Possession of the Society of Antiquaries of London. London, 1866.

LINDSAY, J. L., Earl of Crawford. Bibliotheca Lindesiana. Catalogue of English Broadsides, 1505–1897. Aberdeen, 1898.

PAINE, N. Early American Broadsides, 1680–1800. Worcester (U.S.), 1897.

PERCY, Thomas. Reliques of Ancient English Poetry (ed. Wheatley). 3 vols. London, 1886.

(PERCY, Thomas). Bishop Percy's Folio Manuscript (ed. Hales and Furnivall, F. J.). 4 vols. London, 1867.

PHILLIPS, Ambrose (?). A Collection of Old Ballads. 3 vols. London, 1723–5.

PINTO, V. de Sola, and RODWAY, A. E. The Common Muse. London, 1957.

RIMBAULT, E. F. A Little Book of Songs and Ballads, gathered from Ancient Musick Books. MS. and Printed. London, 1851.

RITSON, Joseph. Ancient Songs and Ballads from the Reign of King Henry the Second to the Revolution (Coll.). 3rd ed. revised W. Carew Hazlitt. London, 1877.

ROBINSON, Clement, and others. A Handefull of Pleasant Delites. (Ed. Kershaw, Arnold.) London, 1926.

ROLLINS, Hyder E. (ed.):
The Black-Letter Broadside Ballad (Publications of the Modern Language Association XXXIV). U.S.A. 1919.
Old English Ballads, 1553–1625, Chiefly from MSS. Cambridge, 1920.

A Pepysian Garland. Black-Letter Broadside Ballads of the years 1595–1639. Chiefly from the Collection of Samuel Pepys. Cambridge, 1922.

An Analytical Index to the Ballad Entries, 1557–1709 in the Registers of the Company of Stationers of London. University of North Carolina, 1924.

The Pack of Autolycus or Strange and Terrible News . . . as told in Broadside Ballads of the Years 1624–93. Harvard, 1927.

The Pepys Ballads (1535–1702). 8 vols. Harvard, 1929–32.

ROXBURGHE BALLADS (ed. Chappell, W., and Ebsworth, J. W.). 9 vols. The Ballad Society, Hertford, 1871–99.

WRIGHT, Thomas. Political Ballads published in England during the Commonwealth. Percy Society, Early English Poetry . . . vol. 3, 1841.

MODERN BROADSIDE BALLADS, eighteenth to twentieth century:

ASHTON, John. Modern Street Ballads. London, 1888.

BARING-GOULD, Rev. S. English Minstrelsie. A Monument of English Song. 8 vols. Edinburgh, n.d.
. . . Contains important introductions on traditional and broadside balladry, evolution of concerts, Pleasure Gardens, etc.

BARING-GOULD, Rev. S. Strange Survivals. Some Chapters in the History of Man. London, 1892.
. . . A series of folklore essays, including chapters on Riddles, and Broadside Ballads.

COLUM, Padraic. Broad-Sheet Ballads. Being a Collection of Irish Popular Songs with an Introduction. Dublin, n.d.

CRUIKSHANK, George (ed. and illus.). The Loving Ballad of Lord Bateman. London, 1877.

HENDERSON, W. Victorian Street Ballads. A Selection of Popular Ballads sold in the Street in the Nineteenth Century. London, 1937.

HINDLEY, Charles (ed.). The Catnach Press. A Collection of the Books and Woodcuts of James Catnach, Late of Seven Dials, Printer. London (1869).

HINDLEY, Charles (ed.). Curiosities of Street Literature: comprising "Cocks", or "Catchpennies", a large and curious assortment of Street-Drolleries, Squibs, Histories, Comic Tales in Prose and Verse. . . . London, 1871.

HINDLEY, Charles. The Life and Times of James Catnach (Late of Seven Dials), Ballad Monger. London, 1878.

HINDLEY, Charles. The History of the Catnach Press, at Berwick-upon-Tweed, Alnwick and Newcastle-upon-Tyne, in Northumberland, and Seven Dials, London, London. 1887.

KIDSON, Frank. The Ballad Sheet and Garland.
(In Journal of the Folk Song Society, No. 7, 1905.)
. . . This valuable article is the first attempt to classify and list the broadside printers throughout Black-Letter and Whiteletter periods. It is sketchy, and suffers from some inaccuracies, but is of extraordinary importance.

LAWS, G. Malcolm, Jr. American Balladry from British Broadsides. A Guide for Students and Collectors of Traditional Song. (American Folklore Society). Philadelphia, 1957.
. . . An immensely valuable book in the field of connections between oral and printed traditions. Laws seems to have been the first to demonstrate the dependence of oral tradition upon printed copies.

LOGAN, W. H. A Pedlar's Pack of Ballads and Songs. With illustrative Notes. Edinburgh, 1869.

O LOCHLAINN, Colm. Irish Street Ballads. Collected and annotated, and adorned with woodcuts from the original broadsheets. Dublin, 1939.

SCOTT, Harold. English Song Book. Collected and Edited. London, 1926.

THE UNIVERSAL SONGSTER or Museum of Mirth, forming the most complete, extensive, and valuable collection of Ancient and Modern Songs in the English Language. London, n.d.

MISCELLANEOUS:

CAMPBELL, Joseph. The Hero with a Thousand Faces. (Reprint) New York, 1956.
. . . A key work in the field of comparative mythology and the significance of archetypal images.

DICKENS, Charles. Sketches by "Boz", illustrative of Everyday Life and Everyday People. London, 1850.
. . . Useful background material of nineteenth-century London.

D'URFEY, Thomas (ed.). Wit and Mirth: or Pills to Purge Melancholy. (Reprint) Folklore Library Publishers, Inc. New York, 1959. (facsimile of 1719–20 ed.).
. . . Important collection of popular songs of various kinds from seventeenth and eighteenth centuries.

EARL, Lawrence. The Battle of Baltinglass. London, 1952.

HINDLEY, Charles (ed.). The Life and Adventures of a Cheap Jack. By One of the Fraternity. London, 1881.

HUGO, Thomas. Bewick's Woodcuts. Impressions of Upwards of Two Thousand Wood Blocks, engraved, for the most part, by Thomas and John Bewick of Newcastle-on-Tyne. London, 1870.

LOVER, Samuel. Legends and Stories of Ireland, London, n.d.
    . . . Contains humorous article on Ballads and Ballad-singers.

MACNICOL, N. (ed.). Hindu Scriptures (Hymns from the Rigveda; Five Upanishads; The Bhagavadgita). London (Everyman's Library), 1938.

MAYHEW, Henry. London Labour and the London Poor. London, 4 vols. 1851.

MORLEY, Henry. Memoirs of Bartholomew Fair. London, 1889.

WAGER, W. The Longer Thou Livest, the More Fool Thou Art (ed. J. S. Farmer). Tudor Facsimile Texts.

(WEDDERBURN, J.). A Compendious Book of Psalms and Spiritual Songs, commonly known as "The Gude and Godlie Balates" (Reprint from 1578 ed.). Edinburgh, 1843.

WILLIAMS, C. W., and SMITH, W. C. Music Publishing in the British Isles from the Earliest Times to the Middle of the Nineteenth Century. London, 1954.

GRAMOPHONE RECORDS

with a Note on the Oral Tradition

GRAMOPHONE RECORDS

BALLAD study illustrates the eternal duality of form and essence. On the one hand, the five large volumes of Professor Child, containing every printed variant and analogue distilled from the meticulous study of three hundred and five ballads and seven thousand books; on the other hand, the clear spine-chilling magic of the true traditional singer. There can be no doubt that Child was guided triumphantly through the maze of his materials by an indefinable insight, but who is to say that the same essential knowledge might not be acquired with greater clarity of experience in one inspired moment? Child's colossal devoted scholarship showed how far the academic world had lost contact with a rich tradition, how far poetry had travelled away from its sources.

Since Baring-Gould and Cecil Sharp it has been recognized that the living performance is the key to the meaning of the folk tradition, an intangible essence that defies formal analysis. Information itself can often prove a barrier to this magic world. *Novalis* says: "All experience is magic, and only magically explicable" and "It is only because of the feebleness of our perceptions and activity that we do not perceive ourselves to be in a fairy world." This magic is the eternal mystery that lies behind and beyond the everyday physical world which is only its first frontier. It is the world sought by artists, dreamers, mystics, priests and congregations. In some sense, too, it is also the world of the perfection of the social reformer and the precision of the scientist. Ultimately it is what we live for and by what we live. In modern times much of this meaning has been lost in the material preoccupations of science and technology, and in the purely formal study of the past. Ballads and folklore have preserved for us the fossils and skeletons of that past, in magical incantation, charms, spells, and the dark legends and ritual of nursery-rhymes, but these are the dry bones of extinct animals as fabulous as the unicorn. For many years folklorists have pursued the form instead of the essence.

But there *is* magic and it may yet be evoked. Much of it is still in the oral tradition of folk singing; it does not live in the words and versions but in the living breath of the singer. There have been attempts to analyse and classify the resources of vocal technique in traditional

197

singing; one might equally try to describe happiness in terms of physiology and anatomy. Far better to give oneself to the *experience* of the true oral tradition in the living performance or in the recordings of folk artists.

This oral tradition is not always an unbroken line, nor is it necessarily found only amongst peasants and primitive races. Even a tenuous contact with a folk tradition may, if one is ready for it, spontaneously reawaken an instinctive taste, perhaps from some underground level of collective consciousness. Listen to the astonishing voice of John Jacob Niles as he sings ancient ballads and see what pictures rise before the mind's eye. It is not so much the world of lords and ladies that is evoked, but the titanic figures and shadows of the archetypal situations which loom behind them. In this light the factual occupational songs and social squibs are a secondary experience. When a poor man sings an old ballad about a knight in a strange land, he is rich in his contact with a magic world. It is the unknown and other-worldly, familiar yet mysterious, that opens the magic door and conjures the bright vision.

The astonishing thing is that the vocal practices of meaningful incantation in tones and inflexions should continue for thousands of years. The form of the piece changes, and who is to argue whether ballads came from sagas, or whether songs are a separate category to ballads? No version of any folk utterance is for ever static. From one ballad develops three hundred and five, and a hundred variants of each. Fifty different songs may only perpetuate one inflexion, perhaps a stress of one thrilling vowel sound, and the rest is elegant variation. From countless intricate plots comes one shadowy archetypal theme. Out of a thousand ballad heroes emerges a man with one face. Out of the sifting of song and ballad comes one primeval magical sound. Perhaps this is the sound of life itself, which the yogis and the Cabbalists say may be heard in the body. From earliest times there has been some divine essence that takes on the tone of its environment; it has worked in the wood, metal, horsehair and catgut of the musical instrument, but best perhaps it comes straight from the body through the throat of a man divinely inspired. Sometimes in such music we may sense how the long past and all that is yet to come exists timelessly with an understanding of all details and all inter-relationships. We may glimpse an eternal present where the rich melodies of life have the rhythms of a dance, a timeless magic centre at the heart of the living moment.

*   *   *

The recordings which follow have been selected to demonstrate ancient and magical sounds from oral tradition and inspiration, authentic survivals and revivals in folk balladry, as well as popular versions of street ballad singing. Unless prefixed "English" the record labels are American. It is only fair to say that the American companies have shown more enterprise in issuing unusual and folk interest items, and most of these are now readily available in England.

Modern records often become unobtainable more rapidly than out of print books. The Riverside folk series has been withdrawn recently[1] and it is impossible to forecast how many other items listed will continue to be available. Fortunately the current interest in folk songs and ballads has resulted in various alternative issues. Of the special items listed, three records may be very difficult to obtain: the Parabrahman *AUM*, the monologue from *Der Ewige Jude* and the Norwegian *Draumkvaede*. There is no alternative for the latter item, a unique recording. There is, however, more than a hint of the meaning of the *Aum* in the *Religious Music of India* Album and in the extracts from *Bhagavada Gita*, while any of the excellent recordings of Jewish cantillation generally available will convey some of the feeling of the record of *Der Ewige Jude*.

* * *

1. "AUM"—the sacred Sanscrit Parabrahman (origin of the Universe) recited by Sri Swami Sivananda at his ashram in Northern India. *With:*

   Reading in English from BRIHADARANYAKA UPANISHAD, 4th Adhyaya, 5th brahmana, recited by Sri Swami Sivananda. In this extract, the sage Yajnavalkya is about to go away into the forest, and instructs one of his wives, Maitreyi, in knowledge of the Self.

   . . . HINDUSTAN Record H.0010.

2. TRADITIONAL HINDU PRAYER CHANTING AND SINGING

   Included in Album "Religious Music of India".

   . . . FOLKWAYS FE.4431 (33⅓ r.p.m.).

   Bhagavad Gita—chant from Chapter II, 54–7, read in Sanscrit and English; Extract from *Ramayana*, etc., read in Sanscrit.

   . . . FOLKWAYS FL.9920 (33⅓ r.p.m.).

3. SPIRIT CONVERSATION

   Recorded in Haiti. (Cult-priest goes into trance in small hut built for the purpose. The high sound in background is a small

---

[1] As this book goes to press I learn that the Riverside discs are being reissued by a subsidiary company Washington Records.

handbell which rings continuously with convulsive tremor of the hand. Priest is asked questions, and allegedly replies with the voices of ancestors, just like any modern spiritualist medium. Both priest and questioner instinctively move from speaking to singing, demonstrating close connections between declamation and song.)

... Included in Album *Folk Music of Haiti*. FOLKWAYS FE.4407 (33⅓ r.p.m.).

4. *Monologue from* "DER EWIGE JUDE". Bei'm Klages Mauer, Yerusholayim—Rowina. This record also demonstrates connections between speech and song. A section from a Hebrew drama uses a technique where range and style of voice alternate between declamation and wailing.

... English COLUMBIA DC.103.

5. NEGRO CHILDREN'S SONGS
... Library of Congress, Folkmusic Division, Disc AAFS.20.
... FOLKWAYS FC.7004 (33⅓ r.p.m.). *Ring Games from Alabama*.

6. OSSIANIC CHANT
An ancient Gaelic style used by the epic bards, with four-tone scale (A, C, D, E). The words tell how a band of Fingal warriors are out hunting and meet a man dressed as a blacksmith, whom they follow; at this smithy, twelve powerful smiths appear, and there is a great battle and slaughter. *With:*
DOCUMENTARY RECORDINGS OF HEBRIDEAN WORKSONG (WAULKING)
... Included in FOLKWAYS FE.4430 (33⅓ r.p.m.).

7. "DRAUMKVAEDE"
This is the "Dream-song" of Norway, first noted in the Telemark region about 1200 A.D. It is a sort of Norwegian *True Thomas* ballad, which tells how Olav Asteson fell into an ecstatic sleep lasting from Christmas Eve to Twelfth Night. When he awakens he goes to church and relates to the congregation what he found as he passed through the Kingdom of the Dead, and what he now knows about Heaven, Purgatory and Hell. (Probably pagan in origin, later Christianized.) Sung by Gudrun Grave Nordlung.
... MUSICA N.900–3, limited edition (issued in Norway).

8. THE RANGE AND RESOURCES OF THE HUMAN VOICE

Vox Humana, the Experiments of Alfred Wolfsohn in extension of human vocal range.

... FOLKWAYS Album FX.6123 (33⅓ r.p.m.).

9. TRADITIONAL CAROLS, SONGS AND BALLADS sung by JOHN JACOB NILES

Niles is a famous collector, a singer whose style differs from standard traditional singers in his instinctive taste and feeling for aspects of ancient tone and inflexion which have largely passed out of the mainstream of oral tradition. He has an extraordinary vocal range which can be studied in conjunction with the *Vox Humana* Album above. All his recordings are of exceptional interest, but the following are especially recommended:

Mattie Groves (Child No. 81)—BOONE–TOLLIVER BTR.23 (33⅓ r.p.m.);

The Cherry Tree (folk carol)—"Folk Songs of Christmas, Vol. 2", CAMDEN CAE.206 (45 r.p.m.);

Down In Yon Forest and *The Cruel Brother* (Child No. 11)—"50th Anniversary Album"—CAMDEN CAL.330 (33⅓ r.p.m.);

The Hangman (Child No. 95)—CAMDEN CAL.219 (33⅓ r.p.m.).

10. BRITISH-AMERICAN BALLADS COLLECTED FROM ORAL TRADITION IN U.S.A.

New England Folksong Series No. 1, Helen Hartness Flanders Collection, Middlebury College, Vermont, U.S.A.

11. TRADITIONAL BRITISH SONGS AND BALLADS IN ORAL TRADITION

Young Henry Martin—Philip Tanner, Folk Singer, English COLUMBIA FB.1569.

The Sweet Primroses—Philip Tanner, English COLUMBIA FB.1570.

The Pretty Ploughboy\Harry Cox, Folk Singer. English Folk
Down by the Riverside/ Dance and Song Society, OC.87/88.

Barbara Allen   \Philip Tanner, English Folk Dance and
Young Rober, Esq./ Song Society, JL.2.

The Barley Mow (Songs from the Village Inn); includes: "Still I Love Him"; "Blow the Candle Out"; "The Foggy Dew"; "The Nutting Girl"; "The Barley Mow", actual recordings from folk singers in public houses—English H.M.V. 7 EG.8288 (45 r.p.m.).

Folk Song Today (Songs and Ballads of England and Scotland); includes: "Bonnie George Campbell", "The Haughs of Cromdale"; "My Son David" (Child No. 13); "Dance to th' Daddie";

"High Barbaree"; "Dabbling in the Dew"; "The Foggy Dew"; "The Twelve Days of Christmas"—English H.M.V. DLP.1143 (33⅓ r.p.m.).

Four Sussex Singers (Traditional Songs by Country Singers: George Spicer, Pop Maynard, Jean Hopkins, Jim Wilson. Recorded by Mervyn Plunkett—English, Collector Records JEB.7 (45 r.p.m.). (Comparable performances by such singers as Harry Cox are available in America in the Album: *Columbia World Library of Folk and Primitive Music*, Vol. III—English Folk Songs.)

12. STREET SONGS AND BROADSIDES

English Street Songs—A. L. Lloyd, RIVERSIDE 12–614 (33⅓ r.p.m.); *Street Songs* (Scots)—Ewan MacColl, RIVERSIDE 12–612 (33⅓ r.p.m.); *Street Songs* (Irish)—Patrick Galvin, RIVERSIDE 12–613 (33⅓ r.p.m.); *Broadside Ballads*—Paul Clayton, FOLKWAYS FW.8708 (33 r.p.m.); not traditional style singing, but traditional versions. The record notes illustrate many broadsides in facsimile from originals in the Newberry Library, Chicago.

13. COCKNEY MUSIC HALL SONGS

Song by Colyn Davies—TRADITION No. 1017 (33⅓ r.p.m.). An English performer with a great feeling for the spirit of nineteenth-century London street balladry.

14. FRAGMENTS OF ORAL TRADITION (American)

Millions of Musicians. Documentary conceived, recorded and narrated by Tony Schwartz. Includes Music in Speech, Rhythm of Words, Calls and Whistles, Rhythm and Motion, Rhythm and Work—FOLKWAYS FD.5560 (33⅓ r.p.m.).

15. THE ENGLISH AND SCOTTISH POPULAR BALLADS (CHILD BALLADS):

Nine L.P. discs (33 r.p.m.) Recorded by Ewan MacColl and A. L. Lloyd, Edited and annotated by Kenneth S. Goldstein— RIVERSIDE R.LP12–621/622; 623/624; 625/626; 627/628; 629. *Lucy Stewart*, Traditional Singer from Aberdeenshire, Scotland, Vol. 1—Child Ballads. Collected, edited and annotated by Kenneth S. Goldstein—FOLKWAYS FG.3519 (33⅓ r.p.m.). *Child Ballads in America* Vols. 1 and 2, sung by Jean Ritchie— FOLKWAYS FA.2301/2 (33⅓ r.p.m.).

INDEX OF NAMES